A VILLAGE VOICE

Collected Columns from The Chapel Hill News *by Robert E. Seymour*

For Liza,
Robert E. Seymour
2003

CHAPEL HILL
PRESS, INC.

These columns were reprinted with the kind permission of *The Chapel Hill News*

Published by The Chapel Hill Press, Inc.
1829 East Franklin Street, #300A
Chapel Hill, NC 27514

ISBN Number 1-880849-50-X
Library of Congress Catalog Number 2002111701

Printed in the United States of America
07 06 05 04 03 10 9 8 7 6 5 4 3 2 1

TO THE READERS OF

The Chapel Hill News

"I hope you will talk to an editor about turning

your collected columns into a book."

B.K., Chapel Hill, NC

TABLE OF CONTENTS

SECTION 3 – POLITICS

SECTION 4 – ISSUES

SECTION 5 – CHAPEL HILL

SECTION 6 – TRAVEL

SECTION 7 – SEASONS

INTRODUCTION

When Editor Ted Vaden invited me to be one of the "Village Voices" in 1994, I would never have thought that I would still be writing columns eight years later. It has been an assignment I have greatly enjoyed. I quickly discovered that it is much easier to write a column once a month than a sermon once a week!

It is hard for me to believe that their accumulated number is near one hundred. Friends have encouraged me to assemble them for publication, and though some of the columns are somewhat dated by their context, I agreed to do so.

I have greatly appreciated the privilege of expressing my views about a wide range of topics. The newspaper has placed no restrictions about the kinds of subjects that might be addressed. Although *The Chapel Hill News* generally covers local news only, there has been no objection to my addressing issues that have national or international significance.

The collection includes columns that are "tongue-in-cheek," as well as serious. Surprisingly, the column that prompted the greatest response was about preserving the Southern tradition of enjoying sweet tea. The newspaper even printed bumper stickers reading, "Southerner for Sweet Tea."

An unexpected pleasure from writing these columns has been the opportunity to dialog with the community. Letters, e-mail, and telephone calls have enlivened my life and put me in contact with a host of new friends. I discovered early on that those who disagreed with me were more likely to write a "Letter to the Editor," while those who said "Amen" were more inclined to call or write a personal note.

I would like to thank Ted Vaden for his continuing encouragement, and Debbie Meyer, who has worked with him in scheduling the columns. I also owe considerable thanks to my friend, Charles Wrye, who generously gave to me his time and professional skills to proofread the material and to make suggestions about the format of the book. It was his idea to include samples of the responses received and to print the text in columns similar to the way they had appeared in the newspaper.

The columns are grouped into topical sections. Some of them—especially the ones that are about politics—are in a time warp, but I hope they will be of interest, nonetheless. In each section, the most recent columns are first, and the rest are dated in reverse chronological order.

A major motivation for proceeding with this project was the idea that it would be a fund-raising venture for The Interfaith Council for Social Service. All proceeds from the sale of the book will go to this agency, which serves our community so effectively.

FOREWORD

In 1995, Robert E. Seymour wrote a column about sweet tea. The article praised the syrupy concoction as a Southern tradition and lamented its decline as a staple on our dining tables and in our restaurants. "This is an action alert to all true Southerners," the column begins. "A part of our cherished Dixie tradition is being corrupted by aliens in our midst."

To Seymour's surprise and mild distress, the column elicited an angry letter to the editor in *The Chapel Hill News*, attacking the good reverend for provincialism: "The man is either senile, small-minded, or biased against northerners." Little did the writer know that she was attacking an icon of Southern liberalism. Her letter, in turn, generated an outpouring of letters to the editor from people rushing to Seymour's defense and chastising the letter-writer, a newcomer to Chapel Hill, for daring to attack a local institution. The sweet tea tempest set off an iced tea-tasting contest among area restaurants—judged by Seymour—and a bumper-sticker campaign initiated by *The Chapel Hill News.* Today, seven years later, I still see "Southerners for Sweet Tea" stickers adorning local vehicles.

This is vintage Seymour. Only Bob Seymour could create a community controversy over an issue so seemingly innocent as sweet tea. Controversy seeks out the retired, but never retiring, reverend the same way lightning finds the tallest tree in the forest. And he welcomes it because only by pushing the bounds, in Seymour's reckoning, do we make the world better. The greatest sin is doing nothing; the second greatest is staying silent.

"If you're not outraged, you're not paying attention," Seymour says in one column. No one can ever doubt that Bob Seymour is paying attention. Pick the issue, local or national, and Seymour weighs in with a voice that is knowledgeable, authoritative, firm and, always, always civil.

When I first came to *The Chapel Hill News* in 1993, I had the good fortune of securing Seymour's friendship early on. I had known him by reputation as the respected retired pastor of Olin T. Binkley Memorial Baptist Church and as a civil libertarian and steadfast advocate for the disadvantaged and disenfranchised. So it was to our great benefit—and our readers'—that he agreed to join the paper as one of the "Village Voices" columnists on our front page, from whence these essays are collected.

In the pages that follow, you'll find essays on the great issues of our time: the death penalty, gun control, national health care, abortion, campaign finance, welfare reform, mental health, aging. Seymour's position, as he says, is somewhere between the middle and far left, and he always articulates it with grace and clarity. Underlying everything are his foundation stones of truth, morality, respect for individual dignity, and integrity.

"Integrity is where words and deeds coincide," Seymour tells us. Example: One essay laments the U.S. Supreme Court's decision upholding the Boy Scouts' banning of gays. While the rest of us in Orange County were talking about Triangle United Way's equivocation over Boy Scouts funding, Bob Seymour acted on his convictions and very publicly resigned his position as a United Way volunteer leader.

Not to be Biblical about it, but Seymour has the prophet's gift of foretelling the future. In his Boy Scout essay, he predicted that United Way's position would be untenable, and sure enough, a year after Seymour's resignation, United Way stopped funding of Boy Scouts. In a 1995 essay, he took Gov. Jim Hunt to task for acquiescing in massive Republican tax cuts, and predicted the state would pay the price in future funding for education and human services. Today's $1.5 billion budget deficit, not coincidentally, equals the amount of the tax cuts, and the burden is being borne by the mentally ill, schoolchildren, and the elderly.

Suffusing much of Seymour's thought is an abiding respect for separation of church and state. He is not the typical Southern Baptist in many respects: One essay, for instance, takes his church to task for boycotting Disney World over homosexuality. But he is doctrinaire in brooking no state inference with matters of the church, and vice-versa. "When our government came into being," he says, "Baptists saw the danger of the state endorsing any religion and were successful in influencing our founding fathers and mothers to require in our Constitution impartiality by the state toward all religious groups."

Not all the issues are so weighty. Seymour takes us on travels with his beloved mate, Pearl, to London, Montana, Natchez, and Vicksburg. He opines on advertising ("visual pollution"), acronyms, the glories of aging, snow skiing (which he still enjoys in his 70s), road rage and civility. "We must somehow learn to differ from each other without destroying each other," he says. "We must learn to use language that is passionate and persuasive but never poisonous."

And, I think the retired pastor in him would say, don't preach. These essays are not commandments from on high, but a continuing conversation with a community that he loves and, he must know, returns the affection.

Bob Seymour is a community treasure. I'm grateful as editor of *The Chapel Hill News* that he saw fit to use our publication to share his insights with the community. I'm doubly grateful that his wisdom now is collected in one place, that we may benefit today and in the tomorrows.

Ted Vaden, Editor of The Chapel Hill News

FEATURES

ARE WE THE GREATEST?

July 18, 2001

Last month I attended a humanities seminar on the UNC campus entitled, "The State of the World." Not surprisingly, in the course of the presentations and discussions, the United States was referred to repeatedly as "the greatest nation in the world." Usually this designation was made because of our incredible wealth and our enormous military strength. Money and power seemed to be the primary indicators of what constitutes greatness. Obviously, in these two categories, we are without equals.

It has occurred to me that a more accurate indicator of greatness might be made on the basis of what we do with what we have. Such a standard would show that we do not rank as high among the nations as we may think. Other countries excel in many areas where we have considerable room for improvement.

Despite our great wealth, it is shocking that we have been unable to devise a healthcare system that includes everyone. Forty-five million Americans have no health insurance. Although we lead the world in medical advances and in the quality of care, because of its high cost and inaccessibility to such a large minority, the World Health Organization ranks thirty-seven other countries ahead of the United States!

Our willingness to tolerate a wide gap between the rich and the poor also compromises our claim to greatness. No other Western nation permits such extremes or such a high percentage of citizens to live below the poverty level. Some CEOs make more in a day than many employees in the work force make in a lifetime. According to the figures from the recent census, one out of every six children still lives in poverty despite our unprecedented economic growth and an overhauled welfare system. Compared to the rest of the industrialized world, we still remain at the bottom of the heap.

We also stand out among nations as the most violent country in the world. We see a steady diet of violence in our mass media, and we expose even our children to violent video games. Foreigners find our easy access to guns incomprehensible and are shocked by homicide statistics, which keep the U.S. at the top of the rankings for murder.

We also are almost alone in the world in our perpetuation of the death penalty. Even South Africa and Russia have ceased government killings. Countries that practice capital punishment are not permitted to become member states of the European Union. We are grouped with such nations as China and Iran in supporting the death penalty.

Our reputation for violence is also heightened by our huge military-weapons industry. We sell more military hardware to other nations than any other country.

Although we like to see ourselves as being a generous and caring people, we do not rank first in what we give to others in foreign aid. In fact, there are twenty countries, mostly European, who share a higher percentage of their GNP than we do. We give away one half of one percent, and much of this "aid" is military weaponry. The most generous nation in terms of the actual amount given is Japan, with France ranked second. The United States is third. At the recent world conference on AIDS, our nation was accused of having an "altruistic deficit disorder," so limited was our response to the crisis. The stonewalling of U.S. drug companies about patents and the threat of suing India and Brazil for making cheaper generic drugs for AIDS's victims did not help our philanthropic image.

Another American tragedy is our neglect of the mentally ill. Some years ago, we emptied many psychiatric hospitals and sent patients back to their local communities in the mistaken assumption that there would be resources and facilities to care for them close to home. Instead, many have ended up homeless on the streets, and others land in jail. In fact, today there are more mentally ill people in prisons than in hospitals!

We pay lip service to education, but here again, we rank extremely low in the salaries earned by teachers. Public school teachers in the United States earn less relative to national income than their counterparts in most industrialized countries, yet they spend more hours in the classroom. We are listed 22nd, with such countries as South Korea, Greece, and Turkey being ahead of us! Our economy has grown at a much faster pace than our investment in basic education. We are also among the lowest of the industrialized nations in the percentage of students who graduate in mathematics and science.

We talk about family values, but we have a higher divorce rate than any other nation. We have made it mandatory for many women to enter the work force but have made it impossible for large numbers to find adequate day care for their children. Persons who care for those at both ends of the life spectrum—the young and the old—are among the most underpaid in American society. This speaks loudly of our priorities.

Sadly, the U.S. has acquired a bad reputation at the United Nations for our refusal to pay our full indebtedness to the organization. We are frequently referred to there as a "deadbeat" nation. We withhold our money when other nations do not do as we demand. At a place where we could demonstrate our ability to lead the world, we all too often seem arrogant and unwilling to do our part.

Are we the greatest? All of the above information calls the claim into serious question.

Dear Robert, ...by world standards the top ten percent of Americans receive excellent care, the middle eighty percent mediocre (managed) care, and the bottom ten percent worse care than average for the Third World.

Where is the public outrage in the U.S.? Indeed, where is the money going? Why is the system so appallingly inefficient? Where is the major media outcry on this? *W.C., Chapel Hill, NC*

Bob: I think I should send a copy of your column to Tom Brokaw. If we are the "Greatest Generation," why are we making such a hash of things? *O.O., Chapel Hill, NC*

Bravo, Bob! Another nail hit squarely on the head! *J.G., Chapel Hill, NC*

AGING INTO THE LAST YEARS OF LIFE

May 30, 2001

The month of May was Older Americans Month. It is an observance that usually gets muted attention, though this year WUNC radio gave the topic primetime coverage. Aging is a sensitive topic for most Americans. No matter what our age, we tend to think that the word "old" applies to those who are at least ten years older than we are. If you are sixty, those who are really old are seventy. If you are seventy, the old are eighty.

I have just returned from the 57th reunion of my Navy unit, and it was somewhat jarring to see how old everyone looked. I was pleased when several friends from more than a half-century ago said, "You haven't changed." Of course I knew it was a lie, but it is the kind of lie we like to believe.

We generally think of senior citizens as the aging segment of our population, but no one escapes the aging process. It begins the moment we are born. I like that bumper sticker which reads, "Aging is the only way to live."

Recently at Carol Woods we welcomed new residents at a social event, and I was asked to say a few words to them about what to expect when we move from the "go-go" stage of life to the "slow-go" stage. You know that you are approaching old age when you begin to realize that you are no longer "a promising young man" (or woman), or when you suspect that you may not be indispensable to whatever it is you are doing. As you move out of the mainstream to the sidelines, you will discover that the world can adapt to your retirement remarkably well.

If your ship has not already come in, you begin to realize that it may never arrive. You will have more nostalgic memories of the past and fewer ambitious plans for the future. You may observe traits in yourself that you remember seeing in your mother or dad. (And I hope you are glad about that!) You will conclude that other people's grandchildren are not as bright as yours are. The passing of the years will seem to accelerate the older you get. Birthdays come closer together.

The "slow-go" stage of life should not be dreaded, for it offers many entitlements. From now on you can accept senior discounts gracefully, for there is no way of concealing your age. You can set your own agenda and do only those things you really want to do. You can spoil your grandchildren and get away with it. You no longer need to be cautious about what you say or the opinions you express. You are free to "let it all hang out," to tell it like it is. You can complain, "We never did it this way before," and you can exclaim repeatedly, "What is the world coming to?" Because many people will assume that your hearing has diminished, you can listen selectively, pretending not to hear things you would prefer to ignore.

There are several "don'ts" you need to respect. Don't cup your hand to your ear to hear better. This has gone out of style. Instead, just smile a lot and appear interested in the conversation. Don't contradict your grandchildren. They probably know better than you do, but even if they don't, you will have trouble reversing their self-assurance. Never neglect to enter engagements and appointments in your calendar; otherwise, you may find yourself scheduled to be at three different places at the same time. Although you may be a splendid storyteller, don't ever tell a story without first searching your memory to make sure you have not told it to the same people before.

There are other things you should know as the "slow-go" stage of life edges toward the "no-go" stage. You should never worry about being taken hostage if you travel to exotic places, because you will be the first one released. There will be times when you will find yourself more interested in going back home than in getting where you are going. Cease worrying about sexual- harassment charges; it will be much harder to make them stick. Expect people to telephone you before nine o'clock at night and ask, "Did I wake you up?" You can still be the life of the party if the party begins at five and ends before eight. You will spend more time looking for things you have lost, but be assured that you have hidden them in a very secure place. Many things that you buy will never wear out.

At last, your health insurance will begin to pay off. Your acquaintances will no longer consider you a hypochondriac. You will spend more time in waiting rooms reading last year's copies of *People Magazine.* Don't be surprised when your children begin to parent you. They will tell you repeatedly to take care of yourself, and they will call and ask, "Where have you been?," similar to the way you used to ask them the very same question.

Relax and enjoy advanced age. You will be able to get away with a lot. People will be more ready to forgive you. Some will even consider you helpless. "Senior moments" may on occasion bring your conversation to a sudden halt because of your inability to recall a word. Of course this can be embarrassing, but you know you are "with it" even though others may wonder.

Aging is like climbing a mountain. The terrain may be steep and your steps may slow down almost to a stop as you struggle to reach the top, but the view from the top is wonderful and well worth the effort.

Bob, I read the Internet edition of the Chapel Hill newspaper with some regularity, and I was pleased and tickled by your remarks re: aging. I'm going to copy it to send to some of my elderly friends here who can use the advice. I'll keep a copy on file to read myself when I become elderly. *B.M., Wilmington, NC*

WHEN IS ENOUGH ENOUGH?

April 11, 2001

When my daughter was very young, I took her to a dime store to select a new toy. She walked up one aisle, and down another, carefully surveying all the merchandise.

Then she said, "Let's go, Daddy. They don't have anything I want."

Her response to the constant pressure upon us to be good consumers is rather rare in our culture, but there is some indication that this may be changing. At last, we may have reached a point in our abundance and affluence that a few people have satisfied virtually of all of their material wants.

Now that our economy is slowing and possibly headed for a depression, we are told repeatedly that, "consumer confidence is down." The hard sell—for the latest fashion, the most expensive car, and a new house twice as large as our present one—is not soliciting the anticipated response. When people stop buying, economists start worrying.

Maybe something else is at work here. Is it possible that a part of our population is beginning to question the conventional wisdom that more is better? When is enough enough?

Surprising evidence of this change came from an unlikely source. In response to the Bush administration's push to do way with estate taxes, nearly one hundred millionaires and billionaires publicly declared they didn't want it! They were quite willing to continue paying at the present level, as much as fifty-five percent of their fortunes! They still had plenty left and felt uncomfortable with the widening gap between the privileged and the poor. Subsequently, over seven hundred more of our richest citizens have signed the protest of the cut in estate taxes proposed in 2001, calling their group "Responsible Wealth." Their action is unprecedented.

Equally significant is the discovery that the majority of the American electorate is not overly enthusiastic about dispensing of our national surplus with a huge tax cut. Polls show that most people expressed greater interest in using this money for education, erasing the national deficit, and protecting the environment. The proposed tax cut was fourth on the list of priorities! This suggests that even citizens who are not numbered among the wealthy realize when they have enough to live a comfortable life and feel no need to acquire more at the expense of the public good.

Perhaps another emerging factor in reduced consumer spending is our rapidly growing senior adult population. Like millions of older people across the country, my wife and I disposed of a large part of our material possessions as we made the transition from a sizeable house to a much smaller dwelling. We have moved from conspicuous consumption to downsizing, and the process continues. We have what we need and are at a stage of life when our "want list" is short. We are not lacking in consumer confidence—we are just content with what we have.

The prevalence of this condition may affect our economy increasingly. A familiar dilemma at Christmas is trying to decide what to give to friends and family members who already have everything! Yet, it is the holiday buying splurge that is essential to our economy. Last year, it totaled over five hundred billion dollars! The frustration of not knowing what to give has led to alternative gift fairs, where customers are encouraged to make a donation to some charity in someone's name in lieu of the customary present. This makes more sense than to give something that is not needed or perhaps not even wanted.

Something else that may eventually affect our economy is our increasing awareness of the intolerable discrepancy between the "haves" and the "have-nots" in the world. It troubles our conscience to know that many of the earth's people live on as little as a dollar a day, while others starve. We are also disturbed when we learn that while the U.S. claims only four percent of the world's people, our growing economy is responsible for twenty-five percent of the globe's carbon dioxide pollution. Yet we refuse to mandate its reduction. A challenge to this imbalance in distribution of the world's goods is summarized succinctly in the plea to "live simply, that others may simply live."

Realizing when enough is enough may also be reflected in the incredible rise in philanthropy. The number of charitable foundations in our country has escalated, and not even a slowing economy has kept them from posting record growth. Last year, foundations gave out more than $27 billion, nearly twenty percent more than in the previous year.

Engaging in conspicuous consumption is what our economy expects of us. Indeed, some may view this as a patriotic duty. But be not deceived. An accumulation of things is no guarantee of happiness, and the most important things in life are not things. You may be surprised to discover that there is greater happiness in giving than in getting. There is wisdom in knowing when enough is enough.

ADVERTISING IS EVERYWHERE

June 28, 2000

A vivid memory of church from my youth is the use of "Courtesy of the Funeral Home" fans on hot Sundays. Since there was no air-conditioning, ushers presented a complimentary fan to worshippers as they entered, and everyone meditated on their mortality as their fans waved back and forth across the congregation throughout the service.

Ironically, the sanctuary is one of the few public places left today where you are not subjected to advertising. Ads bombard our lives, and though we may think their ubiquitous presence has little influence over our consumer habits, their power is both pervasive and persuasive.

Advertising is visual pollution. We need stronger advocacy for advertising-free zones where the commercial clutter is forbidden. One of the delights of the Interstate highway system are those stretches of the road where marketing signs are either out of sight, or discreetly noted on small, standard notice boards, without compromising the scenery.

I am outraged that North Carolina may be on the verge of permitting advertisers to pollute Interstate 40 from Raleigh to Wilmington. The pressure is "on," and only concerted protest is likely to prevent it permanently.

I recall a parody of Joyce Kilmer's famous poem, which has lodged in my memory since childhood:

I think that I shall never see
A billboard lovely as a tree.
And if the billboards soon don't fall,
I'll never see a tree at all!

You realize just how ugly billboards are after traveling in Central Europe, where most countries have banned advertising from their highways. But when you enter Italy, the contrast is jarring, for suddenly, you feel at home. In all directions, billboards vie for your attention.

We can be grateful to Lady Bird Johnson for the ongoing effort to beautify our roads by planting flowers, but unless such projects withstand the aggressiveness of the marketers, "America the Beautiful" will be no more.

Another advertising-free zone that is eroding is public television. Public TV was once a wonderful oasis from those incessant ads which plague the programming of the traditional networks, but now, it too has succumbed to the temptation. This reversal of policy makes you wonder if corporate sponsorship compromises public television's ability to do investigative reporting on controversial issues. If Mobil pays for *Masterpiece Theater*, the producer would likely think twice before approving a derogatory program about Mobil's environmental record.

I am annoyed by the proliferation of advertising in new and unexpected places. Some service stations now play advertising recordings while you pump your gas, telling you what you should buy before leaving. I was angered when ads started emerging from my fax machine. Nearly every morning, I find a printout about a vacation option or an investment opportunity, offers that they insist I can't afford to ignore. I feel violated by these uninvited appeals that have entered my home without my permission.

Name recognition counts for everything in advertising. An ominous event toward this end has just occurred in New York City, where American Airlines has purchased the Round-About Theater in Times Square and announced that it will henceforth be called "The American Airlines Theater."

I find it difficult to understand how young people have been co-opted by industry to become "walking billboards" by wearing trade labels. You see it everywhere: people with Old Navy, the Gap, or Tommy Hilfiger emblazoned across their chests. I find such clothing offensive.

Where will it all end? There is an apocryphal story about an American businessman who arranged an audience with the pope. He told His Holiness that he was prepared to make a multi-million dollar contribution to the Vatican in exchange for one small favor. "And what can I do for you?," the pope asked. The businessman replied, "Just change one word in the Lord's Prayer. Instead of 'Give us this day our daily bread,' change it to 'Give us this day our Sunbeam Bread.'"

I am glad we no longer use mortuary fans in church. But I would not be surprised some Sunday soon to read at the bottom of the worship bulletin, "The Scripture lessons were brought to you today through the courtesy of McDonald's."

WE ARE WORD PROCESSORS

March 15, 2000

I like the story about the man who met an old girlfriend on the street, someone he had not seen since college days. Early in the conversation, he asked about her husband, to which she replied piously, "Oh, didn't you know? Harry is in heaven." The friend replied, "Oh, I'm so sorry." But as he processed what he had just said, he thought, I shouldn't be sorry that Harry's in heaven, so he quickly corrected himself and said instead, "What I mean is, I'm glad." Somehow that didn't transmit too well either, so in a final attempt to say the right thing, he explained: "What I really mean is, I'm surprised!"

Speaking clearly and saying what we mean makes "word processors" of us all. To be understood accurately is the essence of good communication, requiring attentive processing in the mind of the listener, too. As a clergyman, I have often been surprised when people quote back to me what they thought I had said from the pulpit, for sometimes it was the very opposite of what I intended.

We are living in a time when words are used not simply to clarify, but to deliberately conceal or confuse. Something called "doublespeak" has emerged in our culture. People carefully choose words in the hope we will process them in ways that cover up the truth. Much of our public speech has been delegated to "spin doctors" whose task it is to manipulate reporting, frequently trying to put something that is essentially negative in a more positive light.

For example, car dealers no longer sell "used" cars. Now they are "pre-owned." Lobbyists who push for a state lottery have ceased calling it "gambling." Instead, they call it "gaming." North Carolina pig farmers have tried to transform the image of hog-waste ponds by labeling them "lagoons" rather than cesspools. People who don't like to think of themselves as influence peddlers boast about having "privileged access." And Ronald Reagan introduced the phrase "revenue enhancements" to avoid calling for a tax increase.

All of us have become accustomed to processing code phrases, to hearing a hidden meaning behind an audible statement. When someone says, "She means well," we know that the person described has her heart in the right place but she cannot hack it. When an acquaintance is described as, "never having had an enemy," we wonder if he has any strong convictions. When the job applicant states, "I am a people person," we conclude he is no good at administration. When the sports commentator announces, "They didn't finish the job," we realize our team lost the game.

Word-processing skills designed to soften the truth are pervasive. When old friends tell us that we haven't changed, we understand they are really saying, "You don't look as old as I thought you would." When the air carrier announces that there will be a change of equipment, you realize with a touch of anxiety that the plane you were about to board was not fit to fly.

Ironically, sometimes what we say communicates a totally different message from what has actually been spoken. For example, when participants in a heated argument are cautioned to, "Stop before you say something you don't mean," the real message may be, "Stop before you tell each other the truth." And if anybody advises, "Now don't take this personally," you probably should!

Unfortunately, much of our public speech has become the language of deception. In political campaigns, the candidates are tempted to tell the public what they think the electorate wants to hear, while trying to conceal their honest convictions. The Pentagon has become a master at masquerading the truth. The insistence that something is "simply not true" sometimes means, "There may be some details that are incorrect, but you are on to something." Or, "It's not false, but it is complicated." Another convenient cover-up explains, "This has to be looked at in the context of the time at which it occurred; back then, we didn't think we'd get caught." And when information is withheld because it has been "classified for national security," it could mean, "If everyone knew what we know, people would not feel very secure!"

The business world has also developed skills in cosmetic word processing. When Glaxo/Wellcome announced its plan to merge with SmithKline, instead of acknowledging that some employees would lose their jobs, they said to the press, "There will be redundancy in administration." CEOs of large corporations like to call themselves "risk-takers," but their golden parachutes make them among the most financially secure people in America. Industry's "cause-related marketing" translates as self-interested benevolence—for corporations have learned that linking the name of your firm with a good cause which the public supports, pays off.

A huge change in perception because of word processing has occurred in the field of ethics. There was a time when ethicists talked forthrightly about good and evil, but gradually they found it easier to talk about right and wrong. Now the vocabulary is changing again, as some find it more comfortable to talk about "appropriate" or "inappropriate" behavior. The labels "good" and "evil" have been sent to the recycle bin because it is no longer deemed acceptable to be judgmental.

As a pastor, I had to become proficient in word processing. When someone said to me, "I need somebody to talk to," I understood that I was being asked, "Do you have the time?" I also learned that when someone says, "You are a good listener," they are saying, "I believe you care about me." And I soon discovered that most of the parishioners who came into my study and confessed, "I have lost touch with God," were really saying, "I am unhappy in my work," or "My marriage is in trouble," or "I am depressed."

Significantly, a phrase that has moved out of the professional counselor's office into mainstream conversation is, "I hear you saying thus and so...." I hope this means we are becoming more skillful word processors and want to hear one another with greater accuracy.

✉

The Rev. Seymour stated in his article, "People carefully choose words in the hope we will process them in ways that cover up the TRUTH... frequently trying to put something that is essentially negative in a more positive light."

For once, the Rev. Seymour and I are in total agreement. Some of the more notable "doublespeak" phrases from him are:

"Pro-choice"—the negative choice doesn't include killing. Although the "pro-choice" label breaks down when it comes to vouchers, gun ownership, conservative free speech or creation science.

"Gay marriage"— i.e., the union of the same sex is now sanctioned by God because God changed his mind and/or didn't make it clear enough in the Bible....

"State-sponsored murder"—enforcement of the death penalty for brutal first-degree murderers is unjustified, and if you don't agree, you are worse than the murderer...

"Civil Rights"—you missed the true civil rights movement thirty to forty years ago, so now you are making up for it by whining as professional left-wingers and namby-pamby milquetoast liberals. By the way, Jesus is a liberal and wouldn't think of judging anyone... *J.G., Chapel Hill, NC*

✉

Bob: The Oxford English Dictionary begins to give examples of "gaming" in 1501. Of "gamble" it notes: "the vb has not been found till about 1775-1786, though gambler and gambling occur as slang somewhat earlier: gambler in 1747, gambling in 1726."

I appreciate the general gist of your March 15 piece, but guess that gambling was an 18th century version of the very word processing you deplore. *J.P., Chapel Hill, NC*

MILLENNIUM SPARKS REFLECTION ON THE MYSTERY OF TIME

December 5, 1999

I recall wishing as an adolescent that I would live until the year 2000. With only a few days to go, I believe I will make it. But now, of course, I am extending my hope that I will survive well into the next century.

There seems to be some confusion about when the millennium begins. With all the hype about its approaching, many people seem to think it starts this New Year's Day, but that is not the case. The year 2000 is the final year of the second millennium, not the first year of the new one. The new millennium actually does not arrive until January 1, 2001.

Understanding the nature of time is elusive. All of us think we know what time is, but most of us would be hard-pressed to define it. Is time a human invention, or is it in some mysterious way an integral part of reality? When we say, "time marches on," we may be imposing our own perception on the universe. Clocks serve a useful and practical purpose, but they are a human device.

Though we may measure time accurately, we do not experience it as always moving at the same pace. The older I get, the faster time seems to fly. I recall my father saying in his last years that he felt as if he were always putting up the Christmas tree or taking it down! Now I understand what he meant, but, when I was a child, Christmas seemed to never come.

Depending upon what you are doing, time may accelerate or seem to stand still, and there may be days when, as Shakespeare said, "To-morrow, and to-morrow, and to-morrow, Creeps in this petty pace from day to day, To the last syllable of recorded time." Pleasure shortens time, pain lengthens it.

Not all cultures perceive the movement of time in the same way. The ancient Greeks thought it was circular, like the seasons: what will be, was, and what was, will be. The Hindu sees time as essentially stationary, not going anywhere. Whereas, in the West with our Judeo-Christian heritage, we see time as moving forward, and this way of viewing history has given birth to the secular concept of progress, the idea that as time moves forward, things get better and better. Today, however, there are those who are challenging the belief in the inevitability of progress, though the idea is deeply entrenched in the Western mind.

Biblical literature is characterized by yet another way of understanding time, contrasted by the words *chronos* and *kairos*. *Chronos* time is sequential, ordinary time, whereas *kairos* time refers to those occasions in life when things come together in such a way as to provide an opportunity for a providential event, suggested by the phrase "in the fullness of time." Each of us can look back over our lives and recall those pivotal moments when some unique intervention seemed to set the course for our future.

I think the nature of time is best defined as the medium of our human existence, for we are always aware of it, and we experience it in three dimensions, as past, present, and future. Every minute is instantly transitional, as we leave the present in the past and simultaneously enter the future. But all the time we ever actually have is NOW. Thus, the time of our life is life's most fundamental gift. Perhaps this is why we so often speak of time as "the present."

What we do with the present moment is indicated by a host of commonplace phrases that punctuate our everyday speech. We talk about "saving time," "wasting time," "serving time," "making time," and "squandering time." It is our most precious possession, and determining what we do with it is life's most important decision.

As this year comes to a close, some people feel uneasy and anxious, as if there were something ominous approaching, perhaps even the end of time. The anticipated Y2K computer problem as we enter the year 2000 has accentuated such speculation, especially among some religious sects. But now that The National Institute of Standards and Technology and The Library of Congress have both pointed out that the millennium really doesn't start until 2001, all such fears can be postponed for at least another year.

But let's not cancel the celebrations planned for the weeks ahead. Now we are authorized to extend them for another twelve months!

THERE'S NO EASY WAY TO MOVE

August 22, 1999

I have seldom been so completely exhausted. My wife and I have just moved from a house that has been home to us for twenty-seven years. It has been a horrendous experience, both physically and emotionally. We feel like survivors.

On average, Americans are said to move from one place to another about every five years. Maybe if we had done this more often, it would not have been such an enormous and arduous task. It is incredible how much stuff we had accumulated and how overwhelming it was to empty the house of everything.

I am sure it would have been easier if we had been making the transition to a larger residence, but instead, we were cutting back from three thousand square feet to seventeen hundred, and this, of course, meant that we had to dispose of about half of our possessions. Now that the task is over, I feel somewhat liberated, but downsizing is difficult and painful. Deciding what should be kept and what should be disposed of creates considerable ambivalence.

Having two children helped, for they were able to claim some things they could use, but their "takes" did not make a very big dent in reducing the clutter. Furthermore, their tastes do not coincide with those of their parents, so some of the things we thought they might cherish were passed over.

The big beneficiary of our move was the Binkley Memorial Baptist Church yard sale. We literally filled five truckloads with furniture, plants, white elephants, and excess! A part of the china and silver inherited from our families was welcomed at Replacements, in Greensboro. Stacks of piano and organ music accumulated both by my wife, Pearl, and her mother (who was also an organist) were given to the music library at Meredith College, and my books on preaching went by FedEx to the new Wake Forest Divinity School. We had kept a huge collection of magnificent hats, which my mother had worn and for which she was famous. Our daughter insisted on saving a few of these, but the rest went to the costume wardrobe at Playmakers. The Chapel Hill Senior Center was glad to get punch bowls, a hundred or more cups, and serving dishes.

For me, the most painful part of downsizing was pruning my extensive files. Every time I went to the dumpster, I felt as if I were giving up a part of my life, yet I know that most of what I threw away would be of little interest to anyone else. I was pleased that the UNC Southern Collection wanted some of my writings and correspondence. Wading through letters from a lifetime was tedious and much slower than expected. Memories of people and events that I had not thought about for years kept surfacing. It was a bittersweet exercise.

In this day when people are building larger and larger homes, I am convinced that in the future it will necessary to add one room to accommodate the accumulation of family memorabilia. We are being deluged with data! Photo albums, scrapbooks, yearbooks, videos, letters—they all take up a lot of space. (My wife had a closet full of souvenirs, programs, news articles, etc., about Dean Smith and UNC basketball!)

Our basement had been filled with accumulations not only from our immediate family but also the hand-me-downs from both Pearl's parents and mine. And of course, our children had also left behind boxes of term papers, books, and such from their college years. We made some surprising finds. We were especially happy to locate our son's Lego set, for which we had been looking for several years to pass down to our grandson. We found enough candles to open up a candle store! There were also those white elephant wedding presents that were tucked away for the "future" that never came.

The impending move prompted many concurrent projects. We had the rugs professionally washed. We re-finished the dining room table. We parted with the sofa, with which my mother and dad began housekeeping, in order to buy a pullout bed so we would have a place for both grandchildren to sleep when they visited us together. Then we faced the hassle of securing all the necessary "connections" for our new dwelling: the television, the computer, the fax machine, the telephone, and the dog door.

Another major headache is the process of informing everyone where to find us. For weeks we have been sending out change-of-address notices (and also a new telephone number). We are hopeful that the avalanche of second-class merchandising will never find us.

One reason moving is so difficult is that you experience conflicting emotions simultaneously. You are saying "good-byes" and "hellos" at the same time. Neighbors to our old house held a farewell party in our honor, a delightful occasion that prompted flashbacks of nostalgia. But the pain of leaving has been softened by the warm and cordial welcome of the residents of Carol Woods. I am confident we will gradually come to think of this as home, but now I have the odd feeling of being away at summer camp. (I have already made the mistake of driving back to our old house automatically.)

Leaving 609 Greenwood Road was especially hard for our children. Our daughter even seriously considered purchasing the house herself in anticipation of her own future retirement. After coming home for several days to help us through the ordeal of packing and sorting, she left in tears. Our son was also somber as he walked around the empty house for a final look. Both Frances and Rob knew that they were giving up some of the last vestiges of their childhood.

Our dog, Therapy, is gradually adjusting, though he misses his primary vocation of barking at joggers and bikers on Highway 15/501. Now he chafes on his leash when he sees one of the multitudes of rabbits that populate Carol Woods.

It may yet be weeks before all the boxes are unpacked, but thank goodness we will not have to move again! Next time someone else will do it for us.

✉

Dear Bob, Over the time I have come to know you, I have felt an increasing kinship with you, but it really reached a peak when I read your column in *The Chapel Hill News* last Sunday. For we, too, have just gone through the agony of downsizing and moving.... *M.D., Chapel Hill, NC*

REFLECTIONS FROM A FIFTY-YEAR REUNION

July 15, 1998

I graduated from seminary a half century ago, and last month I commemorated that event with fifteen classmates who returned to our Yale Divinity School campus for a 50th reunion. The occasion was heavy with nostalgia, and all of us coveted that complimentary lie generally heard at such gatherings, "You haven't changed."

Of course, we had changed, but it was obvious that aging affected us in widely different ways. Some members of the group did look remarkably the same, but others had an almost totally different appearance, beyond recognition.

We noticed immediately some major changes on campus. Now women make up a high percentage of the student body, but we were there when only the first few had arrived, none of whom considered a pastorate, but anticipated careers in religious education. I recalled a talk made by a previous dean who never accepted the wisdom of opening the door to women. Even though female students were on the front row, he pointedly ignored them by beginning his speech with the greeting, "Gentlemen."

Another significant change is that today's student body is older, with the average age being thirty. Many have come to seminary as a second career, and most are married and more mature than we were. Consequently, there is not much need now for single-student housing, so the campus is in the process of being redesigned, a somewhat painful sight for those of us who greatly valued the sense of community that emerged as we lived together in those buildings.

Students in my dormitory met each morning in a nearby prayer chapel before breakfast. We laughed as we remembered one of our housemates who never made it even once in three years but who often could be heard shouting from his windowsill as we left the building, saying, "You guys worship God at this ungodly hour and expect God to be there!"

One of the most popular professors was Halfred Luccock who taught homiletics (preaching) and who could find something good to say about even the worst of sermons, often tempered his critiques with a sense of humor. One day one of my friends preached a very long sermon to the class, and afterwards, Luccock inquired about the Band-Aid on his chin. He said, "I was thinking so hard about my sermon when I shaved this morning that I cut my chin." Luccock replied, "Next time think about your chin and cut your sermon." On another occasion, a student who was approaching the pulpit to preach his trial sermon complained, "I feel like a lamb being led to the slaughter." And from the back of the room, Luccock continued the Biblical quote, "and as a sheep before his shearers is dumb, he openeth not his mouth!"

During my three years at YDS, our dean was the chairman of the translating committee for the Revised Standard Version of the Bible. One morning he passed me in the hall and said, "Seymour, aren't you from South Carolina?" "Yes," I acknowledged. He continued, "Well, yesterday I received a can of ashes from a Bible burning in Due West, South Carolina, as a protest of our changing the word "virgin" in the passage from Isaiah which reads "a virgin shall conceive" to "a young woman shall conceive."

Attitudes toward me made it difficult to forget that I had come to Yale from the South. Some of my friends seemed surprised to discover that Carolinians wore shoes. Also, my public-speaking professor tried to purge my habit of sounding one-syllable words as if they had two syllables. And of course, I was stereotyped for being a Southern Baptist, a denomination generally regarded there as a sect.

Going to divinity school "up North" was a transforming experience in my life. I never would have gone there had it not been for the war, for I was sent to Yale by the Navy as a candidate for the chaplaincy. There I was exposed to the social gospel for the first time and learned that the role of a good pastor is not simply to "comfort the afflicted" but also "to afflict the comfortable." Norman Vincent Peale was at the height of his popularity in those years, and at YDS there was a general consensus that the difference between Peale and the Apostle Paul was that "Paul is appealing but Peale is appalling!" I was introduced to biblical criticism at Yale and forced to surrender my fundamentalist upbringing, which regarded Scripture as inerrant. The persistence of the inerrancy dogma in our culture accounts for such things as homophobia and the patriarchal model of the family.

Members of the Class of '48 were on the front lines of the civil rights movement. It was impressive to hear the life stories of friends, both black and white, who were a part of that mammoth struggle in the 1960s. We marveled at how much our society has changed since we left New Haven, and we were proud to have had a part in it.

I came away from the reunion feeling most grateful for what I regard as a providential opportunity in my life, the privilege of having been a student a Yale Divinity School.

CAN WE TRUST THE MEDIA?

March 6, 1998

I am disenchanted with the local television news and do not watch it as faithfully as I once did. Inevitably, the lead story is about some crime, and often almost half of the program seems more like a daily police report than coverage of what is happening in our area. Even the national news seems to be moving in the same direction. I thought we would never cease hearing about O.J. Simpson.

It is odd that this should be the case at a time when statistics show that the number of violent crimes has dropped dramatically. Homicides are down by thirty percent in New York City, and are down twenty percent nationwide. Yet, all across the country, crime gets more attention in the news than any other topic. A 1996 Pew study concluded that crime outranks sports, local government, religion, and politics in coverage!

Why is this true? Obviously, crime is rather easy to report and doesn't require very much of the news team. Furthermore, it grabs the attention of the viewer or reader, so publishers and broadcasters often seem committed to the proposition that "if it bleeds, it leads." But perhaps the primary reason is a reflection on the public, which seems so addicted to hearing about violence that it has become a form of entertainment. Thus, the bottom line is marketing. Publishers reason that if the public wants to hear about crime, give it to them, and ratings will remain high.

Unfortunately, this seems to be true. Those few TV stations that have tried to change the format and not play up crime have not done as well financially. But I applaud their effort and hope others will have the courage and responsibility to follow their lead. For example, a few stations have stopped reporting those crimes that are no threat to the viewers. Others have ceased identifying the accused on the basis of race to prevent the danger of racial stereotyping.

Some of the consequences of giving crime top billing are very harmful. Instead of trying to help the public reduce the level of fear, the heavy emphasis on criminal activity increases fear. It creates perceptions that are erroneous and unfair. People from the suburbs hesitate to go downtown because they have been convinced that crime is rampant, when in fact this is not the case. Women are more afraid than men, yet men are more often the victims. And the crimes against women are more frequently committed by people they know, than by a stranger.

I am a newspaper junkie and tend to get most of my news from the press, but I am beginning to have less faith in even our most prestigious papers. In recent weeks, following the alleged scandal at the White House, some of the usual cautions about accuracy in reporting seem to have vanished. Repeatedly we have heard such phrases as "sources say" or "our sources tell us" or "reliable sources" or "lawyers close to the president believe," without any documentation of who these sources are. Even *The Wall Street Journal* reported as fact someone having seen the President and Ms. Lewinsky together; then the account proved totally false, requiring a follow-up apology. Then there was the story of the "stained dress" which never materialized.* Hearsay was reported as fact, as the frenzy for more information continued.

I also resent the tendency to editorialize the news. Some papers were convinced from day one that the public would insist on impeachment, and it was as if they were telling the citizenry that this was the way we should respond. There was a rush to judgment.

I was further offended by the hypocrisy of it all. As the alleged tawdry details of the sexual affair were aired with all of the anatomical references, the same papers tried to appear high-minded by including articles about "what we should tell our children." (I liked the cartoon which showed one child explaining to another that, "Oral sex means that they talked about it.")

I guess the moral to all of this is that old adage that, "You can't believe everything you read in the newspaper (or see on TV.)" Except in this one, of course.**

**Later, the dress did materialize*

***The Chapel Hill News*

SOME RANDOM THOUGHTS ON THE PASSING OF TIME

January 2, 1998

Everywhere I turn I hear it: in casual conversation, news commentaries, public speeches. It has become a recurring phrase in common speech. It is one of those catch phrases that has "caught on" and contributes to the further degradation of our language: "At this point in time...."

Whenever I hear it, I cringe. It has become a pet peeve. It sounds so pretentious and redundant. When I hear someone say it, I wonder why he or she did not simply say "now."

NOW!

As we make the transition from 1997 into the New Year, I expect to hear this phrase even more often. For at such a point in time, we are sobered by the thought of edging closer to the end of the century. There is always something a little bit awesome at twelve o'clock midnight on December 31st. We become acutely conscious of time and the passing of it, and it has become an occasion of taking stock of our lives and the direction we are traveling. We feel that we are at a uniquely pivotal moment, caught between nostalgia for what is past and anticipation of what may lie ahead.

It is not surprising that the New Year has traditionally been marked as a time of resolutions. It seems a good time to make an assessment of our progress toward the promises we have made to ourselves. It brings with it a sense of urgency and the feeling that we need "to get on with it." NOW!

A survey from last New Year's Eve reports that almost half of those who made New Year's resolutions said they had managed to keep them or had at least made some significant progress toward their self-imposed goals. Not surprisingly, the two most common resolutions had to do with health. First, the largest number of people resolved to stop smoking and the next-largest group determined to diet and lose weight. The third most prevalent resolution was to spend less money, an almost impossible assignment in a culture that constantly insists that we consume more and more.

Last year I got an early start on my resolutions. I saw the New Year "in" while in London. I was on a bridge over the River Thames looking up at Big Ben as the famous clock sounded the passing of the old year. It seemed rather strange to realize that the folks back home would not have to commit to their resolutions until five hours later!

The word "now" carries much more weight than does the ponderous "at this point in time." It has a sharp edge to it. It calls to mind that demanding call to attention that I can still hear reverberating in my ears from my days in the Navy, when repeatedly the loudspeaker would thunder: "NOW HEAR THIS!" The word "now" also suggests that familiar counterpart, "never." Life brings to all of us those "now or never" decisions, most of which we dread because we realize what far-reaching consequences our choices may carry. We have all faced those "now or never" dilemmas that open doors of opportunity which would have surely closed if we had not walked through them. It may have been saying "yes" to a proposal of marriage. It may have been accepting an offer of employment that could shape our future. It may have been putting our money into a promising venture that would not be available later.

Most of us feel more comfortable with the phrase, "one of these days...." It promises more lead-time and feels less threatening. I have a long list of things I intend to do "one of these days," but somehow they seldom get done. We are like Scarlet O'Hara in *Gone with the Wind* who, when confronted with circumstances she wanted to avoid, said, "I won't think of it now... I'll think of it tomorrow." We like to postpone things. We assume that tomorrow will always be there and that what we have failed to accomplish today we can surely achieve tomorrow.

There are other things about which our philosophy seems to be, "never do today what you can put off until tomorrow." I feel this way in the fall when the leaves begin to come down and clutter our driveway. My wife wants them off NOW, and every day her impulse is to bring out the leaf blower. Meanwhile, I feel guilty and urge delay. "Why not wait until they all are down and do it once and for all?" I'd rather not do today what I can do tomorrow.

There is another option. The Supreme Court coined a very useful phrase to avoid the threatening NOW. Instead of mandating the immediate end of segregation in the public schools, it urged that it be done "with all deliberate speed." That phrase has a very positive ring to it, but you get the feeling that the brakes are still being applied. I suspect this is probably the most accurate description of the way many of us approach the more difficult goals we set for ourselves in life. We like to feel that we are keeping faith with our ideals, but the fact is we are not as committed as we would like to appear to be.

An illustration of this in my own life is my wife's and my intention to make a move to a retirement community when I reach seventy-five. As that ominous year approaches, I realize that I have a lot of getting ready to do. Downsizing is the name of the game, and the process is underway, but it is painfully slow—though I would like to claim it is being done "with all deliberate speed."

As an older person, I can testify that the entry into the New Year feels somewhat threatening. Many years ago, as a very young man, I heard myself saying that I hoped to live until the turn of the century. Now that I am almost there, I have the somber sense that it is "countdown time." Though I feel like celebrating my longevity, I know that time is running out, and at my age you begin to wonder how many more springtimes you will see and whether or not you will live long enough to see your grandchildren become of age. I also know that "at this point in time," the ships that I might have anticipated "coming in" will probably never arrive.

John Updike's new novel is called *Toward the End of Time*, and it is about a sixty-six-year-old man who has "an unfocused dread of time itself." He is confused by life's hints of transcendence and its meaningless absurdities. The novel suggests that we are all caught in a cosmic drift toward the end of time, but "at this point in time," most of us probably would prefer to think about that tomorrow!

I find myself being more attentive to the obituary columns. As friends and associates enter that Great New Year which we call eternity, I feel as if life is like a game of dodgeball. Death has begun to touch many of those around me, and though I have dodged it thus far, I know that I am increasingly vulnerable and will soon be "out."

But "at this point in time" there is good news: TODAY IS THE FIRST DAY OF THE REST OF YOUR LIFE! So enjoy, and make the most of it.

GRANDPARENTING GAINING MORE ATTENTION

December 7, 1997

> *"Over the river and through the woods,*
> *To grandmother's house we go..."*

The words to this familiar seasonal song remind us of the prevalence of family gatherings during the holidays, and for most of us, call to mind a grandparent whom we remember with nostalgia and gratitude.

Both of my grandmothers died before I was born, as had also one grandfather. But the grandfather who lived long enough to know me had a profound influence on my life. Surprisingly, up until recently, very little research has been done about grandparent relationships within the family structure. A part of the reason may lie in the fact that the generation prior to my parents did not live nearly as long, so many of my peers never knew any of their grandparents. Now the situation has dramatically changed. More grandparents are alive today than ever before, and many children have not only the four who are their blood kin but up to six or even eight, because of the multiple marriages of their mothers and fathers!

Another reason for a lack of attention to grandparenting may be that we went through a period when many professional counselors and therapists encouraged parent-bashing on the part of their clients. Adults were led to believe that their problems were caused by an inadequate up-bringing, and so, instead of accepting personal responsibility for their lives, they found it easier to blame their parents. Understandably, those thus convinced tended to shield their own children from that same influence, the children's grandparents.

Fortunately, the parent-bashing fad seems to be over, and today many professionals are recognizing the grandparent relationship as a most desirable resource for nurturing children. It is a unique bond that is often characterized by an unconditional love that provides bedrock emotional support to children and youth during their most formative years. As I look back upon my own life, I can testify to what my grandfather meant to me. He always believed in me and had time for me. I am confident that his influence more than any other led me to my life's vocation as a clergyman.

We are living in a time when many people become grandparents at a very early age. Indeed, it is not uncommon for people to be grandparents more than half their lifetimes! What a shame it is when adults do not welcome their parents' involvement in the lives of their own children or when grandparents choose to distance themselves from their grandchildren for fear of being judged as interfering. Such scenarios often occur because of fundamental misunderstandings between the generations. Some parents who want their own parents more involved hesitate to ask, saying, "My parents worked hard all their lives, and I don't want to burden them with the needs of my children." And conversely, some seniors say, "I raised my kids, and now I want time for myself." Such attitudes generally leave everyone the losers.

Wise are those grandparents who refrain from offering unsolicited advice, but there are many ways they can be helpful and supportive. Their availability can make a huge difference in the lives of both their children and their children's children. Establishing such positive family relationships depends on good communication and a willingness to be candid and honest about the expectations each generation has for the roles of the other.

Perhaps a part of the reason grandparents and grandchildren seem so naturally drawn to each other is that both the beginning of life and the end of life are protected from the demanding activities that require so much time and attention during our prime years. There is more leisure to share, and both birth and death make us more mindful of the mystery of life and more curious about the meaning of it all. Just as young children are always asking, "Why?," old people ponder ultimate questions as they contemplate the significance of human existence. The closeness of grandparents and grandchildren may also grow out of their shared, heightened awareness of nature, a universe that invites fascination by the young and renewed discovery by the old. The simple things of life inspire wonder in both generations.

At a time when the number of grandparents is rapidly increasing, it is unfortunate that great distances separate many families and that an extended family living nearby ("over the river and through the woods") is the exception. Obviously, it is more difficult to create a close bond with one's grandchildren when they are far away and seldom seen. There are, however, creative ways to keep in touch. The tape recorder, the telephone, photographs, and correspondence can keep the communication endearing and current, all of which prepares the way for anticipated visits.

Another hurdle that complicates grandparenting is broken families. Few things are more painful to older people than to see their children dissolve a marriage and to face the possibility of having limited access to their grandchildren. Today, every state has begun to face this problem by having enacted at least one statute about grandparent visitation. The consequences of a failed family may also lead to grandparents assuming full responsibility for children who can no longer be cared for by their own mothers and fathers. (In Orange County alone, there are more than nine hundred children who are being reared by their grandparents!)

A series of full-page advertisements appeared recently in The New York Times. The ads featured a picture of a grandmother talking to her grandchild. The headline read, "The Power of a Grandma." The ads were sponsored by the Partnership for a Drug-Free America, and the concluding paragraph urged, "Grandma, grandpa, talk to your grandkids. You don't realize the power you have to save them."

At last we are waking up to the potentially enormous influence for good that grandparents possess. Next we need to consider the influence of great-grandparents.

An astounding statistic reveals that forty percent of all those who are over sixty-five have at least one great-grandchild!

WORD GAMES HIT THE ROAD

September 5, 1997

Traveling with two grandchildren in the back seat reminded me of two car games we used to play when I was their age. The games were a great help in minimizing the monotony of the trip and in delaying that inevitable question, "Are we almost there?"

We called one of them "cow poker." Passengers on the right side counted the cows they saw on the right-hand side of the road, and passengers on the left counted those on the other side. The purpose of the game was to see who could spot the most cows, but the competition constantly faced the liability of passing a cemetery, where all the cows had to be buried, and the player who suffered this misfortune had to start counting all over again.

The other game was an alphabet contest in which passengers competed by looking on opposite sides of the highway for products being advertised, starting with the letter "A" and ending with "Z." We seldom, if ever, reached the end of the alphabet, but the game kept us entertained and distracted for many miles.

Neither of these pastimes is viable for Interstate travel today, for you seldom see cattle, and not many of the old country churches with a cemetery behind them are visible from the road. And, fortunately, much of the billboard clutter that once lined every traveled road has been minimized on the Interstate system.

There is, however, one distraction that I would classify as entertainment while traveling today, and that is the license word game. I am continually amazed by the creative way people communicate, much of which is exceedingly clever. I often jot down such license plates and now have a long list of some of the better ones that I invite you to enjoy.

But first, I must share with you one given to me verbally by a friend, and I believe it takes the prize. It reads, IYQYQR. (Read rapidly, pronouncing each letter separately.)

Many of the license-plate messages reveal how people see themselves. Consider the self-image behind each of these:

ONOORY
4EVRKID
AFEXION8
SCROOGE
TREWBLEW
SUMRGIRL
HASBEEN (I wasn't sure whether this referred to the car or the driver!)

One plate read, ORFANANY, and I passed it to see if Daddy Warbucks was behind the wheel.

Another large category of cryptic communication is related to the owner's vocation. Many people like to reveal their identity by what they do. Look at these samples:

IDEZINE—designer
CRE8JOBS—entrepreneur
FIXPETS—veterinarian
DECR84U—decorator
IFLOSSU—dental assistant
ISELHOMZ—realtor
ILOOMAN8—electrician
BNKTELR—bank teller
PLANT RX—deals in herbal medicine
REAL DOC—physician who resents PhD's being called "Doctor"
WVU'EER—literary critic with speech impediment!

Hobbies also get a lot of attention. Nearly every one you can think of is announced on the road. Here are some I have noticed lately: H2OSKI, IWNDSRF, LV2SNSKI, VOLYBOL, ANTEEKER, BUC&BASS, GOLFADK, and SKIUAL8R.

The license plate has also emerged as a platform for giving advice to whomever is in the car following. Maybe these words were meant for you:

EZDOZIT
HAVEHOPE
INNER P'S
2BHEALTHI
CZTHEDAY
JOHN 3:21 (Could be answered by YNOTBBAD?)

Sometimes the message is a flirtation, such as, URAQTPI or RUD14ME?

Not surprisingly, many drivers comment about their automobiles. Some of these are a little ambiguous, such as one that says CARITAS. I wondered if this was an admission of an obsession with cars or perhaps had reference to love (because "caritas" is the Latin word for charity). I was taken aback by one that announced it was STOL'N. A driver of an expensive new car asked those who coveted it, YNVEEME? Another advised careful planning before travel—AAAB4UGO. The plate that said MACATAK gave me fair warning that he would likely be turning at the next golden arches.

There was an article in the *News and Observer* last week about the increasing number of groups asking the Division of Motor Vehicles to put their logo, such as a school emblem, on their license plates. The largest such group is Amateur Radio and a close second is UNC-Chapel Hill, with over three thousand such requests. But I prefer those who use their own creativity, such as HRKTHSND and O HEEL!

Enough of this KILINTIME. I had better be MOZNON.

✉

Dear Mr. Seymour: I write in particular about WVU'EER.... The mascot of West Virginia University is the Mountaineer, and the members of their athletic teams often are spoken of collectively as Mountaineers. In recent years, the generally used appellation for the team members has been shortened to "Eers" (as in "How about 'em 'eers!"). Therefore, you might give consideration to the possibility that the driver of the car with the WVU'EER license plate was a West Virginia University alumnus/and/or fan. *J.E., Chapel Hill, NC*

✉

Dear Mr. Seymour: I would like to chide you about one of your explanations. You suggested that REAL DOC might belong to a physician who resents Ph.D.s being called "doctor." Why not the opposite? Couldn't it be a Ph.D. or a D.D. or a D.Lit who resents M.D.s being called "doctor"? In my dictionaries, the definitions for doctor are: "1. Orig., a teacher or learned man (from the Latin docere, to teach)" and "2. A person on whom a university or college has conferred one of its highest degrees..." It's not until we reach definition number three that doctor is defined specifically as "a physician or surgeon." Definition number five, by the way, is "a witch doctor or medicine man." Maybe REAL DOC practices voodoo. *J.A.E., Chapel Hill, NC*

DISNEY BOYCOTT CREATES TARGET FOR RIDICULE

August 8, 1997

I am beginning to feel defensive about Southern Baptists. Ever since their decision to boycott Disney, I have had people joke with me about it as if I were somehow responsible. A message on my answering machine asked, "What have you got against Mickey Mouse?"

My impulsive response is to make it known immediately that I am no longer a Southern Baptist. Binkley Church was officially expelled from the denomination several years ago following the congregation's licensing a gay divinity student from Duke University to preach. At one level it feels good to be able to distance myself from the Southern Baptist Convention, but at another level I am saddened by what I see happening to the religious body which nurtured me and had tremendous influence in shaping my life and steering me toward the ministry. In fact, I have been a part of the Southern Baptist body for all of my life until very recently.

The thing that I object to most strongly is that the press tends to portray the denomination as a monolithic group, and this lends itself to easy stereotyping. Actually, the Southern Baptist Convention has traditionally been composed of a wide theological spectrum, from rigid, puritanical fundamentalism on the one side to liberal openness and social activism on the other. Actually, that is still the case, though the denomination has fragmented from within, and the more moderate and liberal constituents are backing away from the current conservative leadership.

Southern Baptists number more than fifteen million members, twelve thousand of whom were in Dallas and voted to boycott Disney. The press failed to report that nearly fifteen hundred Southern Baptist congregations now support a subsidiary organization called "The Cooperative Baptist Fellowship." This group is looking more and more like a separate denomination. It is publishing and distributing its own educational curriculums and is supporting missionaries both at home and abroad. But it has not yet mustered the courage to sever the emotional cord with the parent body.

In addition, there is an even more liberal group based primarily along the Atlantic seaboard called, "The Alliance of Baptists." There are over one hundred churches that belong to this group, and though still nominally Southern Baptists, they have virtually separated themselves by taking positions that most Southern Baptist churches would regard as unacceptable. They challenge the belief in the inerrancy of Scripture, and welcome homosexuals into the life and leadership of the congregation and women into their pulpits.

Those who tend to make fun of Southern Baptists or stereotype them usually assume that they are backward and ill-informed. Of course, there are those who are in that category, but do not forget the enormous commitment of Southern Baptists to education. Two of our most respected colleges in North Carolina emerged from Southern Baptist life: Wake Forest University in Winston Salem and Meredith College in Raleigh. In addition to these two flagship institutions, Baptists also support five other colleges in our State: Mars Hill, Gardner-Webb, Chowan, Campbell, and Wingate. There are strong Baptist colleges and universities all over the South, and now that conservative SBC leadership has taken over the denomination's seminaries, the moderates are in the process of founding new seminaries, currently in Richmond and in Winston-Salem.

A consequence of the Disney boycott is to make Southern Baptists appear to be out of step with mainstream America, and I believe this is true. Disney has done far more for family entertainment than any other company, and we should be praising them for that. Disney is now a major player in the New York City effort to clean up Times Square. But of course the issue that sparked the boycott is Disney's respect of and fairness toward homosexuals, and Southern Baptists see this as promoting a "gay lifestyle."

This is unfortunate, for in fact there is no such thing as a "gay lifestyle." Gays are all around us and have as many varied lifestyles as heterosexuals do. There is also the assumption that one chooses to be gay, whereas the most informed medical and psychological opinions teach that it is genetically given, originating at birth. Sadly, the case against homosexuals is bolstered by misuse of Scripture and the failure to see and understand Biblical literature in its cultural context.

Let us not make the mistake of scapegoating Southern Baptists as if they alone are on a crusade against homosexuality. The controversy has engulfed every major religious denomination. In fairness, we need to admit that this issue has fractured the entire Church, unlike any other since slavery.

I am sure that the boycott will have very little effect on Disney. The company touches too many aspects of our lives, including the ABC television network. (Someone has suggested that the primary effect may be for the children of Southern Baptists to join other denominations!) My son and his wife have just taken my two grandchildren to Disney World where they had a wonderful week, and they belong to a Southern Baptist church in Cary. They are not likely to be frightened away from such entertainment by threats of hellfire and animation!

Though I think the boycott is misguided, I believe people have every right to shun anything the marketplace serves up if they do not like it. Personally, I am grateful for any company's extending health benefits to those who need it, and I applaud Disney's affirmation of the gay members of its employment force, many of whom are the most creative people in America. There is surely nothing anti-family in treating people equally and with respect.

There are many Southern Baptists for whom I have great respect, such as Jimmy Carter, Bill Clinton, and Bill Moyers. And locally, we have been blessed by such people as Bill Friday and C.D. Spangler, both of whom have Southern Baptists roots.

Though I can no longer officially claim the label, I cannot belittle my indebtedness to the Southern Baptist denomination. There remains great potential for good there, which I hope will someday become more apparent to all of us.

✉

Dear Bob, Your column in today's *Chapel Hill News* was informative, unbiased and a pleasure to read.... Hope you sent copies to church editors ...in Orlando, Fla. *P.M.S., Chapel Hill, NC*

TELEPHONE TECHNOLOGY IMPEDES COMMUNICATION

June 14, 1996

The invention of the telephone enabled people to communicate with one another as never before, but, ironically, new telephone technology often seems to prevent communication. It is not unusual to dial throughout the day and never speak to a living soul. Instead of facilitating conversations, answering machines and voice mail allow us to play hide-and-seek.

I am weary of hearing that repeated recorded statement, "I am sorry I cannot take your call right now. I am either away from my desk or on the telephone...." Some days I get the impression that no one ever stays at their desk anymore. The recording may continue, saying, "We really value your call; your message is very important to us." Really? I sometimes suspect that the person to whom I wish to speak is sitting within earshot but has decided to screen incoming calls and respond to them at his or her convenience.

Another increasingly common device for use by business and government agencies is answering their calls with a recorded "menu." You are subjected to a lengthy list of options and invited to press a number that coincides with one of the options. The troubles with this are manifold. In the first place, I feel greatly imposed upon to have to listen to so much stuff that is not remotely related to why I made the call, and in the second place, the menu often does not include the matter I want to discuss. Some systems invite you to keep listening with the promise of speaking to an operator at the end, but even this civility is passing. After all options are aired, you may be instructed to "Press nine to have the menu repeated." I hang up the phone fuming. (It is enough to make a preacher want to cuss!)

Now we have progressed to the point of having sub-menus. After you press the entry number for the information you want, you may be offered a series of subsidiary options, which presumably will eventually get you to your goal. The airlines' 800 numbers are a classic example. One punch leads to another, and you may even be told to dial an altogether different telephone number, as the interminable search for the information you are seeking continues.

Whenever I am answered by a friendly telephone voice saying, "Welcome to our fully automated system," my blood pressure begins to rise. I know this means that I will be hearing nothing but canned messages. My new computer arrived accompanied by a guarantee which promised twenty-four–hour support service, but the first time I tried to access it, I was greeted with a recording which said, "It is not timely to speak to you now, but our automated technological support will answer all of your questions." I felt cheated by my inability to set the agenda for the conversation. Instead, I was forced to listen to a long catalog of possible problems, and as anticipated, not one of them related to the help I needed.

I resent being made captive to a barrage of information I have not requested. I encountered one of the worst such systems when I called the North Carolina coast for the schedule of ferry departures. Before finally finding out what I wanted, I had to be informed where all of the picnic tables and rest rooms were at seven different sites!

Churches play the game, too. Some congregations now rely on answering machines in lieu of a secretary, and even if you were calling to report an emergency, you would first have to hear that Sunday School begins at 9:30, the worship service at 11:00, and how to enroll your child in the daycare center. It is a maddening imposition. Generally I hang up before the P.R. pitch is over.

I was introduced to another technological procedure recently, which I hope will not proliferate. I made a call to the Durham YMCA and was asked to "punch 1" to gain access to their directory. Then I was instructed to enter the first three letters of the name of the person to whom I wanted to speak in order to secure that staff member's extension. Not knowing his name, I felt victimized by a mechanical maze.

I thought I had figured out a way to get around such recorded automation by pretending not to have a touch-tone phone. Obviously, with a rotary telephone, you are not able to punch the numbers. But the technocrats have won this battle, too. When I tried this with Duke Power during the recent winter storm, I was introduced to "voice recognition" and invited to speak the number I needed instead of punching it. The technology is awesome, but the frustration level of the consumer is likely to soar.

Two other "services" I deplore are Call Waiting and Caller ID. Few things seem more rude to me than to be in the middle of a conversation with someone and have them interrupt to ask, "Would you mind holding for a minute? I have a call coming in on another line." I do mind, and sometimes I simply put down the receiver. The request makes me feel that my call is of secondary importance. Similarly, the increasing use of Caller ID makes me wonder if my attempt to reach someone has been denied because my number has been revealed where the phone is ringing. (This is the technological counterpart to that other annoying question so frequently asked, "May I say whose calling, please?")

I have several further pet peeves about telephones. My foremost complaint is the rise of telemarketing, which targets our household nearly every evening as soon as we sit down to dinner. If some legal way cannot be found to stop such harassment, I predict we will eventually not need telephone books because everyone will want to protect themselves from such intrusions by getting an unlisted number!

Another development that threatens all of us is the advent of the automobile telephone. A recent study shows that people who use a telephone while they are at the wheel have a thirty-four percent greater likelihood of having an accident. Surely this is not surprising. Obviously, talking on the telephone compromises the driver's undivided attention to the road.

My final "beef" is with AT&T, MCI, and Sprint for their non-stop television warfare. Imagine how much lower our phone bills would be if they were not paying for all those high-priced commercials!

✉

I suspect that Robert Seymour's distress is registered on many angst-meters these days. His column reminded me of this ditty by one L.F. Ayvasian. It was published in the *New York Times* in 1986.

I think that I shall no more see
A telephone that answers me,
That spreads hellos without recording
Instructions canned and unrewarding,
Exactly when my urgent choice

Is first to hear a human voice
Nuanced with banter, gossip, laughter:
Who's married, split, or gone hereafter?
But no, I'm told that at the tone
This fool must speak to someone's phone.
I'd just as soon all summer wear
A nest of robins in my hair!
(I've ripped my phone from off my wall;
Now only God can make a call!)
E.K.W., Chapel Hill, NC

✉

Dear Bob, While I understand the frustration being trapped into automation, I have experienced the other side. From someone who has no less than eight meetings per day, constant interruptions, and at least fifty phone calls, I find voice mail improves my chances of communicating—rather than impeding. At least now, I get messages of people who needed to speak with me. If I have someone in my office, I'd rather be giving them my full attention than constantly interrupting our conversation to answer the phone...

If you call me and get voice mail, please know your call IS important but I am engaged in another situation and not just screening your call! *P, Chapel Hill, NC*

✉

Dear Bob Seymour, I seem to recall that Alexander Graham Bell refused to have a telephone in his home.... Luddites of the world, unite! You have nothing to lose but your computers! *H.M., Chapel Hill, NC*

BILLY GRAHAM IS AN AMERICAN ICON

May 5, 1996

The presentation by Congress of the Congressional Gold Medal to Billy Graham was a formal recognition of Graham's status as an American icon. His name is familiar to everyone, and he is the recipient of widespread adulation and appreciation. He always comes across as a very personable and caring man—and I am sure he is—but I must confess to feeling some ambivalence about his career.

I think his popularity can in large degree be accounted for by the kind of religious message he espouses. It is individualistic, non-controversial, and can be easily exploited by heads of state who have sought his blessing. It is a carry-over of the Revivalism of the 19th century, which seems strangely anachronistic when matched with the technology of 20th-century mass media. It is heavily weighted with nostalgia for a simpler age when evangelists felt that all of our problems could be solved if we could just "win everyone to Christ."

My lifespan and career as a clergyman have coincided with Graham's. I have watched him carefully through the years and from time to time have had opportunity to communicate with him. When I was a student at the University of Edinburgh, Graham came to London for one of his first overseas crusades. On shipboard in mid-Atlantic he told reporters that his mission was to combat the sins of Britain, and in the catalog of sins enumerated, he included socialism. Predictably, a storm of protest erupted in the British press, and public sentiment was livid with anger over the audacity of this young American standing in judgment over their political system. Quickly, Graham's staff sought to repair the damage by insisting that Mr. Graham had had a slip of the tongue and had meant to say "secularism," not socialism.

I felt sorry for him and thought his crusade would be a disaster, but gradually the tone of the press began to change and he won over the British people. On the final night, I happened to be in London and went out to Wimbledon to hear him. It was pouring rain, and I could hardly believe my eyes when I saw a multitude standing under umbrellas to hear this American preacher. Amazingly, seated on the platform was the Archbishop of Canterbury, who offered the final benediction. The next day the newspapers wrote about the campaign and said in effect, "We didn't want this man to come, but obviously, he is a person of integrity, and since we do not have an excess of integrity here, we cannot afford to stomp on it."

My main disappointment with Mr. Graham is his refusal to take public stands on controversial issues. In the early days of the civil-rights movement he kept silent about segregation. He addressed the South Carolina legislature where he failed to challenge elected officials who were applauding such rhetoric as, "Those who believe in integration are dead from the neck up." I wrote to him about this and urged him to condemn the evil system, which we called "our Southern way of life," but he was silent. The replies to correspondence always explain that he doesn't want to be distracted from the main thrust of the Gospel.

Recently, I have had a similar response to an appeal to Graham to take a public stand against the death penalty, a position endorsed by all mainstream churches. But his administrative assistant responded with a polite refusal and explained that there would be no more murders if everyone became a Christian!

I had an unexpected visit with Mr. Graham some years ago when I boarded a plane in Louisville for Asheville. He was on board, and we were seated near each other. Shortly after takeoff, an engine caught fire, and we looked out to see flames belching out of it. It was a tense flight back to the Louisville airport, and I must confess that I felt a little more secure knowing that Graham was a passenger with me. After a safe landing, we talked briefly while waiting to be transferred to another aircraft. He told me he was concerned about losing his luggage because it contained a Bible he had used in a Texas crusade where a local man had promised to purchase it for $5,000. He also spoke of how difficult it was to be a celebrity and to be recognized everywhere he went. He was especially interested in my own educational background and said he coveted my introduction to the writings of Brunner and Barth at Yale Divinity School.

It has been impressive to see how Graham has transcended his provincial denominational background to participate in ecumenical Christianity. He has attended meetings of the World Council of Churches and has managed to keep peace with his broad base of fundamentalist supporters despite these associations with the larger Christian community.

Graham plans a major crusade in his home city this year in the new Panther stadium at Charlotte. Already efforts are underway to ensure a good response. Little is left to chance even after the series of services begin. After the sermon when the "altar call" is given, you quickly see hundreds of people coming down the aisles. For a long time many people did not know that most of those were his counselors who had been requested to lead the way in order to be available to the converts who would follow. Graham always makes an effort to refer the names of those who have made "decisions" to local churches for continuing nurture in nearby congregations, though the impact of this effort has seldom been convincingly demonstrated.

One of Mr. Graham's most difficult times was during the Nixon administration. Graham had been a frequent guest at the White House, even holding private services there for his friend. He was embarrassed by all that was later revealed. Unfortunately, he has not learned from the Old Testament that few of the Lord's prophets consorted with kings.

I am glad that Graham is an honest man and has used his money responsibly in an age when we have seen one television evangelist after another convicted of criminal activity.

And I think I am glad that he has been given the Congressional Medal of Freedom. However, I believe if I were he, I would have felt quite uncomfortable standing next to Strom Thurmond and Jesse Helms, who still symbolize for many of us the evils of an age we are trying to overcome.

Certainly nothing I know about the Rev. Seymour qualifies him to take cheap shots at a person of the stature of Billy Graham. Like the Rev. Seymour, I am a contemporary of Billy Graham and I have often thought how much more he has accomplished with fewer educational advantages. I am not a preacher, but if I were, I think I might be downright envious. *J.G., Carrboro, NC*

Bob's comment on the pulpit-ward rush of counselors at the end of a Graham sermon—which tends to create a "herd effect"—reminded me of a story once told me by the late Wallace Caldwell, who taught ancient history at UNC for many years.

Professor Caldwell had been very curious as a young man about what took place at a Billy Graham revival. His chance came when Billy announced a revival for Madison Square Garden. There was a very full and enthusiastic house, but Wallace managed to get a seat and remained to the end. A savvy New Yorker from Brooklyn, he knew that the quickest way to the street was via an emergency exit, so he went to the front of the arena and asked an attendant for its location. He did not think it peculiar that the man asked his name.

Caldwell was astonished to read in *The New York Times* the following morning that among those who had come forward at Madison Square Garden to receive Christ was Wallace Caldwell of Brooklyn, N.Y. *J.B.G., Chapel Hill, NC*

Dear Bob, As a northern Unitarian, I never thought I'd sit at the feet of a Southern Baptist!

With thanks, respect and affection. *P., Chapel Hill, NC*

Dear Mr. Seymour, You have refreshed my life and renewed my confidence with your Sunday column in *The Chapel Hill News.*

Finally somebody did it! That is, someone spoke frankly about Billy Graham's persistent and convenient refusal to face the crushing here-and-now needs of humanity while preaching that the only real item of religious importance in life is personal conversion to Christianity. He has had nearly a free ride while conveniently failing to take any stand upon thornier issues of human responsibility. His emphasis upon "making a decision for Christ" has always taken complete precedence over "deciding for people's needs," if I may use that phrase. *C.H.H., Chapel Hill, NC*

Dear Rev. Seymour: It must have been very hard for a person of your stature and background to write such a column.... I appreciate your having done so!!! *O.S., Chapel Hill, NC*

Dear Dr. Seymour: I am not comfortable with this letter, but I want to inform you that there are educated, intelligent, and progressive folks who are dismayed by your emphatic statements, which present your opinions to be the unmitigated truth. *S., Chapel Hill, NC*

CAMPING OUT IN OUR FAMILY ROOM

February 28, 1996

On the weekend of the big chill, our home was without power from mid-morning Friday until late Monday afternoon. What started out as an inconvenience rapidly developed into an alternate lifestyle.

From the outset, our biggest frustration was in not knowing what we were facing. We had assumed at the beginning that it would only be a matter of hours before the lights would be on again, but the hours gradually extended to days without any assurance of how long it would last. Of course, the first thing we did was to telephone Duke Power, but the line was interminably busy. Fortunately, we had a battery-powered radio, and that briefed us on the seriousness of the situation, so we lighted a fire, and my wife, Pearl, bedded down on the sofa while I stretched out in my Lay-Z-Boy chair, as if ready for an overnight plane flight. Our dog, Therapy, seemed a little confused by the arrangement but quickly adapted to a corner of a comforter, which had sagged from the sofa to the floor. We were braced to withstand the deepening chill that was consuming the house.

One major concern was to protect my many plants, which are housed in winter in an electrically-heated solarium, so this, along with our dog, precluded our seeking refuge in a motel. I tried without success to purchase a kerosene heater by calling around to all the obvious places, but every merchant had already sold out. The only hope of my plants surviving was to crowd them into the family room with us, until it looked like we were camping out in a jungle.

Food did not pose much of a problem. An outside balcony became our refrigerator and deep freeze, and we were close enough to the mall to get to the cafeteria for an occasional hot meal. On the second day, we were happy to discover in our basement an old Coleman stove which we had used years ago when camping with our children, and we were surprised that it had escaped several decades of yard sales. After minor tinkering, it worked perfectly, and we rewarded ourselves the next morning with bacon and eggs for breakfast.

Our ski togs also protected us from shivering. We pulled out the long underwear and kept on our down ski jackets both day and night. But when the temperature threatened to plunge to near zero, we decided we had to have a supplement to the fire. Our son in Cary, who checked on us repeatedly, made a welcome appearance with a large kerosene space heater and a supplementary load of split logs. (When the instructions for using the heater mandated good ventilation, I reached up to turn on the overhead electric fan!) The family room was then quite comfortable, but the rest of the house was an icebox. It was especially difficult to visit a frigid bathroom, and each time I made the trip, I thought of those people who still frequent outdoor privies in all kinds of weather.

We had forgotten that our water is heated with gas, so we were elated to discover that we had plenty of hot water. This made possible a rejuvenating steam bath, as the tub full of torrid water raised the temperature of the small bathroom to bearable exposure.

This whole experience highlighted how totally dependent we are on electricity. I could not use my electric razor. We had to look for a manual can opener. When the outage occurred, partially cooked food was left on the stove, and wet clothes stopped tumbling in the washer. Clocks stopped and pools of water dripped from the icemaker. We were without music and television. Nothing worked, yet, habitually, I found myself flicking switches as if I expected them to be unaffected by the storm. (Pearl, my wife, was grateful for having received a miniature battery-powered television at Christmas, for this enabled her to watch the UNC vs. North Carolina State basketball game.)

We take so much for granted. Imagine living in an earlier generation before electric power became available! Imagine what it would be like to have to set fires every morning and to monitor them throughout the day and night. I thought about Abraham Lincoln reading all of those law books by candlelight, and I marveled at the heroism of those who make treks to the polar regions and manage to survive the bitter cold living in tents. I also remembered a book I had seen at the Intimate Bookstore not long ago which was titled: *The Good Old Days, They Were Terrible.*

During this protracted confinement, it was especially nice to have access to a telephone. It was our main contact with the outside world. Expressions of concern and offers of hospitality were heartwarming. I believe it is true that when such crises descend upon a community they bring out the best in everyone. We realize our need for one another, and the requirements for basic survival help us put our priorities in order.

I thought a lot about people who live on the edge of crisis all the time, those in Orange

County who do not yet have indoor plumbing and those families living in houses that are impossible to heat adequately because of poor construction and negligent maintenance. I thought of those who were more isolated than we were and did not receive the attentiveness of neighbors or family.

When we finally got through to Duke Power, the answer was recorded, but it lifted our hope to hear that the anticipated time of having our power being restored was five o'clock Sunday afternoon. But five o'clock came and went without its restoration, and darkness soon followed. We despaired at the prospect of another night of camping in and making do, especially when a revised telephone recording from the power company informed us that it might be from mid-to-late week before everyone's electricity would be back in service. We were elated when, late Monday afternoon, our lights came on, and we quickly began to get things back in order, moving stacks of blankets and putting the candles away. But our activity was abruptly halted by losing power again, though for only an additional hour. At last, our claustrophobic camping was over.

People who live in parts of the country where such weather is expected every winter are better prepared to face it than most of us are. But just in case it comes again, this arctic blast has taught me to always have on hand plenty of candles, a supply of dry wood, a good flashlight, and a battery-powered radio. These are basic essentials for survival.

We all owe special thanks to the utility specialists who worked around the clock for days on end to get things back to normal. There is one further thing for which I am especially thankful: I do not have to face all those make-up days in school!

DEPRESSION IS COMMON THREAT TO HAPPINESS

January 21, 1996

The recent holiday season was not joyful for everyone. For some people the preparation was so stressful or the nostalgic associations were so painful that they were plunged into depression. It is estimated that depression touches the lives of as many as thirty million Americans every year. Indeed, depression is so prevalent that it is sometimes called "the common cold of psychiatry."

As a pastor, I was very much aware of the prevalence of depression among members of the congregation. For some it was a normal and temporary reaction to some trauma, such as a death in the family, but for others depression was recurring or chronic, creating acute anxiety for those who battled it repeatedly or continuously.

Joe Buckwalter, a retired local surgeon, was one of those for whom depression was so frequent and so totally debilitating that much of his adult life was lived under the threat of suicide. In a remarkably candid book, which he has entitled, *A Soul Lost Is Saved*, Joe tells his story in the hope that his own experience may be of help to others who are suffering from a similar struggle. He feels quite rightly that depression is a disease that needs to "come out of the closet" to remove the traditional stigma of emotional instability or mental illness. He is right.

My father was a victim of depression after my mother's death. He could not transcend his sense of loss. He lost all self-confidence and his ability to function in the most ordinary ways. This eventually led to his being hospitalized and to extended treatment, but he never fully recovered.

Often, however, depression is not nearly so obvious and may even be unrecognized. Two years ago, I began to experience insomnia for no apparent reason. I simply could not go to sleep at night and dreaded going to bed. Finally, I went to a physician, whose first question was quite properly, "Is there anything in your life that has caused you to feel depressed?" I could think of nothing to account for my behavior, and fortunately, after several months of sleeplessness, I was able to sleep again. I still do not know how to account for it.

Depression may afflict people in different ways. For most people it is like a dark cloud enveloping their lives, tempting them to withdraw into themselves. It often carries with it a sense of low self-esteem or sense of failure from lack of confidence in oneself. Symptoms may be insomnia or over-sleeping, or appetite disorders (eating too much or too little). There is generally a feeling of sadness and a loss of interest in life. The mood of the depressed person is not in tune with his or her circumstances, sometimes causing acute anxiety. As one depressed woman said, "I feel that I have run out of gas and that there is no more fuel available anywhere." Some people suffer from what is called a "bipolar" disorder, characterized by abnormally elevated feelings of well-being followed by episodes of depression. These severe mood swings from the heights to the depths seem to recur for no obvious cause.

Older people seem especially vulnerable to depression. My father was a classic illustration. His treatment was almost exclusively electroconvulsive therapy, a procedure that restored him to near normalcy for several months before it needed to be repeated. Recently, at a workshop on depression at the Senior Center, the response was so overwhelming that the room was packed, and people were standing outside unable to enter because of a lack of space.

There are two schools of thought about the origin of depression. In the past, most psychiatrists thought it was a manifestation of some psychological disturbance and that treatment mandated an attempt to understand the root cause. Today, however, there seems to be a growing consensus that much depression can be accounted for by biology, a consequence of some chemical imbalance within the brain, and that normal functioning can be restored by proper medication. A wide range of new drugs have had dramatic results in helping people keep depression at bay, but they do not seem to be equally effective for everyone.

Depression can be devastating not only to the individual who suffers from it but also to family members who live with it and feel so incompetent to deal with it. Buckwalter's book acknowledges what a major factor the support of his family was in sustaining him through these difficult periods. His story also illustrates how lethal depression can become. Indeed, statistics show that between ten and thirty percent of those who suffer chronic depression eventually kill themselves.

It is time we ceased associating depression with weakness or someone's inability to cope. Simply to tell someone, "You've got to get your act together," is of very little help, if any. In fact, such approaches to depression probably succeed in exacerbating the situation further. It is time we recognized depression to be a disease for which no one should be held personally responsible. And like any other disease, we should seek help whenever we suspect that our lives are being compromised by it.

Joe Buckwalter has done us a service by his confessional account of the hell he has been through. Happily, for him the cloud seems to have lifted, and he is enjoying life again. Books like his can help us understand that depression is a potential danger for anyone, and that today, more than ever before, there is the promise of help and hope.

✉

As a psychologist and former senior administrator at the National Institute of Health, I must take exception to one phrase in his otherwise excellent recent column on "depression."

He identifies depression as "the common cold of psychiatry." He should more appropriately called it "the common cold of mental illness." Psychiatry, as he well knows, is not the only profession concerned with mental illness.

✉

Dear Rev. Seymour, I am writing to tell you how touched I was by your article on depression. You described it eloquently and compassionately. Thank you for explaining this disease and taking away some of the myths surrounding it. *S.B.H., Chapel Hill, NC*

OLD SOUTH TRADITION IS THREATENED

August 6, 1995

This is an action alert to all true Southerners. A part of our cherished Dixie tradition is being corrupted by aliens in our midst. Sweetened tea is becoming more difficult to find, and if the present trend continues, it may even become extinct.

Those of us who grew up in this region know that tea by definition is sweet. We never heard of unsweetened tea, and the very thought of it sounds like an abomination.

During my childhood in South Carolina, we always knew that summer had arrived when pitchers of pre-sweetened iced tea were placed on the table. It was a seasonal thing, like going barefoot and finding "courtesy" fans from the local funeral home on all the church pews. Nothing was more refreshing on a hot July day than iced tea—and it was ALWAYS sweet.

Nowadays, more often than not, if you order sweetened tea, the waitress is likely to say, "We have only unsweetened tea, but sweeteners are on the table." Now every true Southerner knows that unless tea is sweetened when it is hot and being brewed, you can never get it right. Sugar will just not dissolve in cold tea, and the so-called sweeteners always leave a slightly bitter edge.

For a while, I tried to adapt to the New South and sweeten my tea at the table, but it's a losing proposition. Just when you begin to get it almost palatable, along comes a waiter who fills your half glass full again, and then your tea is all messed up, not sweet enough. Now when a waitress informs me that only unsweetened tea is available, I reply, "Then just bring me water."

Sometimes my family is embarrassed when I make an issue of this and say to the server, "Isn't this supposed to be the South?" Generally the server agrees with me, like that waitress in Alabama who replied, "Some Yankees bought this place, and they just don't understand how we like it down here."

Maybe it's unfair to blame the change altogether on the newcomers. During World War II, when sugar was scarce, some Southerners did drink it straight rather than have no tea at all, and no doubt some of them learned to like the compromise. And all this concern about calories has probably lured some people away from the real thing, too.

I have observed that sweetened tea is more likely to be found in places where older people eat. I went to the Piccadilly Cafeteria at lunch the other day and noted that about ninety percent of the people eating there were senior citizens. I also observed that there were more glasses of sweetened tea available on the serving line than any other beverage. These were mostly people of my generation, so after we're gone, I suspect that sweet tea will not be in as much demand there.

You also find it in places where indigenous farmers and laborers work. In all those barbecue places "down East," like at King's in Kinston, sweetened tea is readily available.

You would think that in places that like to feature the Southern ambiance you would also find sweet tea, but there is no consistency. A name like Plantation Inn would suggest that serving sweet tea would be as certain as finding cornbread on the menu, but such is not the case. The two-hundred-year-old Colonial Inn in Hillsborough has slipped a little by offering a choice of sweetened or unsweetened. Insofar as I am concerned, the real test of the new Carolina Inn will be whether or not sweet tea is served. I understand that the new Doubletree managers come from the West, so we may not see it there initially. I hope you true Southerners will campaign with me to make sure they comply with our mores. I am happy to report that the new Carolina Club on campus has not capitulated and gets an "A" rating, for pre-sweetened tea is readily available there.

I have noticed, however, that generally in the more elitist and sophisticated restaurants, tea is sometimes served as if it was something from the bar, and it is NEVER sweet. And instead of serving it in a large iced-tea glass, they bring it to you in one of those small goblets, which never holds enough to quench your thirst. Sometimes it even comes with a straw, all of which looks very strange to us natives.

Fast food restaurants are unpredictable, but one reason I prefer Wendy's is that I know I can get sweet tea there. I have discovered, however, that Wendy's does this because of its sensitivity to regional tastes. Elsewhere in the country, only unsweetened tea is offered.

Despite all this pessimism about the threat of losing our Southern tradition of tea being sweet by definition, there are some promising signs on the horizon. One of the new fads on the West Coast (where everything begins) is serving tea-based drinks that are sweetened by fruit juices. We may yet live to see the day when sweet tea is offered as a gourmet taste. It has taken a while for the rest of the nation to discover all that is good about the South. Also, Lipton is marketing cold tea in cans—and IT IS SWEET! Nothing is more refreshing on these sweltering, sizzling days.

Insofar as I am concerned, on a hot day in the South, no lunch or dinner is complete without sweet iced tea. When I was a student in Europe many years ago, I survived an extended summer camping trip in the Middle East. Because of our concern about the safety of the water, we always boiled it first, and since there was no ice, we drank hot tea only. That was very hard for me. I even dreamed about tall frosted glasses of sweet iced tea—with a slice of lemon and a sprig of mint. (In the Old South, everybody had a mint bed.) That's the way we Southerners were brought up, and that's the way I like it.

You know you're in the South when the waitress brings a pitcher of sweet cold tea to your table even before you ask for it. And only in the South is she likely to come back later and inquire, "Honey, is everything all right?"

✉

Sunday, when I was in Chapel Hill, I happened upon your newspaper. Although I thought the paper was well done and entertaining, I was appalled and offended by the "Village Voice" article by Robert Seymour.

Is that man prejudiced against Northerners, or just a nut? How could you let a person write such ridiculous things and put them on the front page of your newspaper? Is he accusing Northerners of threatening the Old South tradition of sweetened ice tea? Is he actually attacking a group of people because of ice tea?

How can you give this man so much space to do this? He is writing pure nonsense, and you, sire, are allowing it to be gospel by giving him a column. The man is either senile, small-minded, or biased against Northerners. Whatever he is, he is not a journalist.

I was in a restaurant in Chapel Hill and ordered iced coffee. The waiter looked at me as if I had two heads. I did not think ill of him, as Mr. Seymour seems to do of all who disagree with his tastes. I simply explained how to make it, and the waiter obliged.

In speaking with the locals, I learned that Mr. Seymour is an ultraliberal who champions the causes of the poor. He sure didn't sound like a liberal in that article, or is he liberal-minded toward all but Northerners? To find out that Mr. Seymour is supposed to be a reverend is even more absurd. He is a hypocrite. If he spouts such intolerance, I feel sorry for his flock.

Get rid of this guy before you lose those many Northerners who support your newspaper. *M.D.*

✉

Great jumpin' catfish!

Isn't it enough that we have to deal with an increasing lack of civility everywhere these days; must we also face the loss of any sense of humor or perception of same?

I refer specifically to the diatribe against Bob Seymour's very funny column on the increasing absence of sweetened ice tea. Surely, it was clear to any thoughtful reader that the column was written with tongue in cheek. I laughed uproariously... the greater problem here is this growing tendency for taking offence where none is intended and for responding with name calling. ("Senility, small-mindedness, bias" yet!) Surely, we can put our energies to better use. *L.B., Chapel Hill, NC*

✉

Dear Ms. MD, Chill out!

Your response to Dr. Seymour's "Sweet Tea" column was overreaction personified, to say the least.

I am originally from the Northeast, and I always pre-sweetened tea when I was preparing it for iced tea. I make pre-sweetened (while it's hot) iced coffee, too.

Since I know the columnist personally, allow me to assure you that the Rev. Seymour is not biased against Northerners, nor is he a nut, and he is certainly not a hypocrite. When you research "locals," perhaps your "test sample" should be larger to allow the information you gather to be more comprehensive and thus, factual.

I will continue to read *The Chapel Hill News,* continue to see the humor in some articles, and continue to learn of the customs of my adopted home.

Perhaps you should, too. *Lee M. Pavao, Chapel Hill, NC*

✉

Dear Bob, Ignore that grinch—your essay was a delight. As a long-displaced Northerner, I loved it. *Ellie Kinnaird, Chapel Hill, NC*

✉

Dear Robert, Rest assured, sweet tea will be a standard offering at the "new" Carolina Inn... *T.M., Chapel Hill, NC*

✉

Dear Bob, While I have always appreciated your taking the tough stance on so many of society's problems, I have particularly enjoyed your articles which deal with a lighter, and often humorous, side of life. With all of the stresses that confront us from so many sides, it is a breath of fresh air to read these articles from one such as you.

Keep on writing and I will keep on reading—just as I always appreciated your word from the pulpit. *B.V.M., Chapel Hill, NC*

✉

Roses to the Carolina Brewery for responding to customer demand, Southern tradition, and divine intervention by adding genuine Southern Sweet Tea to its custom-brewed beverages... *The Chapel Hill News. Chapel Hill, NC*

LICENSE PLATES OFFER CRYPTIC COMMUNICATION

May 3.1995

In American culture we are so attached to our automobiles that we speak of them as if they were an extension of ourselves. Consider how most of us are accustomed to saying such things as, "I'm parked over there." We mean, of course, not that we are "over there," but that our car is.

Another place where we see this relationship is in the increasing use of license plates to communicate with one another, most often revealing something about our identities. The availability of the so called "vanity plates" has spawned a ubiquitous phenomena and called forth astonishing creativity, as people use phonetics and precious few letters to speak to those traveling behind them.

I have been intrigued with this activity ever since it began to appear and often jot down the ones I consider most clever. I have observed that many such plates announce one's vocation, such as the following:

I CURE YA—physician
3RD EAR—psychiatrist
TAX LADY—accountant
I PERFORM—actor
UNC PHD 2B—graduate student
DAD RN—male nurse

Sometimes, business vehicles indicate the nature of their work, such as LIFECARE on an ambulance and STUFF IT on a van advertising taxidermy!

There are some plates designed to speak to the driver behind them in case the person following disapproves of the way they drive. Suppose you had just uttered some expletive about the person at the wheel in the car ahead of you and then read, UR12. Or more polite, WELXQSME. Or the driver up front may wonder about the driver behind and ask, RUASLEEP?

I passed a car the other day with a license plate that read REDLOCKS, and not until I passed did I understand the message. The woman in the driver's seat had bright red hair. And I recall another plate warning any would-be male admirer, 2FOXY4U.

Other messages offer advice to anyone who will take it. Consider these:

EAT OT ML
NVR 2 LTE
WHYBNVUS?
LAUD HIM

The last one would probably not appear on a Virginia plate because of a ruling in that state against any references to deity. Texas also had a problem with a plate that said JEW, but the car owner won his case by proving that it had nothing to do with religion but was his initials, Jesse Eugene Washington!

North Carolina also screens all requests in an attempt to rule out any wording that might be offensive to anyone. The Department of Motor Vehicles will not allow messages with sexual or racial connotations. I was told that inspectors even hold up the messages submitted to a mirror to make sure there isn't something offensive spelled backwards! Once, someone raised a complaint against a driver whose plate said SNOW, accusing him of referring to drugs, but the car owner was from Boone and sent back a photograph of his automobile with a ski rack on top.

I like those plates that reveal a love affair with one's automobile. For example:

EXSTCY!
MOZINON
JUSCRUSIN
CLOUD 9
SUNEDAZE
NONLEMON

Occasionally, I have noted a political message. One driver wants the world to know that he is FARITE, while a Democrat New Dealer tells us WER4TVA. Perhaps a clergyman drives the car that says GODZGUD and a Rabbi the one which offers the blessing MIZPAH. My guess is that the URTHLING is an environmentalist.

Although a car may carry a North Carolina plate, the driver may be dreaming of being somewhere else. Consider MISS DC or O2BINCAL. If you are interested in securing a personalized plate, they are available if you pay an extra twenty dollars. Simply write to The Department of

Motor Vehicles in Raleigh. Connecticut was the first state to offer this option, beginning in 1937!

Before signing off, I cannot resist sharing the clergy joke, which asks, "Do you know what kind of car the disciples rode in to get to the Last Supper?" The Scripture says "They were all N1ACCORD."

MER C BE!

C YAH.

PET THERAPY CAN SAVE YOUR LIFE

March 5, 1995

I have a new dog, and an empty place in my life is beginning to be filled again.

I shall never forget that day, when I was only six years old, when I was given my first puppy. My Uncle George, who lived in the country, arrived in our driveway with a precious little Collie curled up on the back seat of his car. My parents told me later that I went about the house for days afterwards exclaiming, "Uncle George really gave me something!"

Though I have a warm feeling toward all dogs, collies are by far my favorites. I had a succession of them throughout my adult life, until my last one died several years before my retirement. My immediate impulse was to go out and find another one, but my wife restrained me. She argued persuasively that during retirement we would be traveling a lot and that it wouldn't be fair to a dog to be left alone. Subsequently, every time I brought up the subject, Pearl would say, "No, not now," but one day she added, "perhaps when you reach the age of needing pet therapy, we can get another one." That time has come.

In order to overcome the objection about having to leave the dog at home, I decided to consider a miniature breed that is close kin to the collie, one that might make trips with us. This led me to a litter of Shelties, the small Shetland sheep dogs. It was love at first sight—a little tri-colored ball of fur with piercing black eyes and a black tail with a flag of white on the tip that wagged incessantly. I could not resist him, and I decided immediately that his name should be "Therapy."

I cannot think of any other name that would more accurately describe what this little dog is doing for me. I have seldom felt such affirmation. He looks up at me adoringly and follows at my heels wherever I go. Every time I enter the house, he races to me and prances about my feet to tell me again and again how glad he is to see me. He thinks I am really great.

And he is so trusting and forgiving. The other day when that white tip of his tail got caught in the sliding door, he yelped but seemed to understand that this was an unintentional accident. When I cradled him in my arms, his tail quickly resumed its normal wagging velocity.

As I look back over my life, I realize that I owe a lot to my dogs. They really have been like close friends and family. That first one that entered my life, when I was a child, bore the obvious name "Lassie." I remember her going with me on a fifteen-mile hike to fulfill a requirement for a Boy Scout merit badge, but on the way home, Lassie collapsed and could not go any further. She was an old dog then, and I had to call home for my parents to come to her rescue. Until she died, she apologized for letting me down that day.

I named Lassie's successor "Pastor." I decided that everyone in the congregation had a pastor but me, and I discovered that dogs are empathizing counselors and are able to respect confidentiality. Our late-night walks together diminished the stress of many hectic days. The only time the name seemed awkward was when Pearl went out on the porch to call the dog home.

Then came my first black collie, and his name could be spelled two ways, either Knight or Night. My daughter came up with the name for our next one. The dog was a beautiful bronze creature who was christened "Melon." Thus, she was a melon collie, or you could spell it "melancholy"!

Having a new puppy in the house is like having a new baby. We had expected some crying at night, but happily that has not yet occurred. When the sun comes up, we do begin to hear a whimper, letting us know it's time to arise. Like a baby, he loves his simple toys, such as tennis balls and empty cans. He chews on everything, and his curiosity is boundless. And, of course, there is the matter of toilet training, and we are still cleaning up after accidents. Like a baby, puppies can disturb one's domestic tranquility, but they are worth it all.

A puppy helps you see the world afresh. He sniffs at every leaf and stone, marveling at them. When we walked around a nearby fishpond, it was a delight to see him gingerly put his paw in the water. You and I usually get so accustomed to the awesomeness of God's creation that we fail to see the miracle of it all. My puppy is teaching me to take another look, and I feel renewed gratitude and appreciation for the magnificent natural world around us.

We agonized over whether to install an electric fence to keep Therapy in the yard or whether to build a traditional fence encompassing our backyard patio. When I was told I would have to subject the dog to ten days of "training" to learn the SHOCKING parameters of the electric fence, I decided I could not do that to my little friend. So a picket fence confines him to a smaller space, but he seems content with his playground.

It was also painful to leave him at home for five days while we made a trip West. I spent a whole day checking out kennels in the area, and, believe me, I saw some terrible places where no pets should be left. Several kennels offered only small indoor cages like miniature prisons, and at one the stench was so bad I could not even enter the place where the animals were housed! I finally settled on Shady Grove Kennels, just off Highway 70 near the airport. It is a clean, spacious place, and the management is clearly dog-loving. Therapy said it seemed like being away at camp!

Now that Therapy is an integral part of my life, I feel very much needed as I perform the responsibilities required for his day-to-day care. He also ensures my taking a walk each day. And he offers an infinite outpouring of affection. I am quite confident that Therapy will not only add life to my remaining years but will also extend my life! To those of you who are aging, I heartily recommend pet therapy.

✉

Dear Doctor Seymour: Seven mornings a week, my close friend and I enjoy the nature trails at our Botanical Garden. We often meet other dog walkers, and this past Monday, you were the topic of our conversations. We empathized with your search for a respectable kennel (dreadful) and agreed the "invisible fence" was a no-no. *M.M., Chapel Hill, NC*

✉

I thank Thee
For Thy creatures, Lord!
This dog
That trots joyfully beside me,
Behind me,
Ahead of me;
Inherent in her
Is the devotion of her kind
That through the ages
Has served man,
And adored him.
Now my dog stops
And with loving eyes
Looks up at me;
Her master.
Would that I,
Could as selflessly adore
My Master!
FROM: "AND HE WALKS WITH ME..."
BY ROBERT J. CHURCH
Sent by *J. & J., Chapel Hill, NC*

✉

Dear Bob, I loved your column on your collies. I too have a collie, Bonnie, who is a most sensitive, loving, gentle... even elegant companion. *E.M.B., Chapel Hill, NC*

POSTAL SERVICE PUTS STAMP ON HOLIDAY HISTORY

January 1, 1995

For a while, it looked as if this past Christmas would be the last time we would see the familiar Madonna-and-Child design or the word "Christmas" on any seasonal stamps. In an attempt to avoid the appearance of favoring any particular religion, the decision was made to delete any reference to religion altogether.

Ironically, whenever such a change is made in deference to the principle of separation of church and state, the end result is often to succumb to secularism and to deny the place of religion in American culture and history. I concur that the government must not promote any religion, but in this case, it would seem far better to exercise fairness not by ignoring religion but by celebrating our diversity and issuing stamps acknowledging not only the Christians in our midst, but also the Jews, Muslims, Buddhists, and other great world religions practiced in our country. (Significantly, we now issue an annual stamp marking the beginning of the Chinese New Year; this year, it's the Year of the Pig.) If the revised guidelines had held, future stamps at Christmas would simply say, "Happy Holidays," or "Season's Greetings," but never, "Merry Christmas."

But as you may know, the decision was reversed by the intervention of President Clinton, and next year, the Virgin-and-Child series, which began in 1966, will continue. (Did you notice that this year's artist for the first time is a woman? She is Elisabeth Sirani, whose work is dated 1663!)

Another controversy erupted over the plan to issue a commemorative stamp in April honoring President Richard Nixon. The Postal Service was deluged with letters of protest from people who felt it was inappropriate to feature a leader whose misconduct had forced him to resign from office. Even so, the stamp will appear as scheduled to perpetuate a long-standing tradition that places every American president on a postage stamp. I believe this was the right decision, for despite his tragic flaws in character, there are positive things in the Nixon legacy.

A third controversy centered on the announcement that a stamp slated to be issued in August would commemorate the 50th anniversary of our dropping the atomic bomb on Japan to "hasten war's end." Understandably, the Japanese felt that to place on U.S. letters a picture of the mushroom cloud that destroyed Hiroshima and Nagasaki was insensitive to the suffering and death of the hundreds of thousands of people in their nation—including countless children and women. The Japanese Embassy exerted great pressure to have the stamp removed from the 1995 schedule, and happily, our government agreed.

We can gain some understanding of the Japanese request through events related to our Navy's tragic downing of an Iranian passenger plane several years ago, which killed about three hundred passengers aboard. The Iranian government issued a stamp commemorating this event, showing a rocket being fired from an American Navy ship and the plane plunging to the earth in flames. Our government tried to prevent this stamp from becoming available to American stamp collectors, but it can be found here.

An extended controversy in the Postal Service occurred last year over a stamp that received more attention than any other. It was the "Legends of the West" sheet that depicted our most famous heroes of the American frontier. The controversy centered on the discovery that the photograph of the black rodeo cowboy, Bill Picket, was not in fact Bill Picket but a relative! Upon the discovery of the error, the Postal Service made a frantic attempt to recall all of the sheets about to be put on sale all across the country.

Unfortunately, some post offices had "jumped the gun" and sold the stamps prematurely, thus putting some erroneous ones in circulation and thereby making them exceedingly valuable. Subsequently, there has been a flurry of lawsuits and courtroom decisions, finally climaxed by an unprecedented lottery-type sale through which 150,000 panes containing the so-called "wrong Picket" stamp were to be sold to collectors.

By now you have probably guessed that I am a philatelist. Yes, I have been collecting stamps since I was a young boy. Most of my stamps are used ones, from all over the world, and they are not very valuable, but they have afforded for me much pleasure and provided a source of information I could not have had access to in any other way. Much of it would serve me well for a lively game of "Trivia." For example, my collection includes stamps from the Falklands, East Timor, and Kuwait, and so, when the attention of our nation was focused on these far away places, I knew exactly where they were and quite a bit about them.

A gift of a stamp album to a young person might ignite an interest in a valuable educational tool. Unfortunately, however, if you wish to collect mint stamps (unused ones) rather than used ones, the hobby can become rather expensive. A cost of a complete collection of all the issues projected by the U.S. Postal Service for 1995 will total nearly seventy dollars. Not surprisingly, stamp collection is being pushed for precisely this reason. Post offices around the world are issuing many, many stamps that will never be seen on a letter because they know collectors will purchase them anyway. It is a major source of revenue for some Third World countries.

Even though you may not be a collector, it would be worth your while to visit the new Philatelic Museum in Washington, D.C., the next time you are in the District. It is located in the old post office building next door to Union Station. They have a marvelous display of the history of postal service in America, and you can see all of the artifacts ever offered by this arm of our government. The museum is one of the newest in the Smithsonian group.

Now that 1995 is upon us, the bad news is that the cost of a first-class stamp will increase to thirty-two cents. The good news is that this is still lower than in nearly every other Western country. Although our Postal Service is often the target of jokes and receives constant complaints, it is perhaps the best in the world. I think we should all be grateful for the incredible task they have just accomplished in delivering literally billions of Christmas cards to every remote corner of our nation.

Dear Dr. Seymour, I read the article in *The Chapel Hill News* about your interest in stamps. Enclosed are stamps that may be of interest to some youngster who is starting a collection. *R.E.T., Chapel Hill, NC*

GOVERNMENT

DECLARATION OF DEPENDENCE

July 7, 2002

The proximity of the birth of the International Criminal Court on the first day of July to our celebration of the Fourth of July suggests that the time has come for our nation to move beyond celebrating our independence to acknowledging our need for inter-dependence with other countries. We have reached a stage in our national life when independence may be a liability.

Indeed, our independent spirit is looking more and more like isolationism. Far too frequently, we have forfeited our opportunity to be a world leader and have said instead, "Count us out." We have been consistent in our refusal to ratify treaty after treaty. We refused to sign the Kyoto Treaty on global warming. We nullified the Anti-Ballistic Missile Treaty. We have not yet signed the Comprehensive Nuclear Test Ban Treaty, the Biological and Chemical Weapons Treaty, the Land Mine Treaty, or the Small Arms Treaty. We even rejected the Convention on the Rights of the Child.

In addition, we are doing everything possible to undermine the newly created International Criminal Court. Bill Clinton signed it, but a month ago our president instructed that his predecessor's name be erased. We insist that we will participate only on the condition that no American will ever be brought before the court for trial. Since the new court may now claim jurisdiction over us despite our objections, we are making other threats. We have threatened to withdraw our peacekeeping troops from Bosnia and to withhold our twenty-seven percent of the budget that supports peacekeeping in general.

National Public Radio described our withdrawal from the court as "...like all your neighbors fighting a horrible fire; but the richest neighbor not only stays home, but also turns off his spigot so that others can't use his water."

Congressman Tom DeLay asked the Appropriations Committee to recommend that our military be given permission to invade the Netherlands to rescue any American who might be brought to trial at The Hague where the new court is located!

Is it any wonder that much of the world thinks we are arrogant? We always want to be the exception. There can be standards imposed on other nations, but not on us. Our friends in the European Union are baffled by our behavior and consider our position both appalling and ludicrous.

It is especially ironic that we have taken this position at a time when we are trying desperately to capture, and bring to justice, Osama Ben Laden and demand that the rest of the world help us. In the war against terrorism we have warned, "If you are not for us, you are against us." You would think we would welcome a court designed to try international criminals. This would seem a strong indication of worldwide support in favor of bringing international terrorists to justice. Our refusal to endorse the court casts serious doubt on the validity of our commitment to justice.

It is further ironic that, at a time when globalization often runs roughshod over the sovereignty of nations, we would be against establishing international jurisdiction.

There is a lesson to be learned from our own history. Not long after the original thirteen colonies declared their independence from England, they began to realize that they needed a much closer working relationship with each other than the Articles of Confederation provided. They concluded that they needed a strong central government "to provide a more perfect union." Today, history has brought us into a new era when fifty United States should see their need for "a more perfect union" among the nations.

Unfortunately, we do not have a commendable record in this regard. We have been a reluctant participant in the United Nations, at best. When things have not gone our way, we have repeatedly threatened "to take our marbles and go home." For several years, we even refused to pay our fair share of the UN budget. This became acutely embarrassing when other countries called us "a deadbeat nation."

As the world's only superpower, it is a pity that we seem to exercise leadership primarily in military engagements. The International Criminal Court is on the right side of history. We are not. Patriotic Americans who have pushed for more responsible participation on our part can take some comfort in the words of Woodrow Wilson, who said after we refused to join the League of Nations, "I would rather lose in a cause that will some day win, than win in a cause that will some day lose."

Dear RS: Thank you for your article in *The Chapel Hill News* on July 7. It expresses exquisitely the dilemma that many, very likely most, of us feel about the present administration's deplorable policies in the international arena. It is perplexing. I find myself getting angry about these matters, which is quite useless I suppose; perhaps you do, too. But you have an outlet, which is to craft words that may have considerable effect. You are a good wordsmith. Keep it up, for the impact will be considerable and accumulative.

I wonder if there be effective ways in which to work toward the dethronement of the current holder of the office of president. Seldom have we had such a clumsy leader.
B.C., Chapel Hill, NC

PATRIOTISM BECOMING TOO CHAUVINISTIC

April 3, 2002

I consider myself patriotic. I love this country and believe our democratic ideals hold the best hope for the future of our world. However, I am having difficulty standing united with the increasingly chauvinistic rhetoric we are hearing from Washington. I am alarmed by the strident threats of belligerent nationalism and suspect they are intended to put our nation on a war footing for an indefinite future.

The first sign of this was when Bush used that unfortunate phrase, "axis of evil," in his State of the Union Address. I found it offensive, not only because it was a blanket indictment of the people of Iran, Iraq, and North Korea, but because it seemed to imply that we are always on the side of the angels. Predictably, the response has heightened hostility. Even the moderates in Iran took to the streets and shouted "Death to America." Our European allies were dismayed, and South Koreans felt that their efforts to restore ties with the North had suffered a severe setback. Jimmy Carter was right when he said, "I think it will take years before we can repair the damage done by that statement."

I believe in diplomacy, not confrontation. Such irresponsible name-calling serves only to increase the level of fear and undermines any ongoing efforts to improve relationships. It was not surprising that the nations labeled "evil" responded by calling the United States "the great Satan." No country is all bad or all good. There are always shades of gray. Mark Twain spoke the truth when he said, "Human nature is pretty well distributed among human beings." (The speechwriter who created the "axis of evil" phrase for the president has resigned!)

A second jarring word from Washington was the release of a report from the Pentagon that described situations where it would be permissible to use nuclear bombs. This represents a major shift in strategy. Previously, our position has been to contain and eliminate weapons of mass destruction, but now we are blurring the line between conventional weapons and nuclear ones. The report mentioned by name not only the so-called "rogue" states against whom such weapons might be used, but also suggested potential future use against our current allies, Russia and China. It is a chilling prospect—so much so that *The New York Times* referred to the U.S. in a headline as "America as Nuclear Rogue." We have begun to think the unthinkable, even contemplating pre-emptive nuclear strikes! Instead of discouraging a nuclear arms race, we may now be making every nation feel that a nuclear arsenal is essential.

Of course, we have the world's largest such arsenal, and we should not forget that we have twice used nuclear bombs to destroy civilian-filled cities. Also, we have just learned from the release of the Nixon tapes that he tried to persuade Kissinger to drop a nuclear bomb on Vietnam. Is it any wonder that the world fears what we might do? We are so convinced of our own good intentions that it is hard for us to understand that some countries consider us more dangerous than the nations we condemn.

A further disturbing announcement from Washington was the plan to establish an Office of Strategic Influence (OSI). The purpose of this new agency was to confuse our enemies by deliberately disseminating disinformation. Obviously, this is a euphemism for official lying. Fortunately, this "brilliant" idea has already been vetoed, but it is worrisome that our leadership would even consider such a course of action. (Could the first lie be to deny such an office exists?)

If our allies were aware of our lying to some countries, why would they not think we were also lying to them? Trust is hard to establish, and once you lose credibility, it is almost impossible to restore it. Ironically, many people in the Arab world already refuse to believe the truth, as indicated by the discovery that the majority still does not think militant Muslims destroyed the World Trade Center. More disturbing, however, are the polls that indicate only half of the American people trust our own government.

I am greatly alarmed by what appears to be escalating chauvinism. I am sure all such belligerent expressions of nationalism are meant to strike fear in the hearts of those we call enemies. As a patriotic American, they strike fear in my heart, too.

Dear Bob: ...You far left-wing extremists always want to turn the other cheek.... I think you should rethink your views and not be so judgmental about a President who wants to protect you and your family. You really kill me.

I suggest we rename Franklin Street: "Seymourville" in remembrance of those who started the homeless shelter in downtown with the idea it would help them. Far from it.

...when someone is killed by these people, you will be marching trying to keep him out of the electric chair, which, by the way, is a penalty, not a deterrent.

The next time *The Chapel Hill News* has your article on the front page, I plan to throw it away—thank God it's free.

By the way, you can quote me. *B.P., Chapel Hill, NC*

Dear Bob: Thank you for expressing so clearly concerns we have long had but have been unable to articulate so clearly. Like you, we consider ourselves strongly patriotic, but we have never been able to buy into the doctrine of Presidential Infallibility. *W.L., Chapel Hill, NC*

Right on, Bob. You say this stuff so much better than I do, and I only hope there will be more and more people who start to think more logically and ethically about this dangerous militarism.

Keep those perspicacious columns coming. *N.C.J., Chapel Hill, NC*

"IT COULDN'T HAPPEN HERE!"

January 20, 2002

We Americans are so confident of our freedoms that it is difficult to consider the possibility of ever losing them. When we observe the rise of totalitarian states elsewhere in the world, we are likely to say, "It couldn't happen here."

The people of Germany felt that way. The majority stood by silently as they watched their neighbors detained and imprisoned by the state. The erosion of civil rights continued until eventually everyone was under the control of a dictatorial government.

Germans look back now and wonder how they ever allowed it.

A temptation in a time of national emergency is for citizens to permit a curtailing of normal civil rights in order to increase security. It is a dangerous concession, for what is considered temporary might possibly become permanent. Fortunately, many people in our country are sensitive to this danger, and their protests have already prompted President Bush to consider changing provisions previously granted in the anti-terrorist legislation. For example, word has been leaked from the White House that discussion is underway to require a unanimous jury decision in military tribunals, instead of a simple majority, before condemning someone to death.

We know the phrase, "The price of liberty is eternal vigilance." In a troubled time, we cannot afford to look the other way while denying our own citizens or people from other countries their civil rights. Indeed, it is ironic that while we talk about wanting to spread democracy to people everywhere, we would stoop to military tribunals for non-citizens. But polls show that the majority of Americans sees no problem with the claim that non-citizens do not deserve the same rights that we have. This implies acceptance of inadequate defense of and unfairness to accused immigrants and foreigners.

If a citizen of this country were captured and tried in such a court elsewhere, we would be quick to complain that the procedure is unjust. We even refer to such tribunals as "kangaroo courts." If we approve of such trials, we give encouragement and comfort to those countries where such streamlined versions of "justice" are commonplace.

The anti-terrorist legislation should ring alarm bells for all of us. People are being detained without warrants, denied habeas corpus, and their names are not released to the public. The FBI now has permission to listen to telephone conversations of any suspect, as if people are guilty until proven innocent. Even the privileged exchange of confidential information between an attorney and a client can be breached, thereby opening the way for legal counsel to spy for the government!

Most disturbing, however, is the attitude of Attorney General Ashcroft toward all of this. He warned: "... to those who scare peace-loving people with phantoms of lost liberty, my message is this, your tactics only aid terrorists." Thus, he has attempted to silence any criticism and to label anyone who protests the loss of freedom as being unpatriotic! This is an especially troubling attitude for one whose primary task is a sworn willingness to protect the Constitution. Surely, America will be stronger in the long run if we respect and protect dissent and hold sacred the freedom of speech.

We dare not forget that it has happened here. During World War II, we rounded up thousands of citizens of Japanese descent in the name of national security. We evicted them from their homes without compensation and held them in prison camps, even though not one of them was ever proven guilty of anything!

I was in Washington, D.C., at Christmas and visited the new national memorial that commemorates this tragic episode in our history. It is located near Union Station. As you enter the monument, you are faced with the following stone inscription: "THE LESSONS LEARNED MUST REMAIN AS A GRAVE REMINDER OF WHAT WE MUST NOT ALLOW TO HAPPEN AGAIN TO ANY GROUP."

Yet, some Americans are now ready to support even more stringent anti-terrorist legislation, such as permission to torture suspects in an attempt to force prisoners to talk. These Americans reason that in bad circumstances it's all right to use questionable means to acquire the information necessary for military intelligence. Others are calling for Congress to approve the issuing of national identity cards, which every citizen would be required to keep on his or her person at all times. This is typically required in all totalitarian countries. All such proposals are contrary to the freedom and privacy Americans cherish, and should be resisted. If our government is allowed to use "any means necessary" to make us feel safe, no one will be safe. Benjamin Franklin once said, "They that give up essential liberty to obtain a little temporary safety deserve neither liberty nor safety."

Ironically, the most vocal leadership in this resistance is often regarded as a far-out left-wing organization, The American Civil Liberties Union.

In actuality, the ACLU is one of the most conservative organizations in our nation! Its sole purpose is to protect the Constitution and to defend *any* citizens who are wrongfully deprived of their civil rights as guaranteed in the Bill of Rights. How could anyone object to this? I am grateful for the vigilance of the ACLU and proud to be a "card-carrying member."

✉

Read your commentary recently; you make a real good argument against hysteria-driven jingoism. It was cogent, just like your sermons. Good job.

(By the way, I've "backslided" back into Methodism.) *T.M., Durham. NC*

FEDERAL FUNDS FOR FAITH-BASED CHARITIES?

February 21, 2001

After President Bush announced his proposal for government funding of faith-based charities, many people were surprised to discover that the idea is not new. In fact, faith-based charities have been receiving federal money for a long time. Among the recipients are Catholic Charities, Lutheran Social Services, and The Salvation Army. Franklin Graham, son of Billy Graham, has just acknowledged that his relief organization, "Samaritan's Purse," is also partially supported by government grants. Graham's organization distributes Bibles along with food, and The Salvation Army "invites" residential clients to attend chapel services.

Also, the welfare reform bill signed by President Clinton in 1996 incorporates a provision for the Department of Health and Human Services to link up with faith congregations. In Orange County, the Social Services Department has a part-time employee whose task is to recruit churches to sponsor families for support and encouragement as they make the transition from welfare rolls to independent living.

As a Baptist, I belong to a denomination that has been vigilant in maintaining separation of church and state. Historically, it was the Baptist voice, more than any other, which insisted that America not have an established church. Today most Americans value the First Amendment and agree that the government should not be partial toward any religious group, offering neither help nor hindrance to their mission.

This has been easier said than done. For example, during World War II, the federal government came to the rescue of many small, church-related, liberal arts colleges by placing military units on their campuses for training. I benefited from this by being a V-12 student on a Lutheran campus for two years, wearing a Navy uniform, with all expenses paid to the school by Uncle Sam. This type of relationship was judged legitimate by contracts with the institutions for "services rendered." Without such government assistance, these colleges may not have survived.

The current proposal by the Bush administration apparently intends to extend such financial support broadly, including making money available for charitable work by local congregations. I hope this does not mean that the federal government will scale back its own programs in the misconception that it will ever be possible for faith-based institutions to do what the government is mandated to do. I am also anxious about the even-handedness of fund distribution. The two exclusionary Christian prayers at the Bush inaugural make me wonder if the administration will be sensitive to the other major religions (and minor ones) represented in American life. Many citizens persist in the misunderstanding that ours is a Christian country, whereas, in reality, we are a multi-religious nation with a government that cannot constitutionally favor one expression of religious faith.

My greatest fears, however, are about the effect of federal money on the faith communities. Would the availability of government funds compromise the generosity of people to give? Would pastors and rabbis tend to muffle their prophetic voice lest they jeopardize receiving grants? Would congregations be able to administer the money without proselytizing? Would the submission to government regulations about the use and accounting of the money be a step toward increased government oversight of worshipping congregations?

Finally, there is the fundamental question about any attempt to sever social outreach from the motivational roots of religious belief. In some instances, any such attempt would jeopardize the past effectiveness of the programs. For example, the much-praised success of prison ministry depends upon its redemptive approach to inmates and their personal commitment to God. This is not peripheral to the program; it is basic. Without its evangelical message, it would no doubt fail. Authentic religion can never be severed from worship.

I have serious reservations about faith-based charities because I treasure the First Amendment and am committed to preserving the principle of separation of church and state. Having said this, however, I conclude with a commendation of broad partnerships that I believe can be forged without some of the risks mentioned above.

I submit as a primary illustration the Interfaith Council for Social Service in Chapel Hill. It is the number-one social service agency in our community for the homeless and for individuals and families in crisis. The IFC is broad based. It is ecumenical, receiving assistance from multiple faith congregations and religions. It also receives funds from municipal, county, and state governments, as well as from the federal government. There is never an attempt to propagate religious faith, yet the agency is dependent upon a huge corps of volunteers whose response to human need is motivated by their personal religion.

The largest federal grant to the council came for construction and management of Project Homestart, a facility providing transitional housing for fifteen homeless families. The Department of Housing and Urban Development (HUD) has also linked up with the IFC for the construction of low-income housing: Elliott Woods, Chase Park, and the Adelaide Walters Apartments in Chapel Hill. In addition, the United Church partnered with the government for the construction of Shepherd House and Covenant House. And currently, the First Baptist Church is a recipient of federal funding to build The Manley Estates for low-income elderly.

All this compels me to conclude that there are ways for faith-based groups to join with the government in meeting human needs. However, with the projected expansion of this principle, a renewed vigilance will be required to protect First Amendment rights and to make sure that our basic institutions do not compromise one another.

Dear Rev. Seymour, For awhile, now, I have felt like a voice crying out in the wilderness trying to warn my Christian friends that they really don't want the close government association they scream for.

I agree with you that America is not a Christian nation, but a polyglot of many disparate points of view regarding religion and just about every other aspect of our lives. The sooner we get to understand and accept that notion, the better we all will become.

I would think that other ministers, like yourself, would be equally alarmed at the prospect of government preferential treatment of a particular religion to the detriment of others. To me, that speaks of a government-sponsored religion. Isn't that what our founders were guarding against? *C.W., Chapel Hill, NC*

Dear Bob, I did not realize that the IFC received government funding. Of course, the IFC is not a religious organization but a service organization. As you say, there is never an attempt to propagate religious faith. I don't think government is precluded from supporting an organization because it is also supported by religious organizations or because it uses volunteers "whose response to human need is motivated by their personal religion." I imagine that is true of everybody, for good or ill. A closer question is that the churches themselves organize the volunteers and, I think, have representatives on the Board of IFC and thus really control IFC. Very complex issue. *B.N., Chapel Hill, NC*

Dear Bob, I really liked your piece on faith-based funding. I have been feeling equivocal about this subject, and you covered the pros and cons well—and mentioned some things I hadn't thought about (or known!) Keep up the good work. *J.B., Chapel Hill, NC*

A CHALLENGE TO THE FIRST AMENDMENT

September 9, 2001

The bill signed by Governor Easley to post the Ten Commandments in public schools exposes school districts across our state to inevitable litigation if they comply.

This is not a new idea. A major attempt to display the Commandments on government buildings began with the production of Cecil B. DeMille's biblical extravaganza, *The Ten Commandments.*

(I feel a personal connection with this film because I was invited to audition for a part in the crowd scenes. I was traveling in the Middle East with three seminary friends in 1956, and we visited Egypt where the filming was in progress. All of us had grown handsome beards during our camping adventure and were approached by a member of the casting staff who said they were looking for English speaking people with beards. But we turned down the opportunity to acclaim Charlton Heston as Moses and headed home instead.)

To promote the film, DeMille entered into a partnership with a Minnesota juvenile-court judge who felt that public displays of the Decalogue would influence the morality of young people, and this led to the judge donating more than two thousand Ten Commandment monuments to communities all over America! DeMille exploited this situation to give maximum publicity for the movie. Many of the dedications were timed to tie in with the release of the film, and Heston was sometimes present as a celebrity guest.

In recent years, these monuments have sparked controversy as a breach of church/state separation. Critics charge that the monuments officially favor one faith tradition over all others. Even so, the crusade to post the Commandments continues with renewed fervor by those who remain undaunted by a string of legal defeats. The current campaign is sometimes called "Hang Ten."

In our own state and elsewhere, legislators hope that litigation can be avoided if the Commandments are regarded as an historical document rather than as a religious document. But the purpose cannot be disguised; they are plainly religious. Indeed, the first four commandments describe the duties of believers to worship the Lord God alone, to avoid idolatry, to not use the Lord's name in vain, and to keep the Sabbath day holy!

The First Amendment to the Constitution makes it clear that our government should do nothing to either help or hinder religion. Despite repeated claims that America is a Christian country, we have no established religion. The state should relate to all religions represented in our citizenry with even-handedness, neither promoting nor preventing any faith expression. We define who we are as a nation not by any particular religious heritage but by the founding principles upon which America was constituted.

Now we can boast of having become the most religiously diverse nation in the world. The recent census reveals that there are more Muslims in the United States than Presbyterians! We should be committed to freedom of conscience for everyone and to the right of persons of any religious persuasion to feel included in our public life without discrimination or condescension.

As a Baptist minister, I believe strongly in the separation of church and state. By passing this new law that exalts one religious tradition above all others, we risk making the wall of separation a war zone. If the Commandments are posted in public schools, there will surely follow litigation to have them removed, as indeed they should be.

We are a country that welcomes pluralism, which we acknowledge in the E Pluribus Unum inscribed on our currency. Pluralism does not push for conformity of convictions but respects differences and believes it possible to express such differences in a common civility that embraces all citizens.

There is irony in the fact that legislators would expose their disobedience to the "Thou shalt not kill" commandment by voting against a moratorium on the death penalty. Obviously, a far better place to enshrine the Commandments would be in the hearts and minds of elected leaders than on tablets of stone.

Perhaps an eleventh commandment should be added: "THOU SHALT NOT USE THE LORD THY GOD AS A POLITICAL FOOTBALL!"

✉

It was a sad day when the legislature passed that bill. But, it was even sadder when the governor "couldn't wait to sign it." The real irony is that that bill was the only way he could get his character-education piece through. He didn't really show much character himself. *P.W., Raleigh, NC*

✉

Dr. Seymour: The reference to the death penalty in conjunction with the Ten Commandments is most appropriate, particularly since Mr. Easley, in his recent refusal to commute a death sentence even while recognizing that the attorney was drunk, seems to equate the governorship with playing our Heavenly Father. *J.A.D., Chapel Hill, NC*

DEMOCRACY OR "CORPORACRACY"?

August 27, 2000

I like to think that I live in a democracy, but I am beginning to wonder if this is the case. In a democracy, every vote counts and all citizens have a voice in their government. In America we are losing this. The power of big money is undermining our political system. At both the Republican and Democratic conventions, the real business took place behind the scenes, as large corporations made their influence felt upon our legislators, seeking privileged access. Maybe we should coin a new word and call our government a "corporacracy."

This election, more than ever, seems to be about money. The cost of running for office has become so great that it is impossible to mount a race without big bucks.

There has been a frenzy of fund raising, though, ironically, in Los Angeles the Democrats referred to such efforts as "donor-servicing events." At the Republican convention, one out of every five delegates was a millionaire. It is especially disturbing to learn that the major source of money for both parties comes from about one percent of the American people! The power of money from a few is especially apparent in the film industry. Movie moguls respond to an occasional gentle reprimand by Congress with a steady stream of violence and vulgarity, brazenly polluting family values. Financial largess insures protection.

Such observations make me feel that my vote has been devalued. It is abundantly clear that power of money is stronger than the power of the ballot box. Else, how can we account for the fact that although polls show that the majority of Americans want meaningful gun control and a patient's bill of rights with teeth in it, none has been forthcoming? The National Rifle Association and health maintenance organizations seem to have more clout than all our voices together.

Yes, money does talk. It is naïve to believe that members of Congress can benefit from huge sums of money without it making a difference in the way they vote. Each year at this season, like many of you, I am solicited for political contributions, but I am very doubtful that any dollars I send to Washington will guarantee to me the kind of attention given to the "Big-Money Boys." My small gift will talk with a whisper, while that of corporations will be more like a blast. In effect, we have lost free speech.

The system is corrupt, and it is undermining our government. Those who run roughshod over us with the power of their money are compromising our freedom. The good of the nation is often sacrificed in favor of legislation that promises the privileged more and more money, distancing them further and further from the poor. In this time of unprecedented prosperity, it is a scandal that we will not raise the minimum wage and that those who teach in our schools and care for the very young and the very old receive such small compensation. How can a country with so much wealth tolerate a fifth of its children living in poverty and forty million of its people with no health insurance? The CEOs of some of America's large corporations make more in one week than many of their fellow citizens make in a lifetime.

If we are really serious about restoring decency, respect, and integrity to government, we must be concerned about more than the personal behavior of those we elect. We must eliminate the undue influence of big money in the political sweepstakes. It is sad that so many of our young people have become so cynical about the possibility of political careers. They understand how difficult it is to be an honest politician in a dishonest system. It may be too strong to charge that we have a government based on bribery, but we seem to be moving steadily toward it. We also are moving toward a government that will be less and less attentive to how we vote at the polls. Those who give the money will strong-arm the big decisions.

I was delighted by Colin Powell's courage in his address to the Republican convention when he pointed out the inconsistency of being against affirmative action for the minority poor while allowing blatant affirmative action via money to favor the rich. But I was greatly disappointed in John McCain's failure to even mention campaign-finance reform. After getting a rousing response from coast to coast about ridding our political system of the abuses of soft money, he said not one word about it at the convention!

Of course it is fallacious to suggest that campaign-finance reform is a partisan issue. It is not. Each party persists in pointing fingers at the irregularities in fund raising of the other, but clearly, both are guilty. It has become an addiction for Democrats and Republicans alike.

Nor should we be surprised by the inconsistency of eliminating welfare for the poor while continuing to grant generous corporate welfare for the rich. The never-ending clamor for a tax cut for everyone is deceiving. Look at the fine print, and in nearly every instance, the wealthy benefit disproportionately to everyone else. This is currently the case with the so-called "marriage-penalty tax" and the estate-tax bills. We have lost a sense of fairness.

The power of corporate money further accounts for much of the skepticism about the emerging global economy. Those who protest are understandably suspicious, fearing that globalism invites corporations to exploit both the environment and the poor elsewhere. We seem more committed to exporting capitalism than to exporting democracy. There is validity in the accusation that the business of U.S. foreign policy is business. A founding document of our country states that "just powers" will be granted "from the consent of the governed." Somehow we must return our government to the people so all can have a voice in our shared future. We have drifted a long way from that ideal.

TAX CUTS THREATEN HUMAN SERVICES

February 11, 2000

In the past several decades, we have witnessed continuing attempts to reduce human services to our nation's most needy citizens. In both Republican and Democratic administrations, there has been the assumption that the government should do less and the private sector do more.

As the new election cycle heats up, we are hearing the same monotonous message on both sides of the aisle. It takes the form of a perpetual mantra: "Cut taxes! Cut taxes! Cut taxes!" The most persistent advocates for scaling back funding for human services have been Republicans, but the Democrats are so intimidated by the tax-cut lure that they, too, are sounding the same refrain. Even the president's new federal budget offers cuts in health and human services, education, and housing. But of course those who push for considerably larger slashes will resist Clinton's modest reductions.

Clearly, the issue is a political ploy that both parties feel forced to play. But, sadly, the losers are likely to be those who stand in greatest need while the wealthy get huge breaks, thus widening the gap between the privileged and the poor even more.

Concurrent with this crusade to cut taxes is the naïve hope that there are other means of providing human services without government involvement. The elder Bush believed that "points of light" could relieve government of much of its responsibility, and soon thereafter, Colin Powell was commissioned to launch a national volunteer pool, which was promoted as a substitute for an expansion of government. Now we are hearing from both parties that the delivery of human services is really the job of faith communities, that federal programs could be significantly reduced if the churches and synagogues would take up the challenge of rescuing people who are in desperate straits.

All such suggestions sound altruistic and are complimentary toward our traditional American commitment to volunteerism and the role of religious groups in assisting the needy. But there is something about this that makes me angry. The hidden message seems to be, "Let's cut taxes and YOU provide the human services while the rest of us increase our incomes." Furthermore, all such assumptions that the private sector can meet the gargantuan needs of our society are totally unrealistic.

Consider volunteers. Americans have always been willing to volunteer for a host of good causes, but the recent call for volunteers has not produced the stampede expected. Why? Most of the potential volunteers are already committed, and others who have not yet stepped forward are, for the most part, unable to do so. At a time in our history when typically both parents work and share childcare responsibilities, there is little time left. Furthermore, most organizations that rely on volunteers to rescue those for whom there is no safety net are already pushed to the limit. Habitat for Humanity can never replace HUD, and Chapel Hill's Interfaith Council could never carry the caseload of the county's Department of Social Services.

Both Al Gore and George Bush have seized upon what they see as another alternative to the government's delivery of human services. Their hope lies in "faith communities," a phrase that has a softer and less sectarian sound than the word "religion." It is true that most religious groups have a good track record in helping the dispossessed, but generally people in the pews are already stressed out and involved in what their congregations are doing. There are neither sufficient staff nor resources to do much more. This response has been answered by the promise of funneling federal money into faith-based programs, but to do so would confront us with the controversy over separation of church and state. Furthermore, if churches and synagogues become the arm of the state, the traditional prophetic voice of faith communities is likely to be muffled. Personally, I think we are deluding ourselves if we allow any politician to convince us that religious groups can, or should, take over the government's responsibility for maintaining the general welfare.

At a time when we enjoy unprecedented prosperity, it offends me that we even consider a tax cut instead of adequately addressing the pressing human needs of our nation. With homeless people on the streets of every city and forty-three million people without medical insurance, it is unconscionable to consider returning the tax surplus. With a few people who have far too much, and multitudes who have far too little, we are now blessed with a wonderful opportunity to provide more adequate human services for everyone and move toward a more decent standard of living for all.

It is to the credit of our citizenry that recent polls indicate most of us do not give high priority to a tax cut. The majority of Americans prefer that the surplus be used to improve our environment, education, and welfare. If only our politicians would listen!

LACK OF SUPPORT FOR UN THREATENS FUTURE

November 12, 1995

When an American politician speaks about the United Nations, it is usually to criticize it. Newt Gingrich judges it to be "a totally incompetent instrument." Others are openly insisting that we withdraw from the UN, while some chant, "Get the U.S. out of the UN and the UN out of the U.S." This is a disturbing trend.

The recent celebration of the 50th anniversary of the founding of the United Nations was muted in America. Many local communities let the event pass without notice. In Chapel Hill, the United Nations Association sponsored a program which featured Terry Sanford and the former governor of Massachusetts, Governor Peabody. It was held in Gerrard Hall, where even a small crowd made it look like a respectable turnout.

The future of the world body in large measure depends upon the continuing support of the United States, yet our government is so far behind in paying its dues that the UN is on the verge of bankruptcy. We owe nearly one and a half billion dollars! It was embarrassing for New York to be the host city for the anniversary bash while our nation was being denounced as a deadbeat. We were accused of wanting representation without taxation. Ironically, the three former Axis powers (Germany, Japan, and Italy) are all paid up.

Our relationship to the UN reveals a recurring hypocrisy. At best it reflects an ongoing ambivalence. We talk about it as if it were something outside ourselves, yet as a member of the Security Council we are in a position to veto anything. When it is to our advantage to use the UN to further our own ends, we do so with gusto. The most blatant example of this was the Gulf War when George Bush, Sr., kept saying, ad infinitum, "We must uphold the UN resolution." But when something occurs that we dislike, we threaten to take our marbles and go home—as indeed we did when we severed our ties with UNESCO because we didn't like the political persuasion of its leadership.

Our lame excuse for such shameful behavior is that we feel the UN should be "reformed." Of course it should be reformed, as is the case with the U.S. Government and every other large bureaucracy I know. Yet, when the time comes for the major reforms to occur—such as having some representation from the continents of Africa and South America on the Security Council—we will likely be the first to oppose it.

Every nation in the world now looks to the U.S. for leadership. It may not be a role we want, but it is a role we cannot escape. Our temptation is to go it alone and throw our weight around like the bully on the block. We should be wise enough to understand that countries tend to distrust a powerful nation (as we do China). Therefore, it is all the more important to be multilateral and not unilateral and to bring everyone into the decision-making process.

The United Nations is not a charity, but is an essential tool as a world forum and a place for innumerable cooperative endeavors that no nation can accomplish alone. We seldom hear the long list of achievements of the UN, such as promoting de-colonization. In 1945, there were only fifty-one founding countries. Today there are 185! The UN has protected more than thirty million refugees, encouraged international trade relations, led the international environmental effort, and facilitated global communication. Recently, its role in improving the status of women worldwide was symbolized by the highly successful conference in Beijing.

It is the peace-keeping role that ignites much of the controversy and the xenophobic idea that there is a hidden agenda for the UN to become a world government which would usurp our sovereignty. We need to do a better job of educating our citizenry about what the facts are. For example, many people think that huge numbers of Americans have been involved in these peace-keeping efforts, whereas a "reality check" shows that only four percent of the soldiers have come from the United States.

The League of Nations died because our country refused to become a member. The United Nations will also die unless our support is more consistent and our commitment to the world community continues. Polls still show that the majority of Americans have positive feelings toward the UN, but these attitudes can be eroded quickly. Despite all of its faults and failings, it is truly remarkable that for fifty years the UN has been a steady influence for peace and concord around the world. Whether or not we can survive the next fifty may be directly related to our willingness to be a more dependable partner in the cause.

All across America, there are local chapters of The United Nations Association, totaling nearly two hundred such units. These are groups dedicated to educating our citizenry about the UN and soliciting grassroots support for what it is doing. It is alarming that in many of these chapters, including the one in the Triangle, the majority of participants are senior citizens. Unless we can expand the UN constituency to include the younger generation, it may not survive.

FOREIGN AID VITAL TO NATION'S FUTURE

July 2, 1995

How would you feel toward the wealthiest citizen of Chapel Hill if you knew that he gave no money to the United Way and refused to support any of the good causes intended to make our community a better place to live?

Your response probably would be comparable to the way other nations are likely to feel toward the United States if some people in Washington have their way about the future of foreign aid and how we relate to the rest of the world. Senator Jesse Helms has said repeatedly that foreign aid is "money thrown down a rat hole." And Presidential candidate Pat Buchanan promises that, if elected, he will reduce our nation's foreign aid commitments to zero.

Fortunately, neither of these men is representative of the opinion of the majority of Americans, but unfortunately, many citizens do have serious reservations about this part of our national budget and are uninformed about both the extent of it and its intended purpose. Polls show that judgments are being made on the basis of widespread misinformation.

For example, most people think we are giving away far more money than is actually the case. The fact is, that in comparison to other nations, the amount we give in foreign aid is surprisingly little. Of the twenty-four leading industrial nations, the United States contributes the smallest percentage of its gross domestic product toward foreign aid. The most generous contributors are the Scandinavian countries, and Japan ranks considerably higher than we do. Uncle Sam spends less than one percent of our budget—about $14 billion.

When we think of foreign aid, we usually think in terms of food and economic development. It is not generally known that foreign aid also means security assistance. Half of our American commitment is in military hardware, not bread and butter. Two countries, Israel and Egypt, are recipients of the lion's share of our money, while countries suffering from conditions of severe poverty often receive very little, if anything.

Ironically, the money we give to other countries frequently benefits the economy of the United States more than anyone else, for those to whom the money is sent generally spend it for American goods. North Carolina alone averages an income of over $400 million a year from foreign-aid contracts, according to a recent issue of *Business Week*!

It becomes increasingly apparent that a strong case can be made for the support of our foreign-aid program on the basis of self-serving arguments alone. This may account for the fact that the budget proposed in the House of Representatives cuts aid by only twenty percent and leaves our financial support of Israel and

Egypt at the same level as before. We can see at work here the same principle that we see in domestic programs: taking money away from those who can least afford to lose it and giving it to those who need it less. Most of the reductions are from allotments to African countries at a time when much of the continent is in turmoil and the refugee problem has escalated to an unprecedented numerical high.

We tend to think of foreign aid in much the same way that many people regard domestic welfare—as a multi-million-dollar handout. More careful consideration convinces that it is best understood not as welfare but as preventive medicine, in both its security assistance and humanitarian components. Spending money to help stabilize nations that are on the brink of chaos may pay rich dividends in the future and help avoid firestorms that could be much more costly later.

We look back proudly to the foreign aid of the Marshall Plan that helped Europe get back on its feet after World War II. Surely it makes little sense to have won the Cold War with the Soviet Union and then to offer no help to avoid an even worse situation developing there now! When we assist the Russians, we are also helping ourselves.

Another prime illustration of helping ourselves by extending a hand to others is the Peace Corps. Only a fraction of our foreign-aid appropriation goes to this agency, yet it is an investment from which we reap rich dividends. Americans who work overseas return as informed world citizens whose influence can be immensely valuable in shaping our foreign policy and sharing a more accurate perspective on the rest of our planet. Over two thousand former Peace Corp volunteers live and work in North Carolina!

I am convinced that most Americans are altruistic at heart and feel some sense of moral obligation to help countries in need. I believe an appeal to compassion and responsible world leadership can be as persuasive as the appeals to self-interest. It makes many of us uncomfortable to be reminded of the huge discrepancies of income between the world's rich and the world's poor. We consume by far the largest share of the planet's resources even though we account for only a small percentage of its population.

Where there is privilege, there should be responsibility. To whom much is given, much is expected. I believe most Americans are sympathetic to the biblical principle of sharing and feel the moral imperative of increasing the amount of our giving as our standard of living rises. The prophets of ancient Israel understood that "we are blessed to be a blessing." I hope modern America will also understand and that, instead of retreating into isolation, we will become increasingly generous and feel the pride of being a world power that measures its strength by its ability to care. Just as we measure the morality of our own society by the way we treat the poor in our midst, so should we measure the morality of our country by the way we treat the poor in our world.

PRICE'S BOOK OFFERS INSIGHT INTO CONGRESS

July 29, 1994

Congressman David Price has written one of the best books available about the way Congress works. Unfortunately, it has received very little local attention. Although both *The Chapel Hill News* and *The Chapel Hill Herald* have been asked repeatedly to review it for over a year, there has been nothing in the local press about the publication. I feel this is a serious oversight of a noteworthy event and a failure of our public media to inform its readers about our elected representative. The book is titled *The Congressional Experience* and is subtitled, *A View from the Hill*—meaning, of course, Capitol Hill and not Chapel Hill!

At a time when Congress-bashing seems to be the favorite pastime of the American electorate, this book takes a realistic look at the institution and underscores its strengths as well as its weaknesses. It begins with an account of David's election in 1986 and his own adjustment and setting up shop in Washington. His background as a professor of political science at Duke University made this transition somewhat easier for him than for others, for he anticipated what the "real world" there was like.

Although the party affiliation is less binding at the local level than it once was, it is still very active in Congress. Newly elected representatives are often tempted to stress their solo activity at the expense of the institution, but effectiveness depends in large measure upon party collaboration and loyalty as compared to the role of the "Lone Ranger." Constituents tend to expect too much and should remember that their representative is only one in a body of nearly five hundred members. Inevitably, those who are most successful learn the art of compromise and respect the seniority protocol of the system.

The frequency of elections requires that one continually live with the tension between campaigning and governing. Surprisingly, David sees this as an asset, more positive and productive than distracting and debilitating. Accustomed to the academic life, he might otherwise be tempted to burrow into a work assignment and avoid the limelight. He values the sensitivities and skills acquired by being forced to interpret his legislative efforts to his constituents.

Fiscal irresponsibility was the one thing that alarmed Price most upon arrival in Congress. However, he judged the crisis to be caused not so much by the failure of Congressional procedures and mismanagement as to the unrealistic and profligate economic shortfalls of supply-side economics during the Reagan years and the refusal of the public to protest the situation.

There is an excellent chapter on religion and politics. With a graduate degree from Yale Divinity School, David speaks with refreshing insight about the relationship of church and state. He is committed to Reinhold Niebuhr's realism about the inability to incorporate the full potential of morality in legislation, but he understands that legislation can move society to higher levels of morality. He states that a love ethic can never be perfectly embodied in politics, but it can nonetheless compel its adherents to seek justice as a proximate public expression of love.

Having taught a course at Duke on "Ethics and Public Policy," Price is uniquely qualified to push for further ethical reform of the legislative body. He is disturbed by the ubiquitous willingness of people to believe the worst about public officials and how even those running for Congress are often willing to trash the institution by running against Congress in order to get into Congress. He thinks the press must bear some of the blame for this mood for having smeared the whole institution on the basis of the conduct of a few of its members.

He feels the crusade for term limits is misguided—it takes too long to find one's way into Congress and to be effective; so the whole institution would be seriously weakened if the nation were deprived of the leadership of those whose longevity has served us best. The term-limit proposal seems to assume that experience and expertise count for little. David predicts that if this proposal is ever enacted, the nation will be ruled less by Congress and more and more by staff, lobbyists, and bureaucrats.

He deplores "attack politics," which often succeed in diverting the voters from the real issues and preclude the forging of any sense of national community. (Such as George Bush, Sr., running for president on the issues of furloughed murderer Willie Horton and the Pledge of Allegiance to the flag!)

Congressman Price has faith in politics as an instrument of positive change. He came of age in the early years of the civil rights movement and served as president of the Baptist Student Movement at UNC at a time when campus religious groups were perhaps the most active proponents of change. His background as a professional in political science and theology serve him well, as does also his experience as executive director and chairman of the North Carolina Democratic Party from 1980-1984.

Our congressman says he feels "enormously challenged and stimulated" by his job and feels "extraordinarily fortunate to be where he is." This book is a persuasive testimony to both his intelligence and his integrity.

The book was published by Westview Press. It is one of a series of books under the title, "Transforming American Politics." The book provides an excellent portrait of David Price to his constituents and will serve as a valuable resource in the political-science classroom.

POLITICS

AMERICANS BELIEVE IN FAIRNESS

January 3, 2001

Tomorrow, January 6, 2001, Vice President Al Gore will perform the painful task of announcing the official vote of the Electoral College to a joint session of the House and Senate. Despite the widespread feeling that unfairness ensured the election of George W. Bush, Gore will preside over the occasion with grace. I regret that for me, however, this act will not bring finality to the contest. The abrupt end to the vote counting in Florida has left me bewildered and angry. I feel cheated by being denied information I believe I have a right to have. Did Bush really win the election? The day after the Supreme Court's ruling, *The New York Times* stopped short of saying so. Its headline read simply, "Bush Prevails."

From the outset of the disputed outcome in Florida, it quickly became apparent that the Bush team would do everything in its power to prevail. They were determined that the votes tossed out by the machines not be counted. Obviously, they also thought there was a strong possibility that Gore was the winner, so they made sure any attempt to count the uncounted ballots was suppressed. Even though Gore was significantly ahead across the country with the national vote and needed only three more electoral votes to become president, the Bush people succeeded in getting the media to unfairly portray Gore as the challenger in all the reporting. It was as if the Bush presidency was a foregone conclusion.

In fairness to the five hundred thousand people who gave Gore a substantial lead in the popular vote, I think he had an obligation to question the accuracy of the small margin of victory claimed by Florida for Bush. Calling for a recount is an established approach to fairness in our democracy, and many close races have been settled in this way.

Ironically, George Bush himself signed into Texas law a bill that commended hand counts as the most accurate procedure, and the bill includes the permissibility of including dimpled ballots as votes! An approved voting practice in Texas was judged to be unacceptable in Florida! (What does that say about equal access?) Furthermore, a key witness for the Bush legal team, the man who co-invented the voting machines, testified that a hand count was always more reliable than a machine count!

When the Florida Supreme Court gave permission for the counting to proceed, the Bush team (so vocally committed to states' rights) rushed to the U.S. Supreme Court and insisted that the counting was unconstitutional. Then, by granting a stay, the Court effectively terminated the election process. By stopping the counting, they surely knew that they were running down the clock and that there would be no time left to resume counting following their decision. They handed down their decision two hours before the deadline! This judicial action was tantamount to appointing the president and bypassing the voice of the people. Dissenting, Justice Stevens said, "There is no justification for denying the State the opportunity to try to count all disputed ballots." And faculty from our nation's most prestigious law schools agreed.

I would like to believe that the judgment of the Supreme Court was fair and not politically motivated. The foundation of our nation depends upon the Court's ability to act with neutrality that transcends partisan politics, but, in this case, I cannot give them the benefit of the doubt. They are also human, and as such, are capable of error. A judicial decision does not necessarily coincide with fairness or morality. Of course we have no choice but to accept it, but we are under no obligation to agree with it. (A Supreme Court of an earlier era even approved of segregation as a means of providing "equal access" to blacks and whites!)

The appearance of fairness was not helped by the discovery that Justice Scalia has a son who is employed by the legal team that argued the case for Bush, and that Clarance Thomas's wife was working with the conservative Heritage Foundation and suggesting names of possible appointees to the Bush transition team! Other players in the larger picture which suggested partisan influence from the start were the Florida secretary of state, co-chair of the Bush campaign in Florida, and of course, the governor of Florida, brother to George.

I was also bothered by the unfair treatment of the hundreds of citizens who rallied as volunteers to count votes. These were people like you and me who were judged not to have the integrity to do the task, even though there were participants from both parties who had to concur on every vote counted. The same George Bush who campaigned across the country saying repeatedly, "I trust the people," was unwilling to trust these citizens who readily responded to the call of a civic duty basic to our democracy.

Acting on the principle that the end justifies the means, the Florida legislature made it clear that Florida would choose George Bush regardless of the consequences of any recounting. This arrogant action again compromised any hope of fairness. It was clear that the will of the people would be irrelevant.

The lesson in all of this for us is that life is often unfair. Who of us has not been caught in circumstances that deprived us of something we felt we justly deserved! Such experiences test our mettle. Al Gore passed the test with flying colors in his superb concession speech that gave not a hint of bitterness.

I wish I could be as gracious, but I will continue to think of George Bush as our appointed interim leader until such time as the counting of Florida ballots confirms his legitimacy as president.

Dear Bob: I cannot tell you how upset I am regarding your recent article in *The Chapel Hill News*—"Fairness."... For the good of the country you should stop writing these articles –it lowers your high stature in the community and in my eyes, as Clinton lowered the stature of the presidency of our great nation. While I agree with many of the programs of the Democrats and its esteemed members of Congress, I disagree with your angry article. I think that it was misleading and only showed that you are indeed a "sore loser," which I would not have thought a man of the cloth should show. *R.J.P., Chapel Hill, NC*

Europeans find it difficult to distinguish serious problems in America from the sometimes bizarre "America-as-usual." ...Imagine trying to explain the Clinton impeachment debacle as the political power struggle it really was.

I found Seymour's words very helpful in explaining to my European friends that this is definitely not just "America-as-usual."

Something very serious did go wrong with the election, and many decent Americans, irrespective of political stripe, are, like Seymour, deeply disturbed by it. *J.C.R., Chapel Hill, NC*

✉

Dear Reverend Seymour, It seems to me that people who have the public forum, such as Julian Bond, Jesse Jackson, and others, to include you, should feel a sense of duty to try to unite the country and try to help make any four-year term of any president as productive as possible. What is going on today did not occur in 1960-61, when there was much suspicion of massive fraud in Chicago and quite possibly Texas. Even Kennedy was so concerned about allegations of fraud that, as was reported then and again recently, he contacted Nixon and asked what should be done. Nixon's reply was something to the effect, "You are the president-elect. We cannot afford a constitutional crisis in this country." *P.B., Chapel Hill, NC*

✉

Dear Bob, I think, of all the commentary I have read on this matter thus far, that your view corresponds more closely to mine than any other. You stated the position splendidly. Like you, I have considerable anger about the entire affair. One ingredient more I have, of which I am not overly proud: bitterness. This is an impulse I will endeavor to control, but I have a good way to go yet. Thanks to you, good friend, for stating the obvious and, more importantly, the truth. *R.K., Chapel Hill, NC*

✉

Your article does nothing to heal the emotional wounds caused by this divisive election. You have been given a great responsibility and privilege—a front-page column in the newspaper...

Next time please use your soapbox more carefully. Do your spiritual duty first, and please look at both sides. Have we not had enough of bitter partisan wrangling? I experienced the same bewilderment and anger that you did. I also felt cheated. I have allowed this political process to interfere with my spiritual growth. The whole thing stirs up the worst in my heart. I, and the nation, need healing. We need leaders, healers, wise men. If not from your generation, then where? Peace be with you, pastor.

✉

Dear Reverend Seymour, Politics aside, and I have heard no discussion of this, but might you agree that the most amazing feature of this phenomenon, from an anthropological viewpoint, is the stark revelation that objectivity is not the rare quality we thought it to be, but that it is, indeed, simply an element totally absent from the human psyche? Breathes there one Republican who questions the propriety of Bush's "election." Or a single Democrat who doesn't feel swindled? Are we, then never to know any true color because we see only through colored lenses? *R.C., Chapel Hill, NC*

Like Diogenes, I am still looking for that honest man to lead a nonpartisan discussion. I certainly do not see a reflection of this man in Reverend Seymour's article.

It is disturbing to me that a prominent citizen, like Reverend Seymour, questions the legitimacy of George W. Bush's upcoming presidency when by the laws of our land and the decision of a lawfully constituted body of government, he became the winner.... I would hope that we would all try to see through the haze of our biases and pull together for the betterment of our country, which I spent an Army career trying to help defend. *W.P.B., Chapel Hill, NC*

REFLECTIONS ON THE ELECTION

December 3, 2000

Perhaps by the time this is published we will know for sure who will be our next president. But does it matter? Despite Mr. Nader's contention to the contrary, I believe it does matter. There is an enormous difference, especially in the philosophy of the two major political parties and in the way each views the role of government in addressing the needs of our nation.

These differences are manifested in the way wealth is distributed, in the way regulations are imposed to ensure safety and fairness in the economy, and in the parties' respective understandings of the limitations and power of the Supreme Court. Democrats generally have more faith in the federal government's ability to solve problems, whereas Republicans prefer to trust more solutions to the private sector.

However, during the presidential campaign, both candidates seemed very much alike in their reticence to address some of the most important issues facing our country. Each was so afraid of alienating some segment of the electorate that they would not initiate any discussion of certain controversial matters unless they were confronted with a direct question that they could not avoid. They preferred to keep silent.

Consider the matter of universal health care. Neither Gore nor Bush would touch it. The word "universal" has become almost as threatening as the label "socialized medicine." Both remembered the deathblow given to Hillary Clinton's plan for guaranteeing coverage for every citizen. Although we have forty-three million people without health insurance and are the only major nation in the Western world that fails to offer such protection to all, the two major candidates would talk only about increasing the numbers incrementally and gradually. At a time when there is such widespread dissatisfaction with our present system on the part of both patients and physicians, you would think one of the candidates might have had the courage to propose a universal plan.

Something else that got short shrift on the campaign trail was gun control. Here there was a huge difference in each candidate's position, but the power of the National Rifle Association was so threatening that Gore was put on the defensive. When a question was asked about it, he began by insisting that he would not take away guns. He was so intimidated by the NRA's rating of Bush with an "A" and himself with an "F" that he played down his proposal to license all gun owners rather than pushing it as a campaign promise.

Another issue which screamed for attention but which received only minor mention from the finalists was campaign finance reform. Since both candidates had been so totally co-opted by the present system of soliciting unlimited funds, neither could address the problem with a straight face. In this case, Nader was right. There was no difference between the two parties. Both men made themselves pawns to corporate America. Politics has become a club for the rich, and in this election the amount of money spent reached unprecedented astronomical levels. Recognition of this foul situation probably accounts in part for millions of potential voters not bothering to show up on election day. Senator John McCain made campaign finance reform the primary issue in his attempt to gain the nomination and demonstrated by the enthusiastic response he received that Americans are impatient to change the funding rules. If Bush becomes our president, perhaps he will feel an obligation to McCain and be open to the possibility of considering what McCain proposed.

Sadly, neither candidate tuned in to the fast-growing grassroots movement of people all across the country that are committed to ending executions. Seldom does a week pass without a major article in the press about the inequities of the death penalty or about someone wrongly imprisoned on death row. But both Bush and Gore chose to ignore the momentum for a moratorium and announced their support of the death penalty. One of the most dramatic moments in the debates was when an African-American asked Bush about executions in Texas, where they average putting someone to death about every ten days. Such a record seems shockingly counter to "compassionate conservatism." Significantly, however, the pace of executions was slowed down in Texas as the election day approached, and one death sentence was commuted. It makes you wonder if the timing might have been orchestrated to keep the subject from coming up in the campaign. (A similar suspicion occurred in North Carolina when Attorney General Mike Easley scheduled not a single execution all year until after the election was over, but thirty-six hours after the polls closed, he concurred in a state-approved murder.)

Since the presidential election was so close and both the House and Senate almost evenly divided, let us hope both sides will reach across the aisle for bi-partisan attention to these crucial issues, seldom talked about in the race to the White House.

PIETY ALONG THE POTOMAC

October 29, 2000

Living in a country that has no established religion and with a commitment to maintaining a wall of separation between church and state, it is not surprising to hear someone say, "Religion and politics don't mix." But of course they do. The metaphorical dividing wall is porous and leaks in both directions. Interpretations of the religion clause in the First Amendment are ongoing and will likely always be an important topic in public discourse.

Presidential elections are a time when there is considerable interest in the religious affiliation of candidates, for this gives us some idea of his or her perspective on life in general and on morality in particular. And those who are running for office must be very sensitive to the religious persuasions of their constituents. The strong voice of the religious right in recent elections has motivated most candidates to learn the vocabulary of religious conservatism.

Religion was a primary issue in the election of John Kennedy because of his Roman Catholic faith. Many Protestant groups were fearful that his decision-making would be subject to overruling by the Vatican, and fundamentalists from the South were adamant in their opposition to his presidential bid. They were afraid America would be governed from Rome.

In the current election, we are putting to the test America's readiness to accept religious diversity by having an Orthodox Jew as a vice-presidential candidate. This is an impressive indication of change in American culture, where most people speak casually of our nation being "a Christian country." I have appreciated Mr. Lieberman's talking openly about his faith, but some have judged this to be an inappropriate mixing of religion and politics. Some wonder how his religion would manifest itself in Middle East policy, and American Reformed Jews are indignant over the Orthodox community's challenging their authenticity as Jews.

George Bush is a Methodist, a member of a mainstream, moderate congregation. His testimony to the power of religion to turn his life around and to give him the strength to overcome his drinking problem has played well with evangelical Christians. However, his appearance at Bob Jones University backfired because of the school's record on social-justice issues, especially race. The so-called "personal gospel" still dominates Southern pulpits.

As a Southern Baptist, Bill Clinton has been shunned by the denomination that nurtured him. Southern Baptists have traditionally come down harder on personal sins than social sins. However, the nation as a whole was able to see beyond his personal moral failings to appreciate his record on social-justice legislation. Religion calls us to accountability not only for our own integrity but also for the well-being of our brothers and sisters in the world around us.

Al Gore also has Southern Baptist roots, though he has spoken sparingly about his religion during the campaign. When he returned from Vietnam, he spent a year studying theology at Vanderbilt University in an attempt to come to a better understanding of his faith. It was there that he became convinced of the theological significance of preserving the environment as a divine mandate from its Creator. (In a previous administration, there was a secretary of the interior whose religion believed in the imminent end of the world. Obviously, this conviction would blunt a sense of urgency about preserving the environment for future generations!)

It is interesting that Southern Baptist affiliations have played such a large part in contemporary politics despite the reactionary recent actions of the denomination. I doubt if we have ever had a more devout and overtly religious president than Jimmy Carter. He talked freely about his faith and taught a Sunday school class at the First Baptist Church in Washington while living in the White House. News of his recent withdrawal from the Southern Baptist

Convention because of its increasingly conservative trend was not surprising. His religious commitment has been visible in his post-presidential activities, especially with Habitat for Humanity and his endeavors for peace.

Obviously, when a person enters the political arena, he or she cannot divorce themselves from their religious faith. Therefore, I think it is important to be aware of a candidate's religious background. Some feel very uncomfortable in revealing this and others consider it an altogether private matter. This was the case with Bill Bradley.

One of the dangers of candidates exposing themselves to religious questions or of speaking about it publicly is that their motives may be suspect. Some may judge that religion is being used just to play to certain groups or may conclude that the religion expressed is phony. Or worse, the electorate may wonder if the candidate is vulnerable to zealots who would try to use the elected official to further their narrow agenda.

What is true of candidates is also true of voters. We are simultaneously both religious beings and political beings. When we enter the ballot booth, we cannot leave our religion outside. If our religion is genuine, it will inevitably be a major factor in the way we vote. But because of the principle of separation of church and state, the IRS has warned faith communities that they are likely to lose their tax-free status if they distribute voter guides to instruct their people for whom to cast their ballot.

I am glad we live in a country that tries to be fair in its recognition of all religious bodies without playing favorites. I am also glad that I live in a nation that respects my freedom to vote in the light of my faith-based convictions.

Dear Bob, Loved your column in *The Chapel Hill News* on piety and politics. We don't automatically get that paper, but I buy it at Breadmans, where we eat out often, if I see your picture on the front page! This article is so beautifully articulated and beautifully balanced in perspective. *L. W., Orange County, NC*

MAINTAINING CIVILITY IN PUBLIC DISCOURSE

May 14, 1999

A major change seems to be occurring in our nation. In the year past, we have seen disturbing erosion of civility in public discourse. The impeachment proceedings were compromised throughout by the inability of anyone to hear what others were saying.

The art of persuasion deteriorated into a shouting match. The television talk shows improve their ratings by resorting to stridency and bombast, and politicians who believe that negative campaigning paves the way to election are poisoning the media with personal attacks on their opponents instead of indicating where they stand on the issues.

Even in the local public area we are seeing an increase in incivility. It surfaces in "Letters to the Editor" and in both municipal and Orange County politics. Anyone who considers offering himself or herself for public service knows the danger of becoming a target of acrimony. As a consequence, we are probably losing some of our best potential leadership. With another election cycle on the horizon, I hope we can turn down the volume. We are in serious trouble if the "in-your-face" tactics of the disturbingly popular *Jerry Springer Show* is symptomatic of the direction in which we are moving.

Civility can be defined simply as politeness. It generally manifests itself as a respectful exchange between persons. I say, "Thank you," and you respond, "You're welcome." I ask, "How are you?", and you reply, "I'm fine." Such rituals play an important role in maintaining civility in our personal relationships. Maintaining such reciprocity in the public arena becomes more difficult when we endeavor to reach consensus on complex and controversial issues. This seems especially hard today in our discussion of both politics and religion, and particularly when they intersect.

We must somehow learn to differ from each other without destroying each other. We must learn to use language that is passionate and persuasive but never poisonous. We must learn the art of disagreeing without becoming disagreeable. We should remember that the more rigid we become in our point of view, the more likely we are to be less civil to those who think otherwise. There is a temptation to "write off" anyone who is not a mirror image of ourselves. It is ironic that this is occurring at a time when we profess to value diversity.

I am especially concerned about the politicization of religion, as highly controversial issues fracture our nation. The lines seem so hardened that we hesitate to even bring up subjects for fear of initiating an uncontrollable conversation. The merger of moral convictions with partisan political positions has resulted in harsh judgments and even incites people to violence. Is it possible for us to be more civil in public discourse when we discuss such issues as abortion, school vouchers, homosexuality, and the death penalty? It is unfortunate when religious leaders identify religious integrity with only one point of view. (Someone has said that a fanatic is someone who knows he's doing what the Lord would do if He had all the facts.)

I am active in an organization called The Interfaith Alliance. It is a national group with a local chapter in Chapel Hill. The Alliance is committed to civility in public discourse and is dedicated to the promotion of the positive role of religion in national life. In that spirit, let me make several suggestions about ways to foster civility:

1. Practice the art of listening. In our inordinate lust for certitude, we tend to seek premature closure.
2. Try to see things from the other person's perspective. For example, white people generally see the police as their protectors, but blacks often see the police as their oppressors.
3. Remember that today's enemy may be tomorrow's friend. Though you may differ sharply with someone over the separation of church and state, you may be their ally on economic-justice issues.
4. Don't question another's motives. Give them the benefit of the doubt.
5. Attack policies, not people.
6. Avoid put-downs, such as "Don't be ridiculous!"

Perhaps the most effective model for civility in the public area was Martin Luther King, Jr. Although his entire career was embroiled in heated controversy, he never disparaged, degraded, or demeaned his opponents. King never lost sight of our common humanity. He refused to attack those who abused him.

I recall, as a child, often quoting a saying that was quite common among children when arguments on the playground led to name-calling. In response to a personal insult, we shouted back, "Sticks and stones can break my bones, but words can never hurt me." Now I know better. Words CAN hurt. Indeed, they can become incendiary and sometimes lead to tragic bodily harm.

Words can also have devastating effects on one's self esteem. I had the misfortune of spending my freshman year of college at The Citadel in Charleston, where the plebes are hazed continuously. The captain of our company was a master at verbal abuse. He would call our unit to attention, and as he reviewed the cadets, he would come close to your face and look you straight in your eyes, snarling, "You putrid piece of protoplasm!" Such labels led to lasting wounds from which it took me a while to recover. I have never forgotten.

My friends, we can do better. Let's be more civil to each other.

THE TRUTH ABOUT LYING

October 16, 1998

When I was an active clergyman, one of my responsibilities was to go to the hospital to welcome new babies into the world. This posed a problem for me, for I have never thought newborns were very beautiful, but I felt I needed to say something complimentary about the infant. I solved my moral dilemma by looking first at the baby and then at the mother as I smiled broadly and said, "That IS a baby!" I was truthful but deceitful.

Whenever I travel, I often enjoy conversation with the person sitting next to me, but when that inevitable question arises, "What do you do?" I withhold the whole truth.

My standard reply is that "I teach" (which every preacher presumably does). If I confess that I am a minister, the conversation generally becomes more guarded, or I hear the history of their church relationship, or my seatmates seek counsel about some personal problem they are facing.

All of us are familiar with such dodges, and we generally dismiss them as not being too serious by labeling them "white lies." Society would not be very civil without them. We have all learned how important it is on social occasions to tell people what they want to hear: "How pretty you look!", or "It was a lovely evening." Who would dare say, "Your dress is not at all becoming," or "It was all I could do to get through this tedious evening of making small talk with strangers."

Another category of lying we generally tolerate is what might be called "security disinformation." For example, President Eisenhower told the nation that it was absolutely untrue that we were sending spy planes over the Soviet Union, but when the Soviets shot down one of our U-2s over their air space, there was no way to deny it. Something similar happened in the Iran-Contra Affair with Mr. Reagan. Yet there was no great public outcry that such official lying should warrant any punishment.

When I was in seminary, the field of Christian Ethics was dominated by what is called "situation ethics." We wrestled with complex ethical problems that seemed to offer no easy traditional answers. A classic illustration is that of a Nazi soldier coming to your door and asking, "Do any Jews live here?", and you have a Jewish family hiding in your attic. Are you obligated to tell the truth? Of course not! There are occasions in life when lying is more moral than truth telling.

(Who of us has not said in response to some inquiry, "They didn't deserve the truth"?)

Situations where withholding the truth has been judged permissible are when there is an attempt to protect someone or to avoid unnecessarily hurting them. In the past, more so than today, it was considered unwise to let a child know he or she was adopted, for fear the child would feel less loved. Also, physicians in an earlier age were often reluctant to divulge a full diagnosis to their patients, feeling that it was more merciful to let them cling to hope than to convey a sentence of death.

Another sensitive area where the truth is frequently withheld is in reference to sex. Wherever there is infidelity or adultery, there is always the temptation to keep it quiet to spare one's spouse the pain of knowing. Indeed, some marriage counselors advise that it is best not to "come clean" because of the harm it might do to one's family.

This brings us to our president. Mind you, I think what Clinton did in his relationship with Ms. Lewinsky was deplorable, immoral, and stupid, but I can understand his not wanting to reveal the sordid details of their affair for the sake of his wife and daughter. After admitting to having had an intimate, inappropriate relationship and acknowledging that he deceived the public by withholding the truth, I do not think it was necessary to put the salacious description of all that occurred on television for the world to hear. I am outraged by the capitulation of the media to this mess and saddened that even the newspaper I respect most compromised its honored commitment to "All the News That's Fit to Print."

I also challenge the claim that Mr. Clinton's appearance before the grand jury had nothing to do with sex. It was ALL about sex. If he had been accused of perjury for lying about some business deal in Little Rock, I daresay it wouldn't have received nearly the attention of the sexual scandal. Yes, perjury is a serious crime, and it is prosecuted where there are lies about a serious crime, but our president's infidelity does not constitute a "high crime" against our country. Nor do I believe that when someone lies about his or her sex life that it means they cannot be trusted about other matters.

I further question those who say, "We must treat the president just like everyone else." What ordinary citizen has ever been brought before the public by hostile prosecutors for relentless questioning about their sex lives? If everybody who has withheld truth about a sexual dalliance were threatened by such a court procedure, our nation would be "up in arms!" Surely in the name of truthfulness we are not entitled to a full revelation of anyone's sexual behavior!

Those who see moral erosion in our country because the majority of Americans is against impeachment should understand that this does not mean they approve of what our president has done but disapprove of a seriously flawed judicial process, the political exploitation of it, and a loss of a sense of proportion in dealing with the whole affair.

I hope we can move quickly toward some kind of censure and return to those "weightier matters of the law," such as social-justice issues and peacekeeping.

Dear Bob—I have no more stomach for any more articles on this political lynching of Clinton, but I'm relieved to read your "perspectivising" of the issues. Thanks for your sensible view. *P.P., Chapel Hill, NC*

"HOW COULD I HAVE DONE IT?"

September 13, 1998

I can't get our president off my mind. I try to imagine how it must feel to be in his shoes. He betrayed his wife. He deceived his associates. He misled the nation. As a consequence, his closest supporters have distanced themselves, and political hopefuls rush in to exploit the scandal to their advantage. And of course the press continues to have a field day at the president's expense. He must feel very much alone.

I had such high hopes for him. He looks presidential, and he has the ability to communicate with charm and charisma. He is an effective politician, possessing a remarkable comprehension of the problems and promise of America, and is able to set forth a national agenda accordingly.

Here is a man who even as a boy dreamed of becoming president, and he set his course with unswerving determination to make his dream come true. His lofty ambition was matched by compassion and a commitment to the well-being of all citizens irrespective of their stations in life. He looked forward to leaving behind a lasting legacy for good, but now a dark cloud threatens everything he has accomplished. His career is an American tragedy. His place in history has been permanently compromised.

We tend to put our talented and impressive leaders on pedestals and to forget the likelihood that every hero has clay feet. I recall how excited I was about "Camelot," the promising presidency of John Kennedy, but when I learned much later about his recklessness with sexual liaisons in the White House, I idolized him less. I still feel a sense of reverence at even the mention of the name of Martin Luther King, Jr. so it is hard for me to accept the fact that he was not faithful to his wife. (Though the press knew of these infidelities, they refused to report them back then.)

I daresay that these men, including our president, would claim that they stand with the majority of Americans who value integrity in marriage and deplore lying and deceit. Yet, the record stands. How shall we account for it?

I have lived long enough to understand that we are all our own worst enemies. We do dumb things. We do wrong things. We withhold the truth. We break our own accepted standards even while insisting that everyone else measure up to them. We believe that we are above reproach and incapable of lapsing to the lower level of behavior which we will not tolerate in others. Such an assumption is the seedbed of hypocrisy, and hypocrisy is rampant in our society. I recall the words of a great teacher, who said to those who were about to execute a woman taken in the act of adultery, "Let anyone who is without sin cast the first stone."

My guess is that Bill Clinton has said over and over again to himself, "How could I have done it?" It was such a stupid thing to do: to risk his reputation, to threaten his marriage, and to ruin his presidency—perhaps beyond repair. Yet, it is precisely at this point that I can identify with him. Here we find ourselves on all too familiar ground. Who of us has not said to ourselves on many occasions along life's way, "How could I have done it?" In retrospect, we are shocked by a self-revelation that we wish we could deny. Dismayed, we ask ourselves, "Who was that person who did that? I did not think I was capable of such behavior."

Every clergyman has heard the familiar refrain—the painful confession from people who wonder how, in high heaven, they could have stooped so low to have done what they did. "How could I have done this to my family?" "How could I have been silent and not stood up for my friend?" "How could I have allowed my business to get involved in such a shady deal?" "How could I have suppressed the truth and not called it a lie?"

Is there anyone who cannot look back over his or her life and remember blowing some big opportunity and wondering, "How could I have done it?" Is there anyone who cannot remember hurting the people you love and asking, "How could I have done it?" Is there anyone who has not done something stupidly indecent and exclaimed later, "How could I have done it!" It is when we feel most confident about ourselves and boast, "I would never do a thing like that," that we are in greatest danger. Over-confidence can make us vulnerable to a yet unrecognized Achilles heel.

I listened intently to Clinton's address to the nation after his appearance before the grand jury. I was disappointed in his speech. His anger eclipsed his contrition. I suppose this was understandable, since he had just come away from a humiliating afternoon of questioning. I wish he had waited for at least a day before going public to the nation, for by then his anger might have subsided, and he might have found it easier to say, "I'm sorry." Instead, he attempted to save face and lashed out at his accusers. Frankly, I think he blew it. If he realized this later, he may have sighed, "How could I have done it?"

I had hoped he would ask for my forgiveness. I felt the need to be connected to him, to be available to assist his beginning the long, hard process of rebuilding a relationship of trust.

I would like for him to know that I feel his pain.

LET THE PRESIDENT GOVERN!

February 4, 1998

I voted for Bill Clinton. I saw him as a very gifted young man with considerable potential for leadership. Indeed, I was excited by the prospect of his presidency.

I knew, however, that I was not voting for a perfect candidate. There are not many of those around. I was troubled by his having consented to the execution of a retarded man in Arkansas. Subsequently, I have been disappointed in his inability to deliver on some of the promises he made before occupying the White House. I was angry over his signing the punitive welfare-reform bill.

Now I am troubled over the alleged sexual scandal that threatens to destroy his administration. If the accusations against him about his personal life are true, I would be saddened by such exposures, but I do not understand why some people seem so intent on focusing on his private life or so eager to rush to judgment, even talking about impeachment. I still support Clinton and want to believe the best about him. If he has a personal weakness that has led to infidelities, that is lamentable, but I do not think this is headline news. Nor do I believe that revelations about one's private life are relevant to one's ability to govern.

Do not misunderstand me. I am not excusing sexual exploitation, but if this has in fact occurred, it is not new in high places, and especially in Washington. Some of our most distinguished and revered former presidents had similar liaisons. The public romanticized the marriage of John and Jackie Kennedy, but now we know of repetitive sexual indiscretions on his part. The American people sensed that Franklin and Eleanor Roosevelt did not have a close relationship, and the press was surely aware of Roosevelt's mistress, who was at his bedside when he died. And there is strong evidence that Dwight Eisenhower had an extra-marital relationship during his war years abroad. Yet, none of this surfaced during their presidencies, and although we now know the truth, we hold these men on pedestals despite their private behavior.

What has changed? Today, anyone in public office risks total exposure and the possibility of continuous attempts on the part of the press or political opponents to disclose scandals or invent bizarre scenarios intended to cast a shadow of suspicion upon them. Jerry Falwell even peddled a video about Clinton that accuses him of every sin in the book, including murder! I fear we are creating such a cannibalistic climate in our public life that few people in the future will be willing to step forward as candidates for office. Who wants to run the risk of their lives being ruined? Is there anyone who does not have some indiscretion in his or her past that they would prefer never to have revealed?

There was a time in my life when I was rather pious and severely judgmental toward anyone who "had fallen from grace." I recall how incensed I was by Ingrid Bergman's flaunting her extra-marital affair. I resolved that I would never see another movie in which she starred. Later, however, I realized that her private life did not compromise her ability to act and that viewing her films did not mean that I approved of what she had done, but rather, that I respected her skill as an actress. I was able to make a distinction between her public performance and her private behavior. In much the same way, I believe Clinton has extraordinary political ability irrespective of his private life. I am dismayed by all of the hullabaloo about what he may or may not have done sexually, and I marvel at his ability to meet the demands of his awesome responsibilities while this constant sniping at his Achilles heel keeps him on the defensive.

It is becoming more and more difficult to make a distinction between the tabloids and the so-called "establishment press." Unfounded rumors get top billing. What "he said" and what "she said" is reported in sickening detail. (And we will probably never know who is telling the truth!) In retrospect, we may see what is happening more as a media crisis than a presidential crisis. It strikes me as a judgment against all of us that the report of our president's possible involvement in a sexual affair grabbed the headlines and pushed the pope's visit to Cuba off the front page!

I am also troubled by the methods used to dig up such garbage. Why is Kenneth Starr's Whitewater investigation privileged to investigate the president's sexual history?

Do we approve of the deception used in the taping of the interviews with the alleged sexual partner? I am offended by this kind of entrapment and feel that the deception used to get the information is tantamount to lying.

There is another assault in the making. The novel, *Primary Colors,* is about to be released as a movie. Both the author and the filmmakers insist that this is not a story about Clinton, but inevitably, everyone will assume it is. It is a sordid, libelous account of power hungry politicians who will stoop to anything. I judge this as inexcusably offensive and cynical, tarnishing the image of our democratic institutions.

Why is it that we seem so willing to destroy our leaders and malign our potential heroes? Remember the witch-hunt waged against Martin Luther King, Jr.? He, too, was accused of sexual infidelities, and there may be evidence to support it, but I am troubled by the fact that those making the accusations seemed to have had a perverse pleasure in tearing him down. Fortunately, he weathered the personal attacks, and we, as a nation, will always admire him despite his human frailties.

I pray that Clinton will survive and be given the opportunity to govern without being engulfed by this storm of reported scandals. It is extraordinary that despite all of the allegations swirling around the White House, the president still enjoys a highly favorable performance rating by the American people. This tells me that many citizens feel the same way I do about what is happening. I hope we will see less sensationalism about rumors of improper behavior and more headlines like the following one, which appeared subsequently in most of our nation's papers: "Clinton Proposes $21 Billion over 5 Years for Child Care." I am more interested in the state of the union than in gossip about the president's private life. After his address before Congress last week, a CNN poll reported that his approval rating skyrocketed to an unprecedented sixty-seven percent, and it continues to rise.

Today it is up to seventy percent!

Partisan clerical hacks like the good Reverend have always made excuses for every Caesar from Constantine to Bill Clinton. *F.C., Chapel Hill, NC*

THE ISSUE IS INTEGRITY

October 16, 1996

"If you're not outraged, you're not paying attention."

I cannot recall who made this statement, nor the context in which it was said, but it surely applies to the content and tactics of the current political campaigns.

I am outraged by the implication that we should choose our senator on the basis of whether or not he is prejudiced against gays and lesbians.

I am outraged by those who call our president a liberal (as if it were a dirty word) and then, in the next breath, accuse him of stealing the Republican legislative agenda.

I am outraged by a governor who wants to be known for his advocacy for children, but threatens to sue the government when it moves to protect children from the harm of tobacco.

And the list could go on and on.

Consider the many ads that tell us nothing about a candidate except that he raised or lowered taxes, as if government can be run with no revenue and without ever indicating what programs became possible by raising taxes or which people were hurt by lowering them.

The lack of integrity in all of this is so appalling that it is an insult to anyone's intelligence. My outrage mounts as election day approaches.

There are so many inconsistencies. People who preach the gospel of getting the government off our backs are often the same people who want the government to reimburse them for the loss of coastal property to the hurricane. How can you have it both ways?

Another thing in my craw is the unconscionable pillorying of our first lady and the suggestion that she is not in the same league with Elizabeth Dole. The fact is they are both very competent professional women and are far more alike than they are different. And if family values enter the equation, how can anyone ignore the fact that the president and his wife have reared a child together?

It is hard to find old-fashioned integrity anywhere on the political spectrum. Both presidential candidates, for example, give lip service to campaign-finance reform, yet they have each received huge sums of money from special interests and made irrelevant the money given to them by taxpayers to prevent such undue influence on the presidential office.

Integrity is present where words and deeds coincide. If one has integrity, no discrepancy exists between what one says and what one does. Verbal statements and behavioral acts are not in conflict, for integrity is represented by consistency and wholeness. "Yes" always means "yes," and "no" always means "no." People who possess integrity are authentic people, and what they do is not dependent upon either popular applause or angry rejection. They do what is right because it is right and not because of some calculation of how much it would cost them to follow their conscience.

Integrity is compromised by hypocrisy. We have seen a lot of hypocrisy in Campaign '96. The attempt to give the impression that the Republican convention was inclusive is a good example. There were not more than fifty African-American delegates, and one out of every five persons present was a millionaire and a white male.

Integrity is compromised by expediency. I fault our president for expediency in signing the welfare-reform bill. I think it was a political act, not an act of conscience. And it is impossible for me to believe that former Senator Dole, who consistently pushed for removing the deficit and balancing the budget, could in good conscience be promising a fifteen percent tax cut and pushing supply-side economics, which he had always mocked as self-delusion!

Integrity is compromised by deliberate distortions. This is evident now as both Clinton and Dole claim to have done more than the other to counter the ballooning drug culture, when, in fact, a reality check reveals that neither of them did much.

Further evidence of lacking integrity is the silence of both parties about past performances that they believe did not play well to the nation. What have you heard about national health care from the Clinton campaign? What have you heard about the "Contract with America" from the Republicans?

I have a major concern about the erosion of trust among the electorate toward our government. We yearn for politicians who will talk straight to us and who will not stoop to name-calling and destructive personal attracts on their opponents. The new chapter of The Interfaith Alliance in Chapel Hill, an organization committed to integrity in government, contacted the senatorial, gubernatorial, and congressional candidates in our area and asked them to sign an integrity pledge, saying: "I will not use unfair campaign practices (misrepresenting my opponent's positions) and will condemn the use of campaign materials or practices that cast doubt on my opponent's integrity, patriotism, or moral fitness." Only three candidates signed it: David Price, Harvey Gantt, and Jim Hunt. A letter from Senator Helms' political director said, "You are probably already aware that Senator Helms has been running positive, issue-oriented ads for the last five weeks...." What's happened since?!

Etymologically, integrity is derived from the Latin "integritas," which means wholeness or entireness. It suggests harmony between one's inner life and one's outer life. A person with integrity is someone who "has it all together," whose direction is clear and whose actions are predictable and dependable. The waffling that has compromised Clinton's presidency is now being matched by the flip-flopping of his challenger.

Sadly, in today's political arena, it appears that honesty is no longer the best policy. Many of those running for office have become skilled in the art of doublespeak and seem to believe that willingness to compromise one's integrity is a prerequisite for being elected.

In his autobiography, Jeb Magruder, one of the Watergate defendants, had this to say about himself:

"I was ambitious, but I was not without morals or ethics or ideals. There was in me that same blend of ambition and altruism that I saw in my peers. Somewhere between my ambition and my ideals I lost my ethical compass. I found myself on a path that had not been intended for me by my parents or my principles or by my own ethical instincts. It has led me to this courtroom."

Testimonies like his are an all too frequent tragedy in American politics.

St. Augustine said that the Roman Empire fell for want of order in the soul. Shakespeare advised, "To thine own self be true, and it will follow as night the day, thou canst not then be false to any man." More than anything else, I believe the American people want leaders we can look up to, leaders we can trust, leaders who will appeal to our highest aspirations and not our prejudices, and who will nurture our generosity and discourage our greed, leaders whose principles will be revealed in consistent practice.

I propose that we amend the recurring refrain heard in the last election to read instead, "It's NOT the economy, stupid. The issue is integrity."

✉

Dear Rev. Seymour: The pillorying of Billy Dale by our first lady so that she could favor Harry Thomason's Travel Co., resulting in Dale's loss of job, undeserved harassment, and an expensive trial in which the judge throws the case out in two hours. Should you not be outraged by Dale's treatment?

Refusing by the F.L. to divulge the names of her Health Care Task force. Should you not be outraged by this?

The sudden appearance of the Rose Law Firm billing records in the White House months after they were subpoenaed. Should not you be outraged by this? *B.V., Chapel Hill, NC*

✉

Dear Dr. Seymour: I have continually admired your devotion to your beliefs and the energetic way in which you see to back up your words with actions which are consistent with these words. Your use of consistency between word and deed as the litmus test for integrity is absolutely on the mark. I, too, am outraged at the inconsistency and hypocrisy being displayed by this year's candidates—at almost every level and on both sides of the ticket.

Like you, I am a Democrat. Unlike you, my beliefs are, if we must use labels, conservative. We would most likely disagree on every social and fiscal issue at the philosophical level, but I would bet that the ways we conduct our personal lives are very similar. Herein lies the beauty of the truth that you and I understand about consistency. I admire integrity in people, even when they stand for things I disagree with. I also disdain those with whom I agree on the issues when they show inconsistency. *H.B.D., Chapel Hill, NC*

CHRISTIAN RIGHT A THREAT TO MY IDENTITY

March 31, 1995

A cherished label that I have always claimed as a part of my personal identity is the word "Christian." Increasingly, however, I find myself hesitating to make that association without qualifying what kind of Christian I am. There has been so much media attention to the political involvement of the Christian right that I feel compelled to let it be known that I do not stand with them. On many theological interpretations and most social issues, we part company.

It is ironic that this should be the case, because for many years liberal and mainstream Christians chided the more conservative and fundamentalist groups for their failure to see the social implications of our faith. Some of us had naively assumed that once this happened, we would broaden our Christian influence by uniting around many causes. But now, though we all read from the same Bible, the Christian right often takes a position that is directly opposite to that of the Christian majority.

As a Christian, it offends me greatly that the Christian right has identified itself so closely with the Republican Party and seems to imply that the Democratic agenda is less compatible to Christian concerns. Ralph Reed, the executive director of the Christian Coalition, boasts of mounting their most ambitious lobbying drive ever in support of the Republican "Contract with America" and has pledged for its passage more than one million dollars!

It troubles me that this Christian group would ally itself so completely with those in Congress who seem so willing to give privileges to the affluent at the expense of those who are poor. Although I concur that the present welfare system needs changing, I cannot understand how cutting benefits without ensuring for everyone the basic rights of food, decent housing, and health care, can be acceptable to the Christian conscience. The social programs they support show little evidence of the Judeo-Christian prophetic tradition of justice for the dispossessed.

The Christian right's close alliance with Jerry Falwell and Rush Limbaugh are especially disturbing, for I judge both of these men to be emissaries of divisiveness and hate. Recently I passed a display window of a "Christian Book Store" and was shocked to see Limbaugh's latest book featured there. I was so offended that I went inside and told the manager that Limbaugh's views were an anathema to many Christians, but he seemed incapable of understanding what I was saying.

The area of sexual ethics is another place where I part company with the Christian Coalition. Their rigid refusal to be affirming of homosexuals perpetuates injustice and persecution, and their talk of a "homosexual lifestyle" reveals a total misunderstanding of sexual orientation (as if it were a choice and not a legitimate part of God's creation).

Then there is their rigidity about abortion. I also feel that no one should submit to an abortion lightly, but in a free society, I think every woman should have a right to choose. I also believe there are situations when an abortion may be more moral than to bring into the world an unwanted child or one for whom adequate care would be impossible.

Surprisingly, the Christian right seems to see no inconsistency in its position on abortion and its widespread support of the death penalty. As with the issue of homosexuality, they quote selected verses of Scripture to support their position while ignoring New Testament mandates about forgiveness, reconciliation, and redemption.

As a Baptist, I must also distance myself from the Christian right because of their failure to understand the principle of separation of church and state. Sadly, even the Southern Baptist Convention has forsaken its heritage and advocates prayer in the public school and teaching creationism in the science classroom. The Christian right seems insensitive to the rights of minorities and perpetuates a myth about the Christian beginning of our country. When our government came into being, Baptists saw the danger of the state endorsing any religion and were successful in influencing our founding fathers and mothers to require in our Constitution impartiality by the state toward all religious groups. Today, however, some of those on the Christian right even talk about "the Restoration," an approaching time when the United States will become a theocracy!

It is unfortunate that the press so seldom conveys a balanced picture of the full spectrum of Christians in America. Actually, the Christian right represents a relatively small percentage of those who bear the Christian label. The majority of Christians in our country belong to mainstream denominations, and there are a significant number of others who might properly be described as the "Christian left." I would place myself somewhere between the middle and the far left.

I do not believe any political party is ever likely to embody my Christian vision for society, but, like my Christian right counterpart, I am committed to political activism as a way to bring about change. Though I am uncomfortable when people on the right differ with me on nearly every issue, I concede their privilege to push their agenda in the same way I push mine. However, I do strenuously object to such tactics as selling videos that level unfounded charges against public officials, distributing deceptive voter guides, and exaggerating the effects of policy proposals in ways that unduly alarm citizens. From where I stand, the Christian right seems legalistic, narrow, and often lacking in compassion.

I like that wonderful spiritual, "Lord, I Want to Be a Christian," but when I sing it nowadays, I feel the need to be a little more specific about what kind of Christian I want to be. I want to make it abundantly clear that I am poles apart from my brothers and sisters on the right.

✉

It is plain that Mr. Seymour isn't a Christian according to the Holy Bible. The Bible is God's word and if all would repent of their sins, accepting Jesus as Lord and Savior, the world's problems would be solved. *J.M., Siler City, NC*

✉

Pastor Seymour says that Jerry Falwell and Rush Limbaugh are "emissaries of divisiveness and hate."

Again, false. I have met and personally spoken with Jerry Falwell. He has a large heart, and is a very warm, loving, and compassionate man. He merely believes in moral absolutes and in the firm, immovable principle of doing what is right—regardless of the situation—contrary to hedonistic liberals and the Christian left. *E.Z., Chapel Hill, NC*

✉

Dear Dr. Seymour: I have just finished reading your splendid column in today's *Chapel Hill News*, re the "Christian right." I wouldn't change a word of it. How sanely and wisely you have written this piece! Thank you, thank you.

I am an Episcopal priest.... *L.E.B., Pittsboro*

✉

To the Editors: Thank you for publishing Robert Seymour's columns; this letter is in response to his recent column on the threat of the Christian right.

...When they selectively quote scripture to support their politics, they invariably quote Paul and Hebrew law, not Jesus.

I am of the opinion that the Christian (political) right is so very effective in its mean-spirited misrepresentations of Christian teachings because mainline Christians and others who follow Jesus' teachings are comparatively silent and inactive in the public arena. What is required is that these people speak out clearly and strongly, as does Bob Seymour, every time the right misspeaks.

So, write-on, brother Bob Seymour... *C.G.K., Chapel Hill, NC*

✉

Dear Mr. Seymour, My husband and I are not churchgoers. In fact, he is an atheist of Jewish parents and I am a backslid Methodist, but we agree with what you said. Thank heaven you had the nerve to say it! I know there are many people like us who are afraid to whisper disagreement to these so-called Christians of the coalition for fear we will be put down as anti-Christian. But the whole sick and mean movement has reached vast proportions, and we must not be intimidated. I have sent your column to many people I know, some of whom think vastly different than us, with the hope that they will finally get it. *B.L.E, Chapel Hill, NC*

✉

Dear Mr. Seymour, Your March 31 "Village Voices" column in *The Chapel Hill News* motivates me to doing something I long have intended—-to thank you for your magnificent leadership and caring concern in so many ways for the benefit of all residents. You are indeed a local treasure and an inspiration, and I want you to know that not only I but many others share these sentiments.

My observations are based upon living in retirement in Chapel Hill for the last ten years. I have viewed you from afar, but this in no way lessens my admiration for all that you have done and are doing. May this in some small way encourage you to continue when you are faced with one of the inevitable discouragements a leader encounters. *R.M., Chapel Hill, NC*

DO WE NEED A TAX CUT NOW?

February 5, 1995

I am disappointed in both our president and our governor. Their rapid response to the Republican tax-cut proposal with a tax-cut proposal of their own was clearly an act of political expediency. I would have much preferred their "staying the course" and striving to convince us that other priorities are more pressing. We need leaders who are willing to confront us with reality instead of deciding which direction to take by what appears to be popular.

Most economists agree that this is a terrible time for a tax cut. The economy is good; unemployment is down, and there is no inflation. Yet nearly everyone seems to think it would be political suicide not to jump on the tax-cut bandwagon.

We are making substantial progress in lowering the deficit and have decreased it by eighty-seven billion dollars in the past two years. Ironically, although Congress seems to think everyone is clamoring for a tax cut, polls show that most Americans would prefer getting rid of the deficit before getting a tax break.

Of course, some people insist we can do both, that we can have our cake and eat it too. But we have been down that road once, and it didn't work, so why does anyone think such fiscal fantasy will work now? I am not a believer.

In North Carolina, a tax cut will inevitably mean an inability to meet some long-term goals. Our governor had seemed deeply committed to children and wanted to expand Smart Start to every county. Now there is not a chance that this will happen. And it is probably only a matter of time before the courts will mandate an equalization of funds for the education of every child in the state. As it now stands, many of our children are deprived a decent education because they live in poor areas where there is not enough money from the tax base to upgrade their educational opportunity to that of more affluent communities. If we approve a mammoth tax cut, precious little will be left to meet such challenges ahead. And surprisingly, a sampling of North Carolinians reveals that about half the voters think a tax cut would deny us of what we expect our state to do.

It is also likely that cuts in the federal budget will require states to cough up more money than they have in the past. "Sending responsibility back to the states" may be a euphemism for our picking up the tab locally for things Washington once provided. Indeed, we may end up being forced to give back the funds received from any federal tax cut to finance the shortfall of the state! Consider further the fact that North Carolina's steadily growing population will likely lead to larger demands for tax-supported services.

One of the most inane remarks I have heard is that the people who earn the money should be free to decide what to do with it and know better than the government how it should be spent! Does this mean that groups of citizens will voluntarily band themselves together to maintain our deteriorating national and state parks? Does this mean that people in the Triangle will voluntarily share their income to provide mass transit? Does this mean we can trust citizens to voluntarily pay out of their own pockets money to monitor our environment to prevent pollution?

What we are seeing here is the triumph of American individualism over any sense of community. We place a higher value on independence than we do on the common good. We have difficulty seeing that government is an expression of community. We are slow to admit that there are many things we must do together which will not likely happen if each of us is left to do his or her own thing. Such radical individualism could, in the end, leave all of us the poorer.

Symbolic signs of withdrawal from the body politic are all around us. I see it in new residential developments behind security gates where citizens build their homes. I see it in parents who desert the public schools for private ones or home schooling and deprive their children of the opportunity to learn about democracy by relating to children of other races and economic groups. I see it in people whose income level makes possible good recreational opportunities for themselves but who resist providing funds for recreational facilities for the public at large. I see it in those whose attitude toward the poor seems to be "I've got mine; too bad about you."

My greatest fear is that the tax-cutting frenzy will hit hardest those who can least afford to live on less and who are the most defenseless: the poor, children, and the elderly. I do not believe most Americans would want this. Obviously, we all want more efficiency in social spending—but not at the cost of compassion or ripping the fabric of our common life. (One unfair tax that should be removed, however, is the food tax. Everyone must eat, but the poor are paying a much higher percentage of their income for food than anyone else.)

I hope President Clinton and Governor Hunt will have second thoughts about massive tax cuts and find the courage not to return money to us that is sorely needed to ensure a compassionate, debt-free, and enlightened community.

ISSUES

ELDER "HOSTILE"

August 18, 2002

The word "ageism" is relatively new in our vocabulary. It does not appear in my unabridged Random House Dictionary published in 1966. A more recent edition defines ageism as "discrimination against persons of a certain age group," especially older adults. I predict it is a word that will be familiar to all Americans soon.

Prejudice toward the elderly is likely to increase as we move rapidly toward the graying of seventy-six million baby boomers. Soon, between a fifth and a quarter of the population of North Carolina will be over age sixty-five, and in many rural areas the ratio may be as high as half. There will be more people over sixty-five than under twenty-five.

This demographic shift will occur not only in the United States, but in the world-at-large. The United Nations estimates there will be over two billion older adults by 2050, with more than two million living to age one hundred or older.

Already in this country, the retirement years have become the longest period of life for many seniors, longer than their professional careers. This number will increase, not only because of advancing age, but because American corporations urge many of their employees to move out of the work force in their fifties. The AARP now offers membership to anyone over fifty years of age.

Obviously, this will bring about many changes in American culture and will create new problems of a magnitude never imagined before. One of those problems may be countering ageism, a rising resentment toward older people.

Concurrent with this trend is the way our society has begun to separate the elderly from the rest of the population by luring them into retirement centers, thus creating a new kind of ghetto where older people are relatively isolated from other age groups. Also, assisted living facilities are springing up like mushrooms all across the country, where, instead of fostering traditional home care in an extended family, aging parents and grandparents are housed with their peers.

Age groups, like ethnic groups, are vulnerable to being labeled with false stereotypes when kept at a distance. Long-standing biased images of older people are likely to be reinforced if people have few opportunities to interact with the elderly. The judgment that old age is like second childhood dies hard, as does the assumption that most older people are dependent, less mentally alert, and self-centered.

The media, for the most part, have not yet grasped the impact of the approaching revolution. Television relies on old people for laughs, as seen in the parents of Raymond in the sit-com, *Everybody Loves Raymond.* A recent commercial for Hardee's showed a young man pushing several old men off of a park bench so that he could lure a passing girl to share the bench with him. (Yet, on any given morning in most Hardee's restaurants, you will find a group of old men drinking coffee.) Dementia jokes are on the rise.

As the cost of services for an older population begins to require a larger slice of national resources, ageism will likely spread. Already, there is talk of the "greedy geezers" as the debate over social security, Medicare, and the cost of prescription drugs, moves into the mainstream of the nation's political agenda. Because of diminishing reimbursement for elder medical care, an alarming number of physicians will no longer accept Medicare referrals. Older people will likely be blamed for the budget crises, but instead of complaining to Grandma, the AARP is a more likely target. It is already America's largest political lobby.

One of the stereotypical impressions that account for the fiscal grumbling is the belief that all seniors today are well off. Sadly, this is by no means the case. In North Carolina, over twenty percent of the older citizens live in poverty, and the UN warns that the fastest growing aging population will reside in the poorest countries.

Another factor that may foster a rise in ageism is within families, where the frustration of providing for aging parents and grandparents will add to daily stress and expenditures.

New levels of longevity make it not uncommon for people who retire at sixty-five to be caught in the confining circumstances of caring for parents who are ninety-five. Such situations are likely to lead to repressed resentments that explode in anger, and even violence. In response to rising incidents of elder abuse and discrimination, a whole new division of legal practice has emerged under the heading "Elder Law."

Prevention of prejudice against older people can be countered if we begin to see older people as a resource, and not a liability. By far, the majority of older persons are functional, well and active. Only five percent of persons over sixty-five are in nursing homes. Older citizens can be a valuable asset in such areas as education, nonprofits, and extended employment. Seeing them in this way will depend upon more inter-generational activities such as programs that link seniors and schools or programs that bring other age groups into senior centers. Such deliberate attempts to bridge the generation gap will enable younger people to acquire a more accurate assessment of their elders. Careful, positive planning can help North Carolina prevent a potential "hostile" environment for older people in favor of one that promotes understanding and goodwill.

HOORAY! About time something was written about us oldsters. My gripe is being profiled as a "no brainer." New aides come in here and immediately they start treating me like an altheimer (sic—the heck with it!) patient. Really ticks me off. But they learn mighty quick! Anyway, you made my day! Thanks. *R.H, Nursing home resident*

Hi, Robert, This is Steve over at the Department on Aging. I wanted to let you know that I really enjoyed it; you made many excellent points. If anyone complains about the so-called "greedy geezers," just remind them that people spend most of their money in their last one year to six months of life. That's what I tell them, so they will need all the money they can get. Anyway, again, a great article. *S.R.*

WE NEED A NEW NATIONAL ANTHEM

December 2, 2001

Have you noticed that, in the surge of patriotism following September 11, you seldom hear anyone singing "The Star Spangled Banner"? Instead, we have heard repeatedly "God Bless America." Even members of Congress gathered on the Capitol steps and sang it together. It was also sung at the reopening of the New York Stock Exchange. In a time of national crisis, this is the preferred national song. It seems to be the people's choice.

An obvious reason is that the national anthem is difficult to sing. Its wide range of notes makes it hard for even professionals to perform. Indeed, it is commonplace before civic and athletic events for some celebrity vocalist to sing the national anthem while the crowd simply listens. Amateur singers hesitate to join in.

Patriotic songs have skyrocketed in sales since the attack on our country. And guess what song is at the top of the charts? "God Bless America." This piece seems even more significant when we remember that an immigrant wrote it. It was Irving Berlin's heartfelt expression of love and appreciation of his adopted land. Royalties for permission to perform the song are estimated to exceed a half million dollars since the September tragedy! (Berlin's estate donates all the money to the Boy Scouts and Girl Scouts.)

A further problem with our present national anthem is the militant nature of the lyrics. For this reason, I feel uncomfortable singing it. My wife and I attended the Davis Cup tennis competition in Winston-Salem shortly after September 11th. When the crowd was asked to stand and sing our national anthem, I choked into silence as I anticipated the words, "And the rockets red glare, the bombs bursting in air." In light of what was happening in Afghanistan, it seemed totally inappropriate.

Of course, Francis Scott Key wrote "The Star Spangled Banner" in the heat of battle, when British troops assaulted Fort McHenry at Baltimore during the War of 1812. Once Key's words were linked to a tune, it became immediately popular as a patriotic expression of American invincibility: "the flag was still there."

There is nothing sacred about our current national anthem. It did not even become our official national song until 1931 by an act of Congress. There is no reason why it could not be changed if there is a groundswell of support for an alternative. If so, what song should it be?

Although many might welcome the choice of "God Bless America," I would propose other contenders. I especially like "America." The words are simple, beautiful, and straightforward: "My country 'tis of Thee." But there is a problem with the tune. The tune is the same as the British national anthem, "God Save the Queen." After the atrocity brought upon our nation, it was touching to hear "The Star Spangled Banner" played at Buckingham Palace, but if "America" had been our national anthem, it would have been awkward to echo "God Save the Queen," using the same tune.

My choice for a new national anthem is both easy to sing and has poetic, stately lyrics. It is "America, the Beautiful." It is a celebration of our magnificent land and offers a vision of peace and prosperity instead of bombs and bloodshed. The phrase, "Thine alabaster cities gleam, Undimmed by human tears" strikes a special emotional response in light of what happened to New York and Washington. I especially like the sense of gratitude awakened by singing the song.

As is the case with "God Bless America," "America the Beautiful" also solicits God's blessing. No doubt there might be some citizens who would object to the religious petitions, since we are not officially a religious nation. Political correctness might also require changing the masculine pronouns in reference to God and finding a way to include sisterhood along with "brotherhood." Even so, "America, the Beautiful" is my choice for a new national anthem.

If you watched the recent awarding of the Emmys on television, you know that a groundswell of support for my choice is already underway. Instead of opening this year's ceremony with "The Star Spangled Banner," they sang:

Oh, beautiful for spacious skies,/ For amber waves of grain,
For purple mountain majesties,/ Above the fruited plain!
America! America!/ God shed his grace on thee,
And crown thy good with brotherhood,/ From sea to shining sea.

I can sing this with patriotic fervor.

✉

...I recalled Robert Seymour's recent column in your paper in which he described his pained reluctance to sing the national anthem, the phrase, "rockets red glare, bombs bursting in air", having offended his delicate sensitivities. I don't know this, but I would bet that everyone at the New York ceremony—survivors, friends, fellow officers—would sing the anthem, and sing with tears on their faces, tears of loss and pride for fathers and mothers and friends.

It is a good thing we have a country that accommodates the Seymours amongst us, so burdened with their righteousness. And it is a good thing for us that there are others, who, without "hesitation but with courage and conviction," act and even give their lives to protect us, *B.B., Chapel Hill, NC*

✉

I suggest something easy to sing, not too many words to remember and not offensive in the least, and definitely catchy: "It's a Small World."

It's a small world after all.
It's a small world after all.
It's a small world after all.
It's a small world after all.

Easy, right? And while we're at it, what's the deal with the Old Testament? Talk about violent. We have to fix that thing. And have you heard of this guy Homer? Why are they making my kids read these horror stories in school? Come on, people. We've got talented writers and musicians on welfare who could be re-writing all this old stuff. Think about it. *W.W., Chapel Hill, NC*

✉

Dear Bob, In 1931, the school children of America were asked to vote on which song would become our national anthem. I was one of those school children. I voted for the "Star Spangled Banner." As I grew older, I regretted my vote as the song was obviously hard to sing and had a military theme. I hereby change my vote and let it be recorded in the annals of history. I now vote for "America, the Beautiful." In 1931 Congress adopted the song that America's school children had voted for. I hope Congress will now make the change. *C.V., Chapel Hill, NC*

AMERICA'S MOST DIVISIVE ISSUE

September 27, 2000

No issue in our country is more divisive than abortion. Most people are firm in their convictions about it, and there appears little hope of ending the controversy. It is a complex matter that offers no simple resolution. The question of whether abortions should be banned surfaces before every election, and the one approaching is no exception.

It is important to understand that the 1973 ruling of the Supreme Court permitting abortions was a Constitutional decision, not a moral one. It was not a judgment about whether abortions are right or wrong, but was the declaration that, in a free society, women should be responsible for making this decision for themselves without government interference. The Supreme Court came down on the side of moral neutrality, thereby respecting the plurality of our nation and the wisdom of not forcing anyone to submit to an absolutist position of another in a matter of such a personal nature. Ever since, there has been an intense ongoing dialogue between those who support the decision and those who oppose it.

A major reason for the passion propelling this debate is that abortion is not only a Constitutional issue; it is a religious issue. Where you stand on the matter generally comes down to one basic question: when does a fetus become a human being? Obviously, the potentiality for human life begins at conception, but who can say at what point an embryo becomes a person? Clearly, this is not a legal question to be decided by the courts; it is a theological question, more appropriate to church, synagogue, and mosque.

There is no consensus within the faith community. There are differing interpretations within both Judaism and Christianity, and divergent beliefs from one Christian denomination to another. Some insist that since life begins at conception, it should be regarded as sacred from the outset. Others contend that human life cannot be considered present until the point of viability: that is, when the child in the womb is capable of existing independently of its mother. Most Roman Catholics oppose abortion, for they see each pregnancy as the advent of a soul. Protestants and Jews are generally more supportive of reproductive freedom.

Given the theological dimension of the issue, some religious groups, such as Baptists—who have traditionally monitored the separation of church and state—are wary of the government ever being in the position of arbitrating a theological dispute. For them, freedom of conscience is a primary value.

Though the practice of abortion is both a Constitutional issue and a theological issue, it remains also a moral issue. Anyone facing the reality of an unwanted pregnancy and who is considering an abortion must grapple with the question, "Is it right or is it wrong?" I hope we will never think of abortion as just another way of birth control, and I hope we will never lose the conviction that human life is sacred. I hope that anyone submitting to an abortion will never take it lightly.

However, some decisions are easier than others. When the mother's physical or mental health is in danger, when the fetus is threatened with a genetic deformity, when there has been rape or incest, the decision may not be difficult. It becomes harder when such considerations as the heavy demands upon the existing family are weighed against the potential life of another child, or when it is apparent that the expected child would have little promise of being loved or cared for, or when the expected child would be the child of a child. This is what seminarians refer to as "situation ethics," when one must consider conflicting values and circumstances and try to balance them against each other before making a final decision.

Personally, I think it is unfortunate that those who hold the absolutist position against all abortions are the only ones called "pro-life." I would hope that if a decision is made to end a pregnancy, it is also a pro-life decision, meaning a responsible decision made for the well-being of the living.

I do not think our judicial system is competent to deal with this matter, for situations differ and are usually very personal and agonizing. I believe the possibility of an abortion will always create uncomfortable tensions. It confronts us with a collision of values: the value of human life, the freedom to decide, the respect for conscience, the separation of church and state, the privacy of the individual, the well-being of the living, and the promise of love and adequate care for the unborn.

I wish there were no abortions, but there will always be abortions. If they are banned, the rich will always have access to them, whereas the poor will be left to return to backroom butchery. I subscribe to the succinct conclusion that abortions should be legal, safe, and rare, and that they should be a matter of a woman's personal, responsible decision in consultation with the father, the family, and her faith counselor.

✉

The Rev. Seymour states that all abortions should be "safe, legal and rare." Although abortion may be "legal" since 1973, abortion is far from "safe or rare." Every twenty minutes an abortion is performed in North Carolina—so much for Seymour's wishes. *J.G., Chapel Hill, NC*

✉

Robert Seymour deserves our utmost respect and admiration for not only grappling with a critical political and "moral" issue, but doing so with compassion and the grace of God. He expresses well the tormenting conversation we all must go through no matter on what side of the debate we fall, a fact lost by the fiery nature of advocacy and rhetoric....

"Right to life" and "right to choose" are banner phrases that dilute the very personal and agonizing nature of dealing with these questions. If we accepted our passion on these issues as an indicator of our desire to love, both sides would realize what more we have in common. *D.R., Carrboro, NC*

✉

Dear Reverend Seymour, I am well aware of the rationalizations offered by the pro-abortion lobby in defending its position, which are ostensibly based on compassion for the mother, but I suspect are more often motivated by the desire for social engineering à la Margaret Sangster. To the contrary, I subscribe to principle that extreme cases seldom make good law, and that human life must be defended in all its stages. You, too, agree [that, indeed,] human life is sacred. Being sacred, I maintain that it is an absolute we dare not relativize. The Nazi death camps were the unacceptable price for thinking otherwise.

I will continue to look forward to future articles from your hand, in the expectation of more often agreeing with you than not, and even when not, of finding your thoughts challenging and well worth pondering. *R.M., Chapel Hill, NC*

✉

Dear Bob, Just an overdue note to congratulate you on your 9/27 Village Voices column.... I have never read a more articulate, succinct, and sensible decision—needless to say, I agree with you! *J., Chapel Hill, NC*

BOY SCOUT RULING IS HOLLOW VICTORY

July 26, 2000

The Supreme Court's decision to allow the Boy Scouts to ban homosexual scoutmasters may seem like a victory for Boy Scouts of America, but it is impossible to reconcile this action with the traditional values of the organization. The narrow five-to-four ruling was based on the right of "expressive association" under the First Amendment, but obviously there were strong feelings that the judgment should have gone the other way

It seems important to recognize that the decision was based on an interpretation of the Constitution and that such a ruling does not necessarily coincide with morality. A decision can be both legal and morally wrong. I am convinced that such is the case in this instance and that there will be troublesome consequences for the Boy Scouts organization until they eventually disavow it.

The case arose when an Eagle Scout was forced out of the organization for admitting that he was gay. He had never been involved in any inappropriate or exploitive behavior and had been considered a model scout, but he felt conflicted over violating his pledge that "A scout is honest." He was then judged unfit to belong solely on the basis of his sexual orientation. The Boy Scouts would have preferred that he be dishonest by pretending to be what he was not.

In presenting their case, the lawyers for the Boy Scouts made much of the fact that the scout oath says, "a scout is morally straight." This was revisionism, for when this oath was written, there was no indication that the use of the word "straight" had any reference to sexual orientation.

To argue otherwise clearly implies that one cannot be moral if you are homosexual. Sexual orientation, per se, has nothing to do with morality. It is sexual behavior that determines morality, whether one is heterosexual or homosexual.

The argument further implies that sexual orientation is a matter of personal choice, a view that has been discredited by biological studies. The professional association of American psychiatrists sees homosexuality as a sexual variation, not a perversion. One's sexual orientation is a part of God's creation. It is something that is given from birth and that people discover about themselves.

Apparently the scouts would prefer the "don't ask, don't tell" policy of the military, for it is no secret that some scoutmasters have been gay and that gay boys have been included without making an issue of sexual orientation. Now the stage is set for a witch hunt, and many young scouts will suffer great anxiety, worrying about the possibility of their being gay, not yet knowing.

Few things are worse for adolescents than to be judged "different" or to be rejected by their peers. Indeed, statistics show that one of the primary reasons for suicide among teenagers is the realization that they are gay and thus judged immoral, unfit, and unacceptable. The policy upheld by the Boy Scouts will be a factor in such tragedies. Their exclusion of such boys also contradicts other aspects of Scout Law, such as a commitment to kindness, courtesy, and caring. Even so, the argument before the high court stated that homosexuality is "inconsistent with the values it [Boy Scouts] seeks to instill." Now homophobia can be added to the values list.

Polls now indicate that the majority of Americans are accepting homosexuality without moral judgment. There is also recognition of the error in identifying homosexuals with a definitive "lifestyle." Both homosexuals and heterosexuals have a wide variety of lifestyles, and it is wrong to stereotype either group as associated with only one way of living.

I was a Boy Scout, and I have always admired the organization and supported it financially. Therefore, I am saddened by what I think will inevitably lead to the Boy Scouts becoming increasingly marginalized in our society. We will see erosion of public confidence in the organization despite the current boasting about its recent rapid growth. Many will now see it as intolerant, if not bigoted, and as an organization that practices discrimination.

This emerging perspective confronts many churches with a painful dilemma, for more than sixty percent of the scout troops across our nation are sponsored by churches and meet in church facilities. Can any congregation that would be outraged by the thought of refusing membership to any other minority be comfortable encouraging an organization that excludes this minority? The denominations represented in Chapel Hill that offer gays full participation in the life and leadership of their congregations must surely receive a non-discriminatory pledge from any troop they are sponsoring, thus defying the ruling of the national body.

This also presents a serious problem for the United Way. So long as Boy Scouts receive money from this source, many potential contributors will instruct that their gifts go elsewhere. Already, the Scouts have suffered the loss of United Way support in a number of major cities across the country. There will be more.

There is likely to be some attempt to resolve the problem in the Canadian way, where gay boys are recruited for special troops that are exclusively for gays. This is as offensive to me as separate churches for gays that have sprung up all over America. Such separateness is a visible judgment against Christendom. A similar separation for the Boy Scouts would be a shameful solution.

A warning that if the high court refused to permit homosexuals to hold leadership roles in the Boy Scouts, the Girl Scouts would be forced to admit men as leaders brought a swift response from the executive director of Girl Scouts USA. They already have some men, and there is no prohibition against it.

What appears to be a victory for the Boy Scouts will eventually be seen as a hollow victory. I predict that grassroots pressure will do for the organization what the Supreme Court failed to do.

Ultimately, everyone will be welcome.

...Since the Boy Scouts are a national organization, tolerance of differences should be the value they wish to instill throughout the U.S. If they are allowed to discriminate against gays, what's next?

I hope we will all stand up against this despicable policy and make our voices heard. The real danger is that we will sit back and condone it with our silence. Believe me—our children are listening and watching. *B.C., Chapel Hill, NC*

The Supreme Court ruling to allow the Boy Scouts of America to exclude avowed homosexuals from its leadership ranks is simply an affirmation of the rights that allow private, fraternal organizations to set their own government rules and regulations, not an overt attempt to discriminate against anyone.

In a sociality that seems to be increasingly open and accepting of an "anything goes" mentality, it is important that certain organizations maintain their values and standards, even if these values and standards are not as liberal as some individuals would like them to be. *R.L.G., Chapel Hill, NC*

Dear Revered Seymour, I, too, am concerned with the Boy Scouts' membership in United Way. I am very involved with Triangle United Way, as I direct a member agency and serve on a number of committees. It makes me uncomfortable to know that a colleague agency—which I indirectly support through my United Way efforts and my own contributions—has such an inhumane policy which stands to hurt many young boys. The fact that I direct a member agency also makes it difficult for me to know the best way to speak out against this. *F. H., Chapel Hill, NC*

Dear Bob, I fully respect and agree with your position opposing discrimination against homosexuals in most situations. Nevertheless, I do think that the Boy Scouts have been unfairly pilloried on this issue, and believe that they have used great restraint in defending themselves in a manner that would have hurt the entire homosexual community....

I am certain that the Boy Scouts were addressing a real problem and I believe that they made a ruling that they felt was correct to protect youngsters for whom they are responsible. They do not deserve to be castigated in the same manner that we castigate homophobes of the Christian right. They are to be congratulated for not defending themselves by citing the real issue. I love your provocative column. *J.V.W., Chapel Hill, NC*

Thanks for pointing out the casualties of the BSA decision. While attending NC State University, I lost two friends to suicide.... The reason was as you mentioned in your article. Thank you for speaking up to help save lives.... *J.C.H., Chapel Hill, NC*

PRESCRIPTION DRUG ADS CAN BE RISKY

January 9, 2000

Ever since 1997, when the Food and Drug Administration gave permission to pharmaceutical companies to advertise prescription drugs to the public, we have seen a proliferation of ads in the media.

The ones that appear on television are often misleading and even dangerous. Though required by law to indicate possible side effects, they are stated so quickly that you can hardly comprehend what is being said. Or worse, the information appears at the bottom of the screen in such small letters that is almost impossible to read. The danger of suffering stomach cramps, diarrhea, headaches, and dizziness is downplayed as a minor footnote.

For example, a medication designed to lower cholesterol adds the disclaimer that "it has not been proved that it prevents heart disease or heart attacks," which I would think is the primary reason for taking the drug. Another boasts what the drug might do for you, but a quickly flashed message at the bottom of the screen says, "This statement has not been evaluated by the Food and Drug Administration." Obviously, the sale of the medicine is more important than conveying full information about the consequences of taking it.

The same strategy of following the letter of the law, but making it difficult for potential buyers to become aware of a drug's downside, is used in the printed media. Typically, the advertisements appear on two pages, front and back. On the front, the drug is touted with glowing praise for what it can do for you, but on the reverse side, all the reports about experimental trials and possible side effects are printed in microscopic type, which would require a magnifying glass for most people to read.

I have tried to wade through some of this material and found much of it disturbing. Even the headings are enough to make anyone considering a purchase have cause to pause. There are listed Warnings, Precautions, Adverse Reactions, and Overdosage Dangers. If you read what is written under these ominous headings, you may be tempted to never take any medication again!

The fine print advertising XENICAL to block fat tells you that you are likely to have "gas, increased bowel movements, and an inability to control them." Who would want to subject themselves to that? FLOVENT for asthma includes a chemical that has been known to cause "growth suppression" in adolescents. Who would want to risk this with their child? PRILOSEC reveals that a rat in the trials developed a malignant stomach tumor that was "difficult to interpret." ZYBAN, which promises to help you stop smoking, warns against taking an extra tablet lest you "increase the danger of having a seizure." At the conclusion of all such comforting information, you are likely to find the reassuring comment that the ad "does not list all the risks."

CELEBREX, for diminishing arthritis pain, buries the discovery that "incidence of adverse experiences tended to be higher in elderly patients," who, incidentally, are the persons most likely to suffer from the disease! Those who take RELENZA for flu are told, "It may take a few days to start feeling better." To which I would add, you might start feeling better in a few days anyway!

Fortunately, each of the advertisements insists that you "discuss it with your doctor." One disclaimer for an herbal medicine reads, "This product is not intended to diagnose or cure," yet the heartburn remedy PRILOSEC presumes to suggest that, "You might have acid reflux disease."

In the past, physicians have prescribed the medicine, but with the current surge of advertisements, doctors are now vulnerable to patients telling them what drugs they would like to take. Health professionals may be reticent to deny such requests even though people may ask for medications not needed.

At a time when we have an emerging crisis because of the escalating cost of drugs, it is illuminating to learn how much money drug companies are spending for advertising. In just the first seven months of 1999, the firm that promotes CLARITIN spent a whopping ninety-seven million dollars! Thirty to fifty million for advertising a new drug is commonplace. And now we are confronted with the ads not only on television and in magazines, but in daily newspapers. Recently, PRILOSEC featured a full-page advertisement in *The News and Observer* and offered a rebate to anyone who could give proof of purchase by mailing a prescription label to the manufacturer!

New drugs are entering the market at an unprecedented pace, and their names are often so similar that they are confusing not only to the general public, but to health professionals. Indeed, one of the reasons given for the shocking statistics recently released about hospital deaths is that those responsible for administering the drugs mistake one for another.

As we approach another national election, problems related to the marketing and cost of medicinal drugs should be on every candidate's agenda.

APPRECIATION OF ART SOMETIMES DIFFICULT

October 31, 1999

I was in New York City several weeks ago and went to see Part Two of the Whitney Museum's ambitious show called "The American Century" (from 1950 until now). It explores the American identity as seen through the eyes of artists and also examines the impact of technology and media on both art and culture. All five floors of the museum are committed to this gargantuan project.

I came away both stimulated and depressed, for I observed very little that was a pleasure to see. Instead, the exhibit seemed a severe indictment of our way of life, focusing on the mundane, the materialistic, the ugly—and offering very little that inspires or uplifts the human spirit.

No doubt, I am out of step with the contemporary art world, for I still think of art as having some relationship to beauty. I looked for it in vain. Instead, my response to most of what I saw was revulsion. For example, there was a full-scale sculpture of a nude man on all fours with a trail of excrement behind him. A large photograph of a man with his pants zipper open to expose himself brought whoops of shocked laughter to troops of teenagers as they passed through the showing. And there was an arrangement of a naked light bulb, a seedy looking chair, and a bedpan, entitled "Abortion." (It is to the credit of the Whitney that a warning sign at the entrance read, "Some of the material may not be suitable for children.")

All such exhibits were far more offensive to me than the image of the Virgin Mary covered with elephant dung at the Brooklyn Museum that has caused Mayor Guiliani to stir up public protest and threaten to shut down the exhibit. I suppose that what I saw at the Whitney was considered less controversial because it was simply obscene and not profane. Indeed, I came away with the realization that the line between contemporary art and pornography is blurred, and that what seemed totally lacking at the Whitney was any evidence of the transcendent.

I also have the old-fashioned idea that good art speaks to you without requiring someone to interpret it to convince you how profound it is. Large painted panels of a single color are celebrated for their creativity. In one room there were three huge totally black squares, which said nothing whatsoever to me. I was reminded of the current Broadway play "Art," a delightful comedy about a man who paid a fortune for a huge painting called "White on White." Frankly, it is difficult for me not to suspect that some of this is a spoof and that even the artist is surprised when critics consider it so remarkable. Other panels shown were garish and composites of graffiti, most of which looked similar to drawings my grandchildren do.

Another conclusion about art prompted by my visit to the Whitney is that art is everywhere and that anything can qualify as being artistic. In one room, there was nothing but a pile of red dirt in the middle of the floor. In another, there were slashed pieces of carpet and broken bits of glass which reminded me of the piles of carpet and debris I saw beside the roadways of eastern North Carolina following Hurricane Floyd. Other contenders on display were two deep sinks attached to the wall on top of each other. And there were four vacuum cleaners exhibited, encased in glass. None of this moved me in the least!

I do not consider myself a prude nor a Philistine, for though I disliked most of what I saw at the Whitney, I would never want to censor it or inhibit the freedom of artists to express themselves in whatever way they choose. I think creativity requires freedom of expression, but I could wish that the legacy of our "American Century" in art were more balanced in being less degrading and more uplifting. If art mirrors our culture, it is not a very flattering picture of who we are or what we have made of ourselves.

The next day in the Big Apple, my wife and I went to the Metropolitan Museum of Art to see their exhibit of "Egyptian Art in the Age of the Pyramids." It was awesome and beautiful. I was especially mindful of the hushed quietness of the crowd as people moved through the galleries. It was a reverent kind of atmosphere. I thought to myself that four centuries hence people are not likely to be that respectful of much that our generation has created.

Obviously, I am a prime candidate for a course in the appreciation of modern art!

✉

I was very glad to see that despite your feelings about the Whitney exhibit, you would never want to not have the artists have the freedom to exhibit their work. *D.M., Chapel Hill, NC*

✉

Dear Bob, HOORAY! HOORAY! HOORAY! And thank you, thank you, thank you.

I have been taking art lessons and courses and consider myself to be reasonably knowledgeable in this area of interest. I have had hundreds of discussions with my peers and teachers about "what is art?" To no avail. Every time I go to an exhibition of "minimalist art" or a "happening" I become angrier and more frustrated. Partly because, especially in the beginning, it was self-doubt. Is there something wrong with me that I think that this is a perpetration on the public and an abomination? *E.G., Chapel Hill, NC*

CLASS SOCIETY MORE EVIDENT IN AMERICA

September 26, 1999

The recently released statistics showing the rapidly widening gap between the rich and the poor in America inevitably means that we are becoming more of a class society. The wealthiest 2.7 million of us have as much to spend as the poorest one hundred million put together!

This is a disturbing trend, for several reasons. First, the distance between those at the top of the economic ladder and those at the bottom makes it less likely that they will cross each other's paths. Such separation is a serious threat to a democratic society, for a democracy is based upon a social contract that includes everyone, and the health of this contract depends significantly upon there being contact between citizens. Distance breeds misunderstandings and insensitivity to the plight of others. One wealthy celebrity said publicly, "My lifestyle is so far removed from that of the average American that it is as if I were on a different planet."

The separation of people is becoming more evident everywhere. There was a time when nearly everyone in this country attended public schools, and we regarded this shared socialization as the "melting pot" to ensure cohesiveness in our society, but today private schools are proliferating, and many people in high-income brackets would never consider a public education for their children. I am sure I learned more about democracy in my small-town high school than any other place. Children from the textile mills, the local orphanage, and families of both middle class merchants and CEOs sat side by side in the classroom. (Sadly, at that time, no blacks were admitted.)

Of course, neighborhoods in this country have nearly always been composed of people from one economic class, but everyone could move freely from one neighborhood to another. Today we are witnessing a secession of neighborhoods from the community as a whole. All over the country, gated communities are on the rise. They appeal to the promise of protection and privacy, but the guard at the gate seems to symbolize the impression that these are folks who have withdrawn from the larger community. There is no welcome sign. Those who live there are free to visit people outside, but people who live elsewhere must get permission to visit those behind the gate. There is no reciprocity of contact. For this reason, both Carrboro and Cary have voted not to approve gated communities.

I have some feelings of ambivalence about having just been admitted to a privileged retirement community of senior adults called Carol Woods. It would have been difficult for me to move here if my friends had to get clearance to come to my door. In fact, there is no screening.

People who live nearby are welcome to jog around Harkness Circle, and residents pride themselves on being deeply committed to responsible involvement in the community at large as volunteers in many good causes.

The attempt to move toward more diverse residential communities where people of various economic levels have contact with each other has met strong resistance. In Chapel Hill, where the need for housing for low-income families is so acute, the repeated request of our Town Board to the legislature for permission to make it mandatory for every new development to include a percentage of such homes has fallen upon deaf ears. Fortunately, the developers of Meadowmont have agreed to build a mix of housing, including a few in a more affordable price range for those with limited incomes.

Another place where the masses once mixed and included everyone was at athletic events, but in recent years the egalitarian unity of the fans is being lost. No longer will the mailman and the mill manager sit side by side. Today the wealthy are purchasing luxury "sky boxes" where they will be separated from the crowd and have special privileges denied to others. The brazen request to make an exception to the "no-alcohol" rule for the skybox fans at the new arena in Raleigh is indicative of the trend.

More serious is the inordinate influence the wealthy class has on our judicial and political systems. It is alarming to see how money tips the scales of justice. Those at the top of the economic pyramid sometimes get away with murder, while blue-collar criminals spend long sentences behind bars. A case in point is the current willingness of many Americans to wink at presidential candidate Bush's alleged drug use, the same Bush who as governor of Texas favored felony convictions for others for similar behavior.

The growing disparity between the rich and the poor in America is a threat to our nation. Those with big money have gained increasing control of our government, while the vote of the average citizen counts for less and less. The stranglehold has become so tight that one wonders if we will ever be able to break it. Meaningful campaign-finance reform is long overdue, but there seems little likelihood of curbing the cash flow that influences preferential legislation for the privileged class. Proposed tax cuts will benefit those who need it least and will mean little or nothing to those who need money most.

Except in small towns, class stratification in America has perhaps been more evident in churches than anywhere else. There is some truth in that "old saw" that when Baptists get an education, they become Presbyterians, and if they make a lot of money, they become Episcopalians. But, fortunately, faith communities generally do try to reach out to everyone and understand that genuine community is not likely to occur when people distance themselves from one another. I hope this understanding will become pervasive in our society, for I am convinced that personal contact is our strongest protection from a fragmented America and a prerequisite for the preservation of the social contract that we call "American democracy."

Class stratification in our society has always been defined primarily by money, and if the distance between those who have most and those who have least continues to widen, I fear we will lose our cohesiveness and forget the common good.

✉

Robert, I am unable to sleep and have read your column in this morning's paper. Thank you for those words. I, too, worry about the distancing I see between people of different means in our community—in fundamental ways unlike the small towns we both came from. Class needs to be acknowledged and the widening addressed, but the mere subject is such a bugaboo—even in this university town. It was especially good that you mentioned your own ambivalence regarding Carol Woods. *J.B., Chapel Hill, NC*

✉

Dear Robert Seymour, We thank you for your beautiful articles in *The Chapel Hill News*. We look forward to more of them.

We emphatically agree with you that the growing gap between rich and poor in our country is a serious problem. (It is worse in the U.S., by the way, than any other country in the world.) *A.B. & M.L., Chapel Hill, NC*

AMERICA'S MOST CRUEL POLICY

March 3, 1999

One of the most cruel things we have ever done in this country is to empty our psychiatric hospitals while failing to implement an effective system of care in local communities. We made the mistaken assumption that municipalities would commit sufficient resources to meet the pressing needs. Consequently, many sick people suffer from preventable neglect. We would never permit such negligence of patients with other more traditional medical problems. It is a national disgrace.

One of the major reasons we see homeless people on the streets of Chapel Hill and every other city in America is untreated mental illness. It is no coincidence that widespread homelessness surfaced when the policy of "deinstitutionalization" became standard practice in our psychiatric hospitals. In the name of "freedom" and "constitutional rights," we have condemned people who are incapable of assessing their own conditions. On this point, I part company with the ACLU on its well-intended case for the self-determination of everyone, for I think it is indefensible to permit such human misery in the name of civil liberties. There must be a better way.

Freedom is not such a cherished value when one has only the freedom to choose which garbage bin to search for food or which place on the street promises better protection for sleeping on a freezing night. Homeless mentally ill people are abandoned, not free. The freedom to be psychotic is no freedom at all.

Current laws prevent anyone from being committed to a psychiatric hospital who is not judged to be dangerous to themselves or to others. But surely the lifestyle of the millions who live on the streets of America *is* dangerous to those who try to survive there and civil libertarians falsely presume their mental competence to cope. Adding "helplessness" as a further category for mandatory assistance would seem to be a step in the right direction.

Sadly, all across America, many mentally ill people end up in jail. Sometimes they deliberately create a disturbance in order to be assured of a place to sleep and a square meal. Others commit more serious crimes in their attempts to survive, and jailers everywhere are complaining about their inability to manage mentally ill people who are ending up where they should never be. In reality, we are shifting from the Department of Mental Health to the Department of Corrections. We have moved from prevention to punishment. We should not be surprised that helpless mentally ill people sometimes are sentenced to death row. Indeed, in North Carolina, the last two persons we have executed had a history of mental illness. How much longer can we tolerate such inhumanity!

We have witnessed repeated tragedies when persons with paranoid schizophrenia are isolated and act out what they perceive to be perfectly rational behavior. The Williamson burst of violence on Henderson Street in Chapel Hill brought such a crisis close to home, and recently we have read of another tragedy in New York where a young woman met her death by being pushed off a subway platform and killed by a train.

Such incidents increase the public's fear of meaningless violence, and this is understandable. However, it is important to know that although no one can predict with complete accuracy what the future holds, schizophrenics are rarely violent. And so, we are faced with a difficult dilemma. Obviously, we cannot commit to a hospital everyone who suffers from schizophrenia. Is the only alternative, then, to expose society to this margin of unpredictable risk? And to expose schizophrenics to predictable risks of life on the streets?

Fortunately, there is another option that holds promise both of addressing the needs of the mentally ill and also protecting the safety of the community. It is called "out-patient commitment," a program whereby persons who need medication but who are not reliable in taking it can be required to submit to regular monitoring, with the threat of hospitalization if they refuse to cooperate. We can be proud of the fact that North Carolina is one of the states that has passed such legislation, though it is not always used consistently. This law makes it easier to help people who fail to recognize their own mental states and who erroneously conclude that they are well enough to stop taking their prescription drugs. We need to go a step further and offer a continuum of services, including vocational training, socialization, and communal housing. Such policies are needed not only for the treatment of those who are ill, but also for the support of their families who live with the constant fear of what might happen if their loved one has no access to such services and is left untreated.

As a pastor in Chapel Hill for many years, I have counseled and tried to offer help to scores of mentally ill people. Usually these are individuals who live on the edge. They are not sick enough to be hospitalized, or well enough to function and cope for themselves in normal society. Occasionally, I would succeed in sending persons who had become acutely disturbed to the state mental hospital at Butner, but usually they would be returned to Chapel Hill in only a few days. Crises would keep recurring and trips to the hospital resembled a revolving door. Fortunately, today newly discovered drugs can make a dramatic difference in the ability of mentally ill persons to function reasonably well when they are faithful in taking their medication. This probably means that the policy of deinstitutionalization is here to stay. Large psychiatric hospitals are a thing of the past.

Therefore, it is imperative to lift the level of care in every local community. Whenever a crisis occurs involving a mentally ill person, the blame game usually begins, but there is enough blame to include us all. Our society seldom treats mental illness as seriously as it does other diseases, and limited resources have made it impossible to be sufficiently assertive to reach everyone who needs help. And sadly, diseases of the mind still carry a stigma in American culture, so there is a temptation to try to conceal it. A new commitment to our fellow citizens who endure such suffering is overdue.

IN DEFENSE OF PUBLIC SCHOOLS

January 29, 1999

It is time for everyone who believes in public schools to be more vocal in supporting them. Americans are beginning to believe the lie that public schools have failed. There are persuasive voices all around us urging alternatives that could eventually lead to the dismantling of public education.

The first major assault on public education in the South came with the integration of the schools, when many whites abandoned them and brought into being private academies all over the region. Many of these fledgling institutions failed, but large numbers of them have survived and continue to attract community leadership that public education needs.

There has also been an increase in private schools for the privileged, such as the new one recently opened in Cary where the top administrator was quoted in *The News and Observer* as saying their intention was to attract "the cream of the cream." All such ventures push us closer to a two-tiered educational system, one for the rich and one the poor. They also deprive pupils of exposure to democratic diversity and the experience of relating to people of all ethnic and economic backgrounds, which is so fundamental to a free society.

Then there are private schools underwritten by religious groups that want their children nurtured in a curriculum and by faculty more focused on religious faith, such as the new school soon to be available to the Triangle Jewish community. Parochial schools are somewhat rare in the South, but this alternative is clearly acceptable in a country that operates on the principle of separation of church and state.

Of course, I believe in the freedom of citizens to educate their children in all such private institutions, but I do not think it is the responsibility of the state to create, support, or subsidize alternatives to public schools. Yet, today, for the first time in our history, a slim majority of Americans favor full or partial tuition for all such private or parochial school opportunities.

The plan that poses the most serious assault on public education is the issuing of vouchers to families; this would permit parents to use state funds to send their children to private schools. This plan is the centerpiece of the education agenda of the Republican majority in Congress and is supported by Republican governors in more than thirty states. It has been approved and put into practice in Wisconsin, and although challenged in the courts by those who believe it violates a constitutional principle, the Supreme Court has thus far declined to hear the case.*

Advocates for vouchers argue that public schools need competition, but their ultimate goal may be the privatization of public education. Many struggling private schools are eager for public funding, but should taxpayers be forced to underwrite religious and private education? And as massive monies are siphoned away from public schools, what happens to those students who are left behind? Especially those children with special needs, who are expensive to educate and are seldom welcomed at private schools.

Another alarming trend is the rapid growth of home schooling. In a free society, parents should have the prerogative to educate their own children in the home setting, but the state has a stake in this. Voices from the religious right have been the strongest advocates of home schooling, particularly Pat Robertson and James Dobson. And as we approach the new millennium, there is a crusade underway called "Exodus 2000," urging parents to take their children out of public education and to undertake the task themselves. Many such children will no doubt be deprived of adequate socialization and will likely emerge from such protectionism without the skills to critique the prevailing culture, either for appropriation or correction.

Here in North Carolina, we have launched an alternative educational system, under the guise of experimental education, by permitting the creation of charter schools. Though these schools are funded by the state, they have little accountability to the state. Many of these ventures are meeting in inadequate facilities, and half of the teachers do not hold licenses to teach. Furthermore, nearly half of these schools are primarily of one race and look very much like state-approved re-segregation.

Perhaps it is too early to pass judgment on the quality of education that is occurring in the charters, but it is not too early to urge that their number not be increased until adequate evaluation is made. Many feel that the charter movement is a first step toward getting state support for all private schools. It is imperative that North Carolina keep faith with the stated philosophy for charters, that their purpose is to enrich education, not to impoverish traditional public education. Otherwise, we may be on the verge of radically changing public education in our state in a way that will do irreparable harm.

Many parents who are pulling their children out of the public schools are doing so because of false fears and inadequate information. We have all been shocked by violence in the nation's schools, but statistics still show that schools may be the safest place children can be. Those who think religion has been banished from the schools should know that though there can be no official prayers, students are free to pray at any time and that there can be religious clubs after school, just like any other extra-curricular activity.

We are fortunate in Chapel Hill to have one of the best school systems in the state, but here, too, our schools need strong support. I applaud Governor Hunt's Smart Start program and President Clinton's efforts to provide funding for school construction in areas of the country where money for such purposes is difficult to acquire locally. I am wedded to the conviction that the future of our democracy may well depend upon the preservation of a strong system of public education.

Did you know that despite all of the public school bashing that seems so prevalent, a study by the Rand Corporation concludes that

American schools have steadily improved over the past twenty years? Your support can ensure the continuation of this trend.

** In 2002, the Supreme Court declared vouchers to be constitutional*

Dear Bob, Thanks for the note and your GOOD column. Our public schools are getting better and better. And we MUST keep them strong. Thanks for your leadership. *Jim Hunt, Raleigh, NC*

VISUAL ENTERTAINMENT ERODES OUR MORALITY

August 7, 1998

I do not consider myself a prude, but I am willing to run the risk of being called "an old fuddy duddy." For I have come to the conclusion that a major cause of the corruption of American culture is the visual media, both films and television.

In her recent autobiography, Katharine Graham remembers her mother testifying before a congressional committee in the 1940s about the film industry using its resources for "a progressive vulgarization of the public mind and for the debasing of public morals." The trend continues.

Remember the shock when Rhett Butler, in the movie, *Gone with the Wind*, was allowed to say to Scarlett, "Frankly, my dear, I don't give a damn!" That sounds almost quaint today when compared to the foul language that punctuates the dialogue of so many contemporary films.

My wife and I went to see *Good Will Hunting* after Robin Williams won an Academy Award for his role in it. The language was so offensive that it distracted from the story line. Every other word was the "f—-" word. It was the kind of speech that would have warranted washing out one's mouth with soap in a previous generation.

Now that I am retired, on occasion I turn on the television in the afternoon and stumble onto the "soaps." I was not prepared for what I saw and heard. The plots all seem to revolve around infidelity and intrigue. Promiscuity is portrayed as the emerging standard of morality in sexual relationships. The same is true of many TV sitcoms. A recent episode of *Frazier* drew laughs as five people stayed overnight in a ski lodge and competed to see who would sleep with whom for a one-night stand.

When Dan Quayle criticized *Murphy Brown* for glamorizing the birth of a child out of wedlock, he was judged by many people to be "not with it." Now that the show has terminated, Candice Bergen says she sides with Quayle and reports that she felt very uncomfortable when her scriptwriters put her in that situation. She worries about family values and the visual media's impact on public morality.

With public morality on my mind, I decided to go see *There's Something about Mary*, which was billed as "the sleeper film of the summer season." It merited a full two-page ad in *The New York Times* but was thoroughly panned by PBS's film critic. I have seldom seen anything so crude, vulgar, and insensitive as this picture. The audience is expected to laugh at the physically handicapped, the mentally retarded, and cruelty to animals. I would hesitate to describe here the two sex scenes in the film that elicited the most hilarity from the viewers. The audience response disturbed me almost as much as what was on the screen. I was so repulsed that I felt compelled to exit before the movie ended.

The most disturbing indictment of the visual media is the way it glorifies violence. Just seeing the previews of *Lethal Weapon* was more than I could stomach. The concern expressed by Congress about such gratuitous violence several years ago seems to have had little effect on the industry. The rating system was supposedly improved, but this gesture seemed to give the filmmakers a green light to serve up more mayhem than ever.

Why are we surprised when children shoot children? The average TV-watching kid has witnessed eight thousand murders and over one hundred thousand acts of violence by the time he or she leaves elementary school! Psychologists say there is absolutely no doubt that higher levels of viewing violence correlate with increasing acceptance of aggressive behavior in our culture.

I play a little game with my TV remote that might be called, "find the gun." I flip through the channels to see how long it will take me to locate an act of violence. Inevitably, within two to three minutes, there is someone on the screen with a gun in hand. If Hollywood refuses to use its freedom responsibly, where does this leave us? Maybe it is time to call the carnage from violence "a health epidemic" and to use this as leverage to bring more pressure to bear upon the filmmakers. We would not tolerate having dispensers on our television sets spewing deadly germs into our living rooms!

And speaking of health, have you noticed that, at a time when cigarette smoking is denounced for its demonstrable adverse danger to health, many of your favorite actors still reach for a cigarette in almost every scene? CBS suggests that this is no accident but is probably an indication of a "deal" between the industry and Hollywood. In light of all the lying we have heard from cigarette manufacturers, it is easy to believe there is a collusion to encourage fans to emulate the habits of their favorite stars. The silent message conveyed is that smoking is a grown-up thing to do or a sign of sophistication.

Hollywood can also be faulted for those anti-establishment films that favorably portray the drug culture as a way of protest. The most recent of these was *Fear and Loathing in Las Vegas*, which features a protracted parade of drug snorting and swallowing and presents this lifestyle as an understandable response to the Vietnam War. Adolescents who tend to find counterculture activities attractive may be inclined to "just say yes."

This headline in the newspaper caught my eye: "U.S. Culture Hurts Foreign Youth." It is my contention that we are all hurt by the kind of garbage that is increasingly masking as entertainment. Hollywood defends itself by claiming that it is only reflecting reality. I contest this judgment as a partial truth at best. Visual media are eroding our moral standards.

✉

Dear Dr. Seymour: I just have to muse at how we can be so alike in our beliefs and so different in our politics. Either I am a frustrated liberal trapped in a conservative's body, or you are really a conservative living in a town where the good work you do would not be possible if you admitted your conservatism, because no one would listen to you...

We true conservatives—not the politicians, redneck, and racists—believe in an interconnectedness between all the various "groups" who would work to erode the Judeo-Christian principals upon which our society was built and to which it must return if we are to have hope. Thank you for accurately identifying one of those groups in your column today. I shall look forward to your future columns on the music industry, militant gay organizations, and the Al Sharptons of the world who seek to divide us in order to increase their personal power and wealth. *H.B.D., Chapel Hill, NC*

✉

Cheers to the Rev. Robert Seymour for his forthright column on the steady erosion of our moral standards by films and television. I congratulate him for expressing what many of us must feel as we watch the ever-growing use of profanity, sex and violence in our visual media...

What can we as parents, grandparents, and concerned citizens do...? The question becomes more complex when we also oppose censorship and the abridgement of freedom of speech. When I think about how to approach Hollywood and the New York film and TV producers about this issue, I am forcibly reminded of Joseph Welch's question to Senator Joseph McCarthy at the Senate hearings on Communism: "Have you no decency, sir?" *D.P.B., Chapel Hill, NC*

✉

Dear Bob: A gentle old person asked if I'd like to have lunch with him and go to a movie. I asked him to make the choice of film, since I have not kept up with what's showing. He picked the one advertised as "hilarious."...As with your reaction, I was not only dumb-founded that any such had been written and produced, but distressed that a number of the audience thought it was funny. *J.B., Chapel Hill, NC*

DEATH PENALTY SENTENCES ARE NOT FAIR

June 7, 1998

There are many reasons to get rid of the death penalty, but perhaps the most persuasive reason is that it is unfair. Many people commit similar crimes, but the punishment is not the same. Our justice system works like a lottery. Many factors determine who is executed and who is allowed to live. There is no consistency in capital-crime sentencing.

Consider the following:

Rich people can get away with murder. I challenge you to name a single wealthy person who has been put to death.

If you are a celebrity or can exploit your popularity or manage to inspire widespread sympathy, you are likely to be spared paying the ultimate price for your crime.

If you are a white person and kill a black person, you will probably be allowed to live, but if you are a black person and kill a white person, you will probably die. In America, there is still abundant evidence that we value a white life more than the lives of people of color. You cannot rule out racial prejudice among members of a jury as a major factor in influencing their verdict or in the sentencing decision. Many more African-Americans have been condemned to death than whites.

If you are unable to afford adequate legal counsel, your chance of being executed is much greater than that of those who can afford to employ the best. Indigent prisoners are at the mercy of court-appointed lawyers, many of whom have had little or no experience in defending someone accused of a capital crime. Our present procedure is comparable to asking a physician who is in general practice to perform brain surgery.

Some counties have the reputation of being much harsher in their sentencing than do others. The kind of justice you receive depends in some measure upon where your case is heard.

The appeal procedures following a conviction are inconsistent. The role of the appellate court is to inhibit a rush to judgment and to look for irregularities in the jurisdictional process, but often the public denounces such attempts as "legal technicalities."

It is not uncommon for persons who are sentenced to death to be denied any possibility of being spared, because most politicians today feel it is necessary to appear "tough on crime." Political expediency is often a primary reason for an execution.

If you are against the death penalty, lawyers will not allow you to be seated on a jury that is hearing a capital case. Thus, from the beginning of the trial, the cards are stacked in favor of execution.

If you are mentally ill—and the majority of convicted criminals show some deficiency in mental health—you will probably be put to death regardless.*

If you come from a dysfunctional family and have been abused or neglected as a child, you are likely to held fully responsible for your fate, thus taking the punishment not only for the crime you committed, but also for the crimes committed against you.

The American Bar Association (whose members are primarily responsible for administering the system) has voted to request a national moratorium on the death penalty until each jurisdiction can ensure that death penalty cases are administered fairly and impartially. Four specific areas were noted as falling far short of fairness:

1. Competency of counsel in capital cases. The ABA found that in most cases grossly unqualified and under-compensated lawyers failed to give adequate defense.

2. Weakness in the habeas-corpus system. Prisoners are being denied their proper right to appeal to state and federal courts.

3. Discrimination on the basis of race. The court system is infected with biases that are found in our society-at-large.

4. Execution of mentally retarded people and juveniles. (A bill has just been introduced in the Texas legislature to lower the age level for executions to eleven!)

It is significant that the ABA is not asking for the abolition of the death penalty but rather that there be a cessation of executions until ways can be found to ensure fairness and end the arbitrariness of present procedures. There is a widespread judgment, however, that such an assignment is doomed to failure and that the only acceptable resolution of the problem is to join all other Western democracies in abolishing the death sentence permanently.

In the recent Playmakers production of *The Threepenny Opera*, the murdering thief was sentenced to die. He was a charming rogue, and as he stood on the gallows with the rope around his neck, you could feel the resistance of the audience to carrying out the sentence. Then, at the last moment, an actor stepped forward and said, "since this is not real life he will be allowed to live," and everyone breathed a sigh of relief.

Real life is in Raleigh, where 180 people languish on death row as their execution date approaches. How long will we tolerate this judicial procedure without total revulsion?

I believe most North Carolinians are fair-minded people. If for no other reason than its demonstrable unfairness, this barbarous practice of premeditated murder by the state should be stopped.

** In 2002, the Supreme Court ruled that mentally retarded persons cannot be executed.*

Dear Bob: My relatives in Norway look with astonishment and revulsion on two things in the United States: our death penalty and our gun culture, with all the killings. The abolition of death penalties and the control of handguns and automatic machine weapons seem impossible in today's climate, but your article goes a long way in getting out the facts about the death penalty *A.S.L., Chapel Hill, NC*

THE HEALTHCARE "INDUSTRY" OFFENDS ME

April 5, 1998

In my judgment, one of the worst tragedies of our time is allowing the healthcare profession to be taken over by business. It is a prime illustration of the increased secularization of our culture. Much of modern medicine, which began as a holy calling, is now managed by those whose priority is profit. Making money is eclipsing the original motivation that was rooted in compassion for the sick.

It is no accident that medicine as we know it emerged in Western civilization. It grew out of the conviction that illness is something alien in God's world and that we are called to do everything we can to overcome it. In the Christian tradition, healing was a vital part of the ministry of Jesus. Consequently, people entered the profession from a sense of calling and holy obedience. This accounts for the fact that in nearly every third-world country, one of the first efforts of missionaries was the founding of hospitals to alleviate the suffering of the people.

To a large degree, the same is true in this country. The faith community started many of the best hospitals in American cities, and significantly, many of them are named "Mercy Hospital." Some of them were staffed, and still are, by religious orders—and by people who would never have considered seeking to make a profit from the misfortunes of others. For them, their work was a ministry.

Because of this background, it offends me today to hear the vocabulary of the business community applied to the healing professions. When I go to the hospital, I want to be regarded as a "patient" and not seen as a "consumer." When people refer to healthcare as an "industry," I bristle, and when they talk about "marketing" medicine, it sounds blatantly inappropriate.

Today the mood of healthcare "providers" is fierce competition, and this priority often compromises the traditional emphasis on empathy and compassion. Those hospitals that were once supported by the faith community are faced with painful choices, and many are being taken over by businesses whose mentality is altogether different from that of those who had previously operated them.

The threat of a takeover is compounded by the fear that those healthcare institutions, which once offered generous care for the indigent, will no longer be willing to do so. This was a major concern in Raleigh when The Wake Medical Center was courted by a number of companies. The hospital feared that poor people from eastern North Carolina would no longer be welcome there.

The irony of all this is that the takeover of the medical profession by business was intended to lower the cost of healthcare. It has not happened. It is disconcerting to read about the high salaries paid to the CEOs of healthcare companies. You begin to wonder if you will receive the care you need, when the priorities shift from the patient to that of profit making for stockholders. Nearly every day in the press you read about people who feel that their health has been jeopardized by a business decision overriding a physician's recommendation. It was a strange day in America when it required an act of Congress to ensure that pregnant women would be guaranteed more time in the hospital for the delivery of their babies! The pride we once had in our superior medical establishment is being replaced by a mounting anxiety about the quality of care we are receiving.

I attended the recent community meeting convened by the Coalition for the Public Trust, the group advocating the establishment of a charitable foundation in exchange for permission to Blue Cross to become a for-profit business. Apparently, both parties feel that a mutually beneficial agreement is in the making whereby the people of North Carolina may be blessed by as much as fifty million dollars a year to fund healthcare causes while Blue Cross retains all its assets. It sounds like a good deal for everyone, but I confess to having felt a sense of sadness at the meeting. For too long I have thought of Blue Cross as an organization committed to insuring and serving citizens at the lowest possible cost. It will be difficult for me to think of it now as motivated to make as much money as possible in a competitive market.

Happily, some counter movements are surfacing in the field of medicine that do not march to the beat of the business drummer. Significantly, most of them are emerging from faith communities. The hospice movement came into being to provide more compassionate and less expensive care for the dying and to bring an end to the patient's fear of succumbing behind white hospital curtains in the presence of strangers. And more recently, parish nursing is becoming a part of the organizational structure of many local congregations across the country. Also, the chaplaincy movement, which brought the pastoral care of Christian clergy and Jewish rabbis to the hospital setting, does not yet seem threatened by the downsizing efforts of big business, but one wonders if these ministries will survive in the long run. Furthermore, even at such a prestigious place as Harvard Medical School, students are now being taught to respect the importance of spirituality and the practice of prayer for the sick as a factor in the patient's overall well-being.

Obviously, we are caught up in the midst of radical change in our healthcare delivery system, and it is too early to see where it will all end. I predict that both the "consumers" and the physicians will become increasingly disenchanted with the business mentality that now prevails and that, eventually, we will turn to government-supported, universal healthcare for everyone.

✉

Dear Bob, Of course many of us are distressed at the "business" turn of many services which seem to us inappropriate as for-profit ventures. Among them also are child-care centers, adult care facilities, schools, and senior centers. I simply do not believe it is possible to provide the quality of care or service human beings deserve AND provide a return to stockholders! *L.B., Chapel Hill, NC*

A LOTTERY MAKES LOSERS OF US ALL

June 6, 1997

North Carolina does not need a state lottery. What we do need is moral leadership in Raleigh that would stand up against the stampede to create one.

At first the governor was opposed to the lottery, but now he has capitulated, with the condition that the money gained by this method be used for Smart Start. He would look with favor on institutionalized gambling if it is for the sake of our children. Our governor should know better. In other states where a lottery has been operating, the windfall of large sums of money promised to further education has been largely illusive.

Now it appears that our legislature is ready to approve a statewide referendum so that you and I can decide for ourselves. This is an irresponsible way to avoid a highly charged issue. Our elected leaders should be willing to deal with the merits of such a proposal without passing the buck to the voters. They all know that when a state legalizes a lottery, it seduces its citizens with false promises of riches. Could it be that our legislators are unwilling to take a stand on this matter because of the intense pressure put upon them by the powerful lottery lobbyists?

Let it be said clearly: a lottery is immoral. It is ironic, at a time when politicians talk so much about family values and character education, that we should even be discussing the subject, much less seriously considering it. Ironically, in some of the thirty-eight states where lotteries now exist, they are advertised a "good family fun." But they are exploitive, addictive, and corrupting.

The appeal of a lottery undermines the work ethic. It caters to the principle of "something for nothing" and encourages false hopes about "when my ship comes in."

Obviously, this is a bogus hope, for statistics show that winning the lottery is about as likely as being struck by lightning.

Playing a lottery also caters to the human tendency to enjoy the thrill of doing something risky.

Indeed, for many people the risk appeal will be so irresistible that they will put in jeopardy far more of their assets than they can afford to lose, and a few will unwittingly risk everything they have by becoming compulsive gamblers. There is abundant evidence that gambling in any form lures some people to participate beyond their ability to control it. It is addictive. And instead of its leading to winning great wealth, it sometimes leads to losing everything. The thrill of risking all they have leads people to obsessive gambling which they are powerless to stop. (There is a national organization for compulsive gamblers called Gamblers Anonymous, similar to Alcoholics Anonymous.)

The worst effect of a state lottery would be that those who can least afford it are likely to play. It is a cruel method of exploiting the poor. In other states where lotteries are played, low-income neighborhoods are often targeted by agents who prey on the poor by timing their ads to coincide with the receipt of monthly welfare and Social Security checks. People who have little or no discretionary income will be tempted to believe that they can escape their dire situations by buying lottery tickets instead of food. The lottery becomes a kind of voluntary tax upon those who are the most vulnerable to poverty and hardship. How can we respect any government that would put at further risk its least secure citizens and then have the gall to piously proclaim that it is doing it for "the public interest"!

Furthermore, it is a well-known fact that wherever gambling exists in any form, it frequently makes friends with corruption and crime. Surely there is enough corruption in government already without opening the door wider for more. In answer to the argument that people are going to gamble anyway, so why should not the state profit from it, I would answer that I prefer my vice to be available without government assistance.

Another strange argument in support of a state lottery is that the state needs money. If this is in fact the case, why were we able to cut taxes during the last legislative session, and why do we hear continuous pleas for more tax cuts now? Are we suggesting that it is better to offer more tax cuts for affluent North Carolinians and proceed with the lottery as a less painful way to support state programs? Surely it is more moral to pay for the needs of our state with a fair taxation that distributes the burden proportionately according to all citizens' ability to pay.

We are also being told that we need a lottery because so much money is going out of the state to buy lottery tickets from nearby states. With Virginia and South Carolina and Georgia moving in this direction, how can we afford to hold out? We seldom hear that a state lottery would likely take a large chunk of money outside the state to pay the lottery operators who will probably be located elsewhere. I suppose those who reason that we should begin a lottery in order to compete with our neighbors would also conclude that if the states that border us establish state-run bordellos, we should legalize our own to keep the business at home.

Few doubt that if the people of North Carolina are asked to decide whether or not they want a lottery, it will pass. Why? Because the lottery business will blanket our state with a persuasive campaign to convince us that it would be a good thing. Once it has passed, we will continue to be blitzed with advertising encouraging everyone to play. Indeed, we may even be made to feel that we are not good citizens if we are not buying tickets. And the gambling mentality will be entrenched in the minds of our children, who are not likely to be aware of the dangers that lie further down the road to which it leads.

I hope there are some leaders in Raleigh who will have the courage to speak out with a resounding "NO!" We do not need this corrupting influence in our state. Let's leave this racket to the mob and not try to make a virtue out of a vice by a government takeover.

A DANGEROUS ECONOMIC TREND

February 28, 1997

In the recent Martin Luther King, Jr., holiday observances that I read about or attended, I was struck by the emphasis given to King's concern about economic inequality in America. Since his death, the chasm separating the rich from the poor has steadily widened in our society. The rich are getting richer, while the poor are falling further and further behind.

It is alarming to learn that one percent of our population owns almost fifty percent of the wealth, and that twenty percent of our citizenry claims eighty percent of our economy. People at the bottom of the scale are trying to survive on slivers from the economic pie, instead of slices, and others are struggling to meet their basic needs with merely crumbs.

In the last year alone, there has been a skyrocketing increase in the number of billionaires in our country, now totaling 135! The average net worth of persons listed in the annual *Forbes* 400 richest residents exceeds one billion dollars! We have a rapidly growing new class in America: the super-rich, whose income has ballooned to almost unimaginable proportions, while the income of the majority has increased very little or stagnated.

This has led to erosion of the middle class, with a few being elevated to the privileged while many others have been added to the ranks of the working poor. A commentary on what is occurring was symbolized by one of our former congressmen identifying himself as a member of the middle class, with an annual income of over $200,000! The gulf separating those who receive the highest salaries from those whose pay is lowest is beginning to appear not simply indefensible, but obscene. The average annual wages of the typical chief executive officer in American corporations exceeds $2,000,000, while the average teacher in America's public schools receives $22,000. The technological revolution and globalization of our economy have resulted in enormous accumulations of money for a few but has led to little or no increase in income for forty-five percent of the work force.

Resistance to addressing this trend was dramatically revealed by how difficult it was to get Congress to increase the minimum wage of those at the bottom of the economic ladder, some nine million people. Ironically, even after the new $5.15 per hour minimum wage becomes a reality, it will have less actual purchasing value than did the minimum wage in the 1970s. I shall not soon forget the question asked by the moderator of CNN's *Crossfire* to the Republican congressman from Oklahoma who fought so diligently to defeat the increase. The moderator asked, "Congressman, doesn't it make you feel a little uncomfortable to be against paying someone more than four dollars an hour when you are being paid sixty-three dollars an hour?"

A new phenomenon in America is the advent of the so-called "working poor." These are people who have full-time jobs but who still need assistance in order to pay the rent and put food on their tables. How can we say that we value work if we are not willing to pay for it? Surely people who work for a living are entitled to a living wage!

I am confident that if he were alive today, Martin Luther King, Jr., would insist that we cease talking about minimum wage and begin advocating a "living wage" for everyone. There are those who would like to downplay the economic emphasis of his message and to forget that his death coincided with his crusade in Memphis to secure decent salaries for the garbage collectors there. King moved beyond his concern for racial divisions in our society, as he realized that an even greater threat to our social contract was the divide between the affluent and the poor. The Poor People's March, which he anticipated prior to his death, was intended for both black and white poor to protest together.

All of this is relevant to implementing the new guidelines for welfare reform. While some people who have been on public assistance may be moved toward self-sufficiency, it is most likely that many others will be pushed into desperate destitution. With the scaling down of the availability of food stamps to the working poor, and with the mandate for people to work where there are no jobs to be found, the gap between the haves and the have-nots may become more extreme than ever before. Why is it that we persist in trying to give greater tax breaks for the rich while assaulting the indigent? We are witnessing the emergence of a hard-nosed America. I saw a bumper sticker in Atlanta last week that read, "Feed the Homeless to the Hungry."

In his Inaugural Address, our president boasted that our economy is good. We would do well to ask, "Good for whom?" It is not good for the elderly in Chapel Hill who live on fixed incomes and who must on occasion decide whether to buy their medications or pay their rent. It is not good for part-time employees who get no benefits. It is not good for those who have a minimum-wage-paying job and must live in the community shelter until they can accumulate sufficient funds for a first-month's payment for a place to live. It is not good for those who live in our inner cities, which look like the Third World and where no "help wanted" signs appear. It is not good for one out of every four American children who are reared in poverty. It is time we faced the fact that the rising economic tide in our country has failed to lift all boats.

The trend is dangerous and, if it continues, will undermine our democracy. A healthy democratic society is one in which the two ideals of equality and freedom are kept in balance. But the freedom of unbridled capitalism tends to compromise equality and causes the social contract, which hold us all together, to unravel. Evidence of this happening is not hard to find. I am convinced that this accounts for much of the cynicism now being voiced about our government. People are waking up to the fact that we are shifting to a system where our votes have diminishing value, one in which moneyed special interests have privileged access to the corridors of power and call the shots.

My wife and I attended an estate-planning workshop offered recently by a financial firm in our community. As we left, a friend said to me, "It sure sounded like the system is rigged for the benefit of the rich." Of course, he was right. And it was interesting to note how many times the workshop leader said, "Let me tell you about a little trick that will enable you to avoid taxes."

Nobody likes to be played for a sucker. We have heard many calls to sacrifice for the common good. I predict that such appeals will begin to fall on increasingly deaf ears unless we can do a better job in this country of distributing our enormous wealth. Someone has said, "Justice is the virtue that renders to each his or her own." This definition convicts America as an immoral society until we do a better job of closing the gap between the super rich and the desperate poor.

✉

Dear Bob, I am certain that when the Rev. Martin Luther King, Jr., started preaching his "gospel of economics" that he became truly dangerous to the powers that be, and brought about his murder.

The trouble is that none of these evils can be changed until we have complete reform of the way political campaigns are paid for. And unless reform comes about soon, there is little hope for our much-vaunted "democracy."
A.S., Chapel Hill, NC

WELFARE REFORM AND PREJUDICES AGAINST THE POOR

September 18, 1996

In all the talk about the need to "change welfare as we know it," one reason, which to my awareness has not yet been mentioned, is our prejudice against the poor. The welfare reform bill is really not about entitlements because the entitlements of the middle and upper classes have not been touched. Nor has corporate welfare suffered significant reduction. Only the poor are being targeted for severe cuts in benefits. Though many would argue that "it is for their own good" in order to liberate them from dependency, there can be little doubt that the welfare reform bill was in part punitive in purpose.

Americans do not like to consider the possibility that our economic system has failed. We perpetuate the fiction that anyone who wants a job can get one. We prefer to overlook the dark side of capitalism and refuse to face the reality that there is nowhere near the number of entry level unskilled jobs in our society that would be required to employ all the able-bodied people now on welfare.

And so we tend to assume that the fault is not in the system but with the poor themselves. The most deep-seated prejudice against the poor is that the poor are lazy or deadbeats. In this land acclaimed for opportunity, we persist in believing that anyone worth his or her salt can make a living, and we consider welfare a reward for weakness. The Horatio Alger myth dies hard. Most Americans tend to look down upon the poor as a class, as if their circumstances were of their own choosing. It is surprising that we cling to this judgment at a time when more and more jobs that were traditionally open to laboring men and women are being taken over by technology or moved overseas. The welfare reform bill becomes a mockery unless it guarantees the availability of a job. Initiative and ambition add up to nothing where jobs are nonexistent.

Of course, there are some poor people who do not work because they are lazy, but this is as true among the rich as well as the poor. In fact, most poor people would prefer to work, but they are either lacking in sufficient education, or are ill trained, physically or mentally handicapped, or elderly.

Welfare reform is often a code phrase for racial prejudice. There is a widespread perception that most welfare recipients are black, although statistics show that by far the largest number are white.

In the Old South, many people salved their consciences about widespread poverty in the black community by appealing to another prejudice that dies hard. We romanticized their condition with the myth of the "happy darky," who was like a carefree child who loved to sing and dance and sleep in the noonday sun. Surely, no one enjoys being cold or hungry or ill housed! Television sit-coms such as *The Beverly Hillbillies* also pander to stereotypes, suggesting that poor people are amusingly innocent and naive.

All of these attitudes toward the poor add up to the persistent suspicion that they are somehow undeserving. Instead of considering the possibility that there may be something wrong with our system, we prefer to believe there must be something wrong with the poor. We look for ways to blame the victims, to confirm our belief that they are at fault, to conclude that they have brought their situation upon themselves. Like Job's comforters, we look at them accusingly, convinced that some failure on their part accounts for their condition. Then, not surprisingly, when we try to alleviate their problems, we become punitive.

Those of us who are not poor prefer to think that whatever success we have achieved has come to pass because of our initiative and hard work. We are slow to conclude that we may be where we are because of the good fortune of our birth and ancestry, our inheritance from our family, and the good breaks that came to us unsought along the way. It is far more reassuring to assume that we have earned our place in society than to press home the question of how deserving we might be. The corollary of this, of course, is that the poor man has made his bed, too, and must lie in it. The truth is, however, that not many of us would be where we are today if we had received only what we have deserved.

The prejudices I have described surface in Chapel Hill when people complain about the homeless shelter being downtown. Initially, it was impossible to find a location for the shelter because citizens considered poor people to be "undesirable." When an offer was made to build a shelter adjacent to the police station, it became clear that many people equated poverty with crime. Those in economic straits were perceived as a criminal threat; therefore, offering them lodging next to law enforcement was judged to be an ideal place. Accusations that the shelter is the root of all downtown crime continue, despite the fact that repeated investigative reporting shows that only a small percentage of those arrested there are among the poor and homeless. But the prejudice persists and must be challenged again and again.

Unfortunately, the punitive aspect of the welfare reform bill will hurt innocent children more than anyone else. Informed estimates anticipate that over one million more children will be thrust into poverty. This is a strange scenario coming from a Congress and a president who talk incessantly about their concern for families and the well-being of children.

I was disappointed in President Clinton for signing the seriously flawed welfare reform bill, and I am now less enthusiastic about voting for him. I understand that in politics it is often necessary to practice the "art of compromise," but in this case the price seems too high. I know that sometimes you must accept a half loaf when you cannot get a whole loaf, but with this bill, many Americans may be left with no loaf at all.

✉

Robert Seymour got it exactly right in his "Village Voices" piece. Americans seem to love to hate the poor. At least that's what our current political leaders counted on for their efforts to slash programs that have provided basic assistance to the poor since the 1930s. Perhaps some of us hate the poor more than others. Charles Murray, who got rich by writing his books, *Losing Ground* and *The Bell Curve*, helped some people believe that the programs that assist those in abject poverty actually created poor people. Some of our political leaders took up Murray's theme and worried that the welfare programs we had were "... luring people into a kind of spiritual poverty by destroying their families and their incentives to work." Imagine programs that actually trick people into being what everyone seems to hate—being poor. *D.G., Chapel Hill, NC*

MARKET MENTALITY IS CONSUMING OUR CULTURE

August 18, 1996

The old adage that, "the business of America is business," seems to be truer today than ever before. Aspects of life never previously seen as business enterprises are now routinely considered as such.

I recall the first time the president of Mars Hill College said to the trustees, "We must find better ways to market our institution." The word seemed inappropriate to me. I had always considered an education to be something we offered to people as an opportunity and not as a product to be sold. Similarly, as a member of a focus group convened by the North Carolina Symphony, I was surprised to find it led by MBA students who were considering new ways to *market* the concerts.

The intrusion of the market into public television has compromised what was once a sanctuary for advertisement-free viewing. And now there is a bill before Congress to seek corporate support for our national parks so that visitors can tour the Great Smokies in the awareness that this scenic domain "*has been brought to you through the courtesy of McDonald's.*"

Obviously, the world of sports has already succumbed to commercialism and has become a big business. The baseball strike made it clear that what really matters is how much money the owners and players make, with little or no consideration of the fans. Players are marketed to the highest bidders at exorbitant salary levels that lead inevitably to increased cost of tickets, thus making it more difficult for working-class people to attend the games. The European press complained loudly of the oppressive commercialism at the Olympics. Some referred to the Atlanta event as the "Coca Colympics."

The most recent capitulation to the market mentality is the medical establishment, where it appears we will all be the losers. The CEOs of HMOs are drawing enormous paychecks and in some cases are rewarding their employees for withholding treatment of patients in order to increase their profits. The critical decisions affecting your health are now being made by persons trained in business, not by physicians. It is a frightening development that I pray will be short-lived.

The most serious takeover by business is our government. The most influential forces that shape our nation are large corporations who make huge gifts to political candidates in order to have privileged access to those who enact our laws. Your vote has been diminished in value, for the average citizen has little clout in persuading elected officials when compared to that of the BIG BOYS. Unless we legislate meaningful campaign-financing reform soon, we will have less and less reason to go to the polls. Politicians of both parties talk a good game, but there is no serious movement in Congress to change the status quo.

The power of corporate influence in our government is reflected in the current rush to privatize everything from public schools to prisons. It is assumed that efficiency and reduced costs are the only considerations that matter and that the business community is more capable of achieving this than are government agencies. Many fail to understand that government was never intended to be a business, and that it has concerns beyond the bottom line. Government has the responsibility for the protection and well-being of all its citizenry, and accomplishing this may not be furthered by the guidelines of a market mentality. It is not always true that, "What is good for General Motors is good for the country." Though commerce is essential to our society, it must be our servant and not our master. Capitalism knows how to amass wealth but knows little about justice.

In Chapel Hill, we are seeing this privatizing trend played out in the controversy over the jobs of university housekeepers. Privatizing might save money, but in the process, many low-income people may be hurt by losing their benefits and by being expected to work for less pay. Surely, a state institution has an obligation to see to it that all of its employees are paid a living wage and are not vulnerable to exploitation.

A comparable debate is underway in Raleigh over the proposal to sell Wake Hospital. The county commissioners see this as a way of saving money, but there is little doubt that such a move would deprive many indigent people from eastern North Carolina of adequate medical care. Privatizing tends to be more interested in profits than in people, whereas government institutions should always put people first.

Another trend pushed forward in legislative halls across the nation is the deregulation of industry. Business is complaining loudly about governmental rules and restrictions put in place to guarantee the safety and health of its citizenry and the protection of our environment. We are told that businesses can be trusted to regulate themselves, and some of our leaders seem to have a childlike faith in the power of the market to cure all the nation's ills. Adam Smith's belief in the "invisible hand" to bring about the best for everyone is pervasive, but past experience should be sufficient to show that deregulation often leads to environmental disasters and human tragedies.

Look at the nursing-home business, for example. Does anyone think that adequate safety measures would exist there without legislation to mandate them? It is easy to understand why the concept of the free market has always been the preferred ideology of the privileged, but the drive to do whatever you can to make money leads reasonable people to act reprehensibly.

Sadly, even the church is under constant pressure to be run like a business. Most people tend to judge a church as being successful if it pledges a large budget and is a growing congregation. All across the country "church growth conferences" recommend ways to increase the membership, often at the expense of compromising the Gospel. For example, some encourage churches to seek cultural homogeneity instead of diversity because members like to associate with people like themselves. Let it be said here loud and clear: *the mark of a successful church may be an unpledged budget and a loss of members.* The consequences of faithfulness may be costly and not compatible with the bottom-line values of business.

Ironically, one of the newest and fastest growing businesses in America is the business of operating not-for-profit agencies. Armies of consultants are now available to assist charitable and service organizations to reach potential donors and to invest and distribute their funds. Philanthropy has become a big business, and often these professionals have little or no appreciation for the causes that they are employed to assist.

I see all of the above as convincing illustrations of a major change in our country. The market mentality is consuming our culture.

Dear Bob, I want to know how we can "market" the important ideas expressed in *The Chapel Hill News* this morning. The unholy trinity of marketing (a poor euphemism for selling), competition, and profit threatens to engulf us. *G.W., Chapel Hill, NC*

Dear Amor, J.B. mailed me the latest out of Tekoa, and even if I did not agree with it wholly, I'd call it great stuff, timely and welcome. Now, if we can just bring the Democrats and Clinton "back on track." *W.W. Finlator, Raleigh, NC*

AFFIRMATIVE ACTION ALSO MEANS FAIRNESS

October 11, 1995

I am proud of President Clinton for taking the high road on affirmative action and for resisting the clamor from California to terminate it.

I believe fairness is a value to which most Americans are committed, and affirmative action is an attempt to assure fairness for all. Just as we think it is unfair for Japan to lock out American products from competition in their market, so is it unfair for anyone who is qualified for a position to be kept out of the mainstream in this country.

We are moving from a society in which women and blacks were legally excluded to a society in which women and blacks are legally included.

The legacy of oppression and prejudice is not likely to be overcome unless some legislation is aimed at transcending it. Our culture has a long history of preferential treatment for white males.

Just as public-accommodation laws assure fairness in service to all, so do affirmative action laws seek fairness in the availability of jobs for all. Establishing a level playing field for everyone takes time and requires intentional efforts to achieve it. A legacy of two hundred years of slavery and one hundred years of segregation cannot be overcome in one generation.

We have made considerable progress toward becoming an inclusive society, and affirmative action can claim much of the credit for nudging us in the right direction. American women are no longer confined to the traditional female vocations of secretary, teacher, or nurse. And we are witnessing a rapidly growing middle class of African Americans who can now be found in nearly every place in our corporate life. But we have by no means arrived at a place in history when all doors are open and race and gender are no longer barriers to one's acceptance.

Consider just two illustrations of inclusiveness that have made an enormous difference in our mind-set. Nearly every news team on local television stations all across the nation now has both blacks and women represented, thus projecting an image of teamwork and equality into our living rooms night after night. And in every municipality in America, minorities are employed on the police force, thus attempting to give everyone some sense of ownership and respect for the laws imposed upon them.

The assault on affirmative action has been characterized by political demagoguery intended to confuse the electorate. Affirmative action has been called "reverse racism," a "quota system," and "social engineering." Unfortunately, though not surprisingly, there have been some abuses, but affirmative action has nothing to do with forcing people to employ those who are incompetent or unqualified. It is an attempt to ensure that persons who are equally qualified have equal opportunities. Mr. Clinton is right in saying that the answer to any abuses should be "mend it, not end it."

Some talk show hosts would have you believe that the most discriminated-against group in our country is white males. Many of them are angry, but their anger is misdirected. Rather than face the real causes of their diminishing employment opportunities, they have looked for a scapegoat. The frustration they feel is more related to the down-sizing of corporations, the proliferation of low-paying jobs, and a technological revolution in the workplace, but they blame affirmative action.

It is true that some talented young blacks are also calling for the end of affirmative action because they feel that their achievements may be belittled by the charge of favoritism, but recent polls show that over ninety percent of African Americans support affirmative action, as do over fifty percent of whites. It is especially significant that eighty percent of the Fortune 500 leading corporations want affirmative action continued.

An ironic twist to this controversy is the direction of the Supreme Court. With two women and one black justice on the bench, the court is questioning the constitutionality of affirmative action, yet these minorities would probably not have been appointed had there not been such strong sentiment about the unfairness of an all-white-male court.

Obviously, the success of affirmative action requires the availability of job training and access to the best educational institutions in the nation. How can anyone believe that a child educated in a run-down inner-city school should be able to compete with students from an affluent suburban school? As I look back over my own life, I must acknowledge that I had great preferential treatment over my African-American peers. Indeed, the majority of whites in America are born into families with privileges and inheritances that few in black America can equal. This makes the achievements of minorities all the more impressive and suggests that there is considerable talent yet to be tapped to move our nation toward greatness.

The purpose of affirmative action is to achieve a truly democratic society, where neither race nor gender will be a handicap. The goal is fairness, to open all doors to anyone who is qualified. We will all benefit by making it possible for every citizen to contribute his or her full potential to the well-being of the whole. It is much too early to end affirmative action.

After President Clinton made the address in which he stated, "I have always believed that affirmative action is needed to remedy discrimination and to create a more inclusive society that truly provides equal opportunity," The New York Times said it was "a sermon the nation needs to hear." I add a hearty AMEN!

SPORTS TEACH WRONG VALUES

May 28, 1995

I am not an avid fan of competitive sports, but if I were, I believe I would have become cynical by now and be less inclined to cheer. The old-fashioned value of sportsmanship is rapidly succumbing to greed. Money is the new name of the game.

It saddens me to see Rasheed Wallace and Jerry Stackhouse leave the University of North Carolina. You wonder what the future holds for amateur sports as we helplessly watch professional recruiters cannibalize collegiate teams. You also worry about what will happen to these young men as they are exploited by the promises of big money. You fear that they may not yet be mature enough to grasp the full consequences of the decisions they have made.

You could feel the ambivalence expressed by Stackhouse when he said that his two years at UNC had been the happiest in his life. What a pity to sacrifice two more such years! Not only does this mean a delay in completing their educations (perhaps permanently), but it also entails sacrificing the affirmation of their fans and compromising their loyalty to UNC. Furthermore, it leaves their remaining team members feeling somewhat deserted and facing a highly uncertain next season. But foremost, it requires removing themselves from the positive mentoring and tutoring of one of the best teachers and role models in basketball, Dean Smith.

Characteristically, Dean Smith has voiced no resentment or disappointment, and perhaps he feels none. Instead, he has supported Wallace and Stackhouse in what they want to do and is trying to ensure that they be well cared for and will eventually complete their educations. If I were in his place, I am not sure I could respond so graciously, for I hear something in all of this that speaks loudly of ingratitude. I also feel that the university has been used and that, more so than ever, a part of the hypocrisy of collegiate sports is exposed. In the minds of many, the game is more important than education, and for some of the players, a school's athletic program is seen primarily as a proving ground for self-promotion and being drafted to a professional team.

The recent impasse in professional baseball also revealed how unimportant sportsmanship is in big-time athletics to both players and managers.

On principle, I would have stood with the players in the dispute, but the haggling over such huge sums of money made me want to call down a plague on both their houses. I am pleased that many former fans have refused to show up this season, for they were taken for granted. No one really cared about their stake in the strike.

One cannot help but wonder what influences may have led Michael Jordan back to the basketball court. When he announced his decision to return to the Bulls, the stock exchange showed a sudden rise in the value of Nike shares. And when Jordan was issued a new jersey number, T-shirt companies had an opportunity to double their money. Sometimes it appears that Jordan is perceived more as a product to be marketed than as a person to be admired.

Another aspect of the money game that disturbs me is the increasingly high cost of tickets. This means that many people who used to enjoy sitting in the stadium can no longer afford to do so. In the past, most competitive sports have had a broad base of fans among blue collar people, but today many of these enthusiastic supporters must stay home and watch all the action on television. So long as players continue to sell themselves to the highest bidders, our competitive sports will become more and more elitist and accessible only to those who get tickets through large corporate donations or are independently wealthy. (The customers who helped the corporations make their money are excluded.) The financial factor is also evident when you compare the number of blacks on the team to the small percentage of blacks among the spectators. Most simply do not have sufficient discretionary income to afford this luxury.

Traditionally, athletes have become heroes for the young. Players were people who personified the coveted values of good discipline, courage, and a respect for the rules. Money has become such a corrupting influence that this possibility is no longer assured. Big money has a way of making people consider themselves to be above the law and to conclude that celebrities can get away with anything. How sad to see Pete Rose denied his place in the Baseball Hall of Fame for gambling! How tragic to see Mike Tyson jailed for rape and O.J. Simpson on trial for murder! How shocking to learn that Tonja Harding was willing to participate in a conspiracy to knock out her Olympic competition! Obviously, these are not the people we want our children to emulate.

The frightening part of this is that it mirrors our culture. Many of our athletic idols are falling off their pedestals because we have given them the impression that nothing is more important in life than money, and that if you have money you can have everything. How sad. And whereas teamwork was once the epitome of the game, today many players appear to be out for themselves alone. Let us mourn for what we have lost.

Despite all, I daresay athletics will continue to be BIG in American culture, but it will never be the same. Fans will stand in awe of the mental alertness, physical prowess, and mechanical skills that players demonstrate, but they will more and more see them only as expert performers rather than as persons of character or heroes for the young, to be respected for the quality of their lives. No longer can we assume that the sports arena is a place where old-fashioned values can be found. Morality is being replaced by money and greed.

Reverend Seymour, Well said... and thanks for doing so! *John Swofford, Chapel Hill, NC*

Because of my own experience as a schoolboy sixty years ago, I always think positively of the impact of athletics on my life as I was growing up. With nostalgia I recall how much we enjoyed the recreation, the camaraderie, the release of energy, and the excitement of competition. It was fun.

We probably didn't realize it at the time, but sports were an important part of our education. Participation in athletics was character building...

Sadly, I must agree with Dr. Seymour that the potential good in sports is frequently overshadowed by aggressiveness and greed. *H.P., Chapel Hill, NC*

Mr. Seymour seems to think that he knows what is best for Mr. Wallace and Mr. Stackhouse, and he doesn't stop there. He goes on to say that Wallace and Stackhouse are "compromising their loyalty to Carolina," their fans, and teammates and suggests that they are ingrates.

To the contrary, Wallace and Stackhouse are merely exercising their right to play [sic] the trade that they have developed by hard work and use of their God-given talents. They have the opportunity to obtain financial security for themselves and their families perhaps for the rest of their lives. The last time I checked, the NBA was a legal entity offering legitimate employment. Who are we to begrudge a young man a chance to secure his future?...

I'd like to know what Mr. Seymour pays his bills with. *R.F., Chapel Hill, NC*

Dear Rev. Seymour,

I am surprised that more promising college athletes with NBA and NFL potential do not leave earlier. This current system is basically "athletic socialism," taking the money made off the backs of college football and basketball players and redistributing it to help colleges fulfill title requirements and other things. At UNC, people cry when housekeepers may get shorted out of a couple hundred dollars a month, yet no one cares when college athletes like Stackhouse make universities great sums of money and are not compensated any more than a free college education... *P.W., Chapel Hill, NC*

Dear Bob—Just a note to tell you how much I appreciated your column on athletics and the university last week. I share many of the same concerns, and you expressed them so well; wish it had appeared in our paper. *M.S., Chapel Hill, NC*

PUT BIBLE'S SEXUAL ETHICS IN PERSPECTIVE

November 2, 1994

Earlier this month, I participated in the "Opening Doors" conference at Chapel Hill High School, an event sponsored by the Alliance of Gay and Straight Students. It was planned to increase understanding of the issues of sexual orientation and to affirm those persons who believe themselves to be gay, lesbian, or bisexual.

I was very much impressed by the obvious preparation that had preceded the conference and by the level of leadership of all the speakers and resource people on the program. I was especially pleased to see a large number of public-school teachers present among the two hundred people who attended. I felt proud to be a citizen of a community where this kind of learning opportunity was made available.

The discovery of one's sexual orientation most often occurs in the teenage years, but the controversial nature of the topic has generally prevented offering support for young people who gradually realize they are different from their peers. A 1989 study for the Department of Health and Human Services concluded that at least thirty percent of youth suicides are committed by lesbian and gay teens. Few things can be more traumatic at that stage of life than the inability to conform to the majority.

I was one of five clergy on a panel to discuss religious beliefs about sexual orientation. Consideration of this subject is on the agenda of every major religious group in America, and although there is divergent opinion, there is an emerging consensus. At last there is a willingness to talk openly about a topic seldom previously addressed.

I am convinced that the fear and prejudice often directed toward gays and lesbians today would be considerably less if the church had done a better job of teaching people how to interpret scripture. It is not surprising that those religious groups which consider the Bible to be the literal word of God and who never question its authority about anything are also the ones who have the most difficulty accepting and including homosexuals in the faith community. Nor was it surprising that the people in the group where I was a presenter asked for help in reconciling their experience with "what the Bible says."

Actually, there is very little in Scripture that addresses this topic, and every reference where it is found needs to be understood in its cultural context. In the Old Testament, for example, there is an uncompromising and oft-quoted condemnation of homosexuality in Leviticus. The text is a part of the old Holiness Code, a book of rules and regulations that are no longer considered completely binding, even for the most conservative Jews; yet this one verse has been used like a weapon by persons who overlook other verses in the same context. Furthermore, it is clear that a primary reason the Hebrews rejected homosexuality was their need for population growth, whereas today we live in a world that faces an urgent need to curtail population growth.

The other Old Testament reference often cited in the controversy is the story of the destruction of Sodom. It can be persuasively argued, however, that the cause of God's judgment against the city was not its sensuality but its inhospitality to strangers. This interpretation gains credence from Jesus, who once said to his disciples, "When you enter a town and they do not make you welcome... it will be more tolerable for Sodom than for that town."

There is no statement at all from Jesus about homosexuality. People quote the Apostle Paul. This in itself is somewhat ironic because the same people never advocate Paul's view of heterosexual relationships. Paul felt that marriage was a concession to weakness and that one is better off to remain celibate. In his "Letter to the Romans," Paul cites as symptoms of idolatry a long list of unacceptable forms of behavior, including homosexuality (along with such sins as greed and gluttony). This passage must be seen against a background of pagan culture where sexual exploitation of both men and women was commonplace. It should also be noted here that Paul assumes homosexual acts are committed by persons of heterosexual orientation, having no understanding of this as a sexual variation.

I personally feel that the most helpful verse of Scripture that might be interpreted in a way relevant to the issue of sexual orientation is found in Genesis, where we read, "God created them male and female." Each of us is created with a combination of male and female characteristics, and we are at different points along a spectrum with considerable diversity and variation. This point of view coincides with the professional opinion of contemporary psychiatry.

It is deeply troubling to me that the faith community has been so oppressive against gays and lesbians that in nearly every city in America we see new congregations being formed to accommodate them where they can be appreciated for the persons they are without fear of exclusion. This represents a new form of segregation that I see as a severe judgment against mainstream places of worship. Yet I am convinced that this is only a transitional phenomenon, and that thirty years hence we will look back and wonder how this could have generated such heated controversy.

Already, the issue of sexual orientation is on the front burner in every major denomination and most seminaries. Eventually, every local congregation will be forced to discuss it forthrightly and come to terms with it. And in the end, I believe we will gradually come to the point of considering sexual orientation as irrelevant as whether a person is right-handed or left-handed.

Meanwhile, I am proud to live in a community that cares enough about its young people to offer a conference designed to help them in their struggle for sexual identity.

✉

To those who have chosen or will choose to engage in homosexual behavior, I urge you to question what Mr. Seymour says—not the Bible. False prophets can come from all segments of society and being misled by anyone who believes man should be exalted instead of God can have eternal consequences. God loves you, and your sins can be forgiven. *P.S., Chapel Hill, NC*

✉

Regarding religious condemnation of homosexuality, The Rev. Robert Seymour... presented an enlightened view of the changing attitude of many religious leaders toward homosexuality. He pointed out that the only section of the Bible that specifically condemns homosexuality is one sentence in Leviticus.

This section also forbids the eating of pork and shellfish, and calls for burnt offerings of animals as a part of prayer. We don't follow these commands today, and we should have a more enlightened view of the statement against homosexuality as well. *M.S., Chapel Hill, NC*

✉

As an African-American gay male, I had to respond to Robert Seymour's article of Nov. 2. It was one of the most moving and meaningful editorials that I have heard from a minister regarding the subject of homosexuality. The article should be mandatory reading for all seminarians, teachers, and lay people.

As a church organist for many years, I would have been proud to have played in a church with a minister of your compassion and understanding. May God continue to bless you. *D.L., Durham, NC*

✉

Dear Mr. Seymour, I am writing to personally thank you for your knowledgeable, compassionate, and timely column in today's paper. How refreshing to read a message of such inclusion, from either side of the sexual orientation debate.

You, as a respected pastor, are in a unique position to single-handedly carry a message to thousands of readers who would not be receptive to that message from even thousands of gay and lesbian activists. Your single voice may very well lead others to reassess their own positions of exclusion. Thank you for using your voice as you have. *G.L., Chapel Hill, NC*

DEATH PENALTY MORE REAL IF HERO FACES IT

July 3, 1994

The indictment of O.J. Simpson for a vicious double murder has stunned all of us and made it almost impossible to contemplate the possible scenarios that may lie ahead. Of course, in the eyes of the law he remains innocent unless he is proven guilty, and it is too soon to know what approaches the prosecutors and defense team will take. But it is conceivable that he will be found guilty and face the death penalty.

If it should come to this, many people for whom Mr. Simpson has been an American hero would be repulsed to see him put to death. Indeed, some people who have supported the death penalty in the past may have second thoughts about it. It would be almost unbearable to see a man who has been so much admired come to such a terrible end.

Even the suggestion that many people might react in this way in itself reveals the unevenness of the practice of capital punishment. How can we be indifferent when some criminals are put to death but find ourselves resisting the very thought of this fate for O.J. Simpson?

Unfairness in its application is a major reason for opposing capital punishment. Although two people may commit identical crimes, one may be put to death and the other allowed to live. Such inequality before the law has been more apparent here in the South than anywhere else in the nation. Statistics show that we have been more ready to execute black people than white people and that when a black person murders a white person, he or she is more likely to be put to death than when a black murders another black.

The O.J. Simpson case reveals a further inequality. We can be sure that his defense team will be the best that money can buy, and because of its forensic skills, it is very possible that even though Simpson may have committed the crime, he could walk away as a free man. At one end of the justice system are the rich and famous, but at the other end are the poor and powerless whose fate is determined by court-appointed lawyers who may have no experience or competence for such trials.

There are many good reasons to oppose murder by the state. The most obvious one is that death is irrevocable. There is perhaps no greater tragedy than to discover convincing evidence that an innocent person has been executed—and there are a number of such cases on record.

I was intrigued by the recent efforts of Phil Donahue to secure permission to put North Carolina's recent execution of David Lawson on national television. Much of the support of the death penalty is based on the assumption that it serves as a deterrent to would-be criminals. Those who really believe this to be the case should demand that executions be public. There was a time when convicted murderers were hanged in the public square in Raleigh, and thousands of citizens turned out for the spectacle. Surely no one wants to return to this! But if we really believe that putting someone to death is a way of inhibiting crime, why do we now execute people in seclusion and secrecy at two A.M. when most people are asleep?

My primary reasons for opposing capital punishment are my respect for human life and my Christian faith. It is impossible to justify putting anyone to death on the basis of the teachings of Jesus. Some church members are surprised to learn that nearly every mainline denomination is on record as being against capital punishment. Yet, one of the ironies of public sentiment today is that some of the strongest support for the death penalty comes from fundamentalist Christians. Jesus overruled the principle of "an eye for an eye and a tooth for a tooth." My faith also teaches me that our final act should never be judgment but redemption and that the last word with God is mercy, not justice.

I suspect that support for the death penalty would wane considerably if the public could be assured that dangerous criminals would be kept behind bars and not soon freed to commit further crime. I hope we will gain more faith in our justice system and see some of the past abuses corrected. The "get-tough-on-crime" mentality of America at the moment makes it difficult for anyone to consider the death penalty dispassionately.

It is significant that our two recent retirees from the Supreme Court, Justices Powell and Blackman, are both now on record as opposing the death penalty and regret their part in perpetuating it. Justice Powell says it takes too much courage or too much callousness to treat death as routine. He believes that doubt and inequality will plague our system of justice so long as people are sentenced to death.

Chapel Hill's Paul Green spent much of his life seeking the abolition of the death penalty. One night on the eve of an execution, he made this public statement while standing outside the prison:

"So let our beloved State of North Carolina take leadership in still another good cause and abolish this old, outmoded barbarity from its statutes. Let us be the first Southern state to do so, as we have been first in other good and noble things.

The spiritual influence flowing from such abolishment could help purify and exhilarate life around us. A strong public moral achievement always does just that. And no one ever loses."

Murder is a terrible act, and we must never forget the victims of the murderer's deed. Nor should we ever forget that murder by the state is murder, too. Before David Lawson died in our gas chamber a few weeks ago, he said, "I hope that North Carolina will some day be sorry it put me to death." I share that hope.

THE ONLY THING WE HAVE TO FEAR IS TOO MUCH FEAR

June 5, 1994

One of the most frequently quoted statements of Franklin Roosevelt is, "The only thing we have to fear is fear itself." Of course, he was right. Too much fear or too little fear can be dangerous, but there is nothing intrinsically wrong with fear. It can serve us well, as long as it does not become excessive.

I think of our former president's statement often as I see the rising level of fear of crime, both locally and nationally. I grew up in a Southern community where we didn't even consider it important to lock the doors to our homes, but nowadays people all across the country are building homes behind barricades with gate keepers on duty around the clock to protect them from danger.

You may be surprised to know that, in fact, we are not suffering so much from a crime wave as we are from a media blitz about crime. F.B.I. statistics show that the crime rate has decreased by three percent for two successive years, yet we are being served a steady diet of reports of violence on television and in the printed media. Whereas we once knew only about violence close to home, we now know about crimes committed all across the nation. The Center for Media and Public Affairs reports that the three major networks aired more than twice as many crime stories last year as in 1992. By seeing and hearing so much more about violence, we are under the impression that there is more violence.

Another contributing factor to our increasing fear is that so much of the crime seems senseless and is committed at random. As long as such crime was committed primarily in the inner city or in drug-infested neighborhoods, many people were not upset about it, but when it seems to be happening close to home, we are outraged and unbelieving. Chapel Hill responded in this way to the tragic murder of the woman jogging on Estes Drive, but previously many of us had remained passive about crimes committed in areas we never frequent.

Although the "crime wave" may not be as threatening in reality as we imagine it to be, the rising level of fear has in some ways served us well. It seems to have been necessary for us to experience this consciousness-raising about crime in order to pass long-overdue legislation to combat it. Passage of the Brady bill and the bill banning the use of assault weapons are unprecedented steps in the right direction. Locally, the "Buy Back the Hill" effort has also helped sensitize us to the ubiquitous presence of guns. Congress has even secured a pledge from Hollywood to cut down on the violence we view; however, I personally consider it a bit naive to think Hollywood will take our concerns seriously.

It is also helpful for all of us to be more alert and to be aware of the possibility of becoming a victim. Many summers ago, I was mugged in New York City. Three men put a knife to my throat and demanded my money. New York has never looked the same to me since that happened. I used to roam the streets without ever a thought of crime, but now I watch the people around me and try to avoid places poorly lighted, and I seldom go out alone. It has not, however, prevented me from going to New York, nor should it.

My wife and I went to a ballet at the renovated Carolina Theater in Durham recently, and when we parked in the adjacent parking deck, we worried about returning to our car after dark. It was reassuring to see policemen stationed at every level of the deck after the performance was over. What a pity it will be if people fail to use this wonderful new facility because of their fear of going downtown in the evening.

I do hope, however, that the current level of fear will engender further legislation curbing the proliferation of guns on our streets. According to *The New York Times*, last year, nearly one million handgun crimes took place in America. That is the bad news. The encouraging news is that despite this nearly fifty percent rise in their use, the rate of violent crime last year was about the same as it was in 1973. But while fewer people are being attacked, more of the attacks that do occur involve handguns. I hope we will insist that the federal government must rein in the number of gun dealers. There are more of these in the Triangle area than there are McDonald's restaurants, and almost anybody, with virtually no screening whatsoever, can get a gun license for the asking. I support the proposal in Congress to make it much more costly and difficult to get such a license. I would also like to see all handgun users required to have a license.

Though some of our fear is having beneficial results in making a safer society for all of us, we must guard against the danger of the level of fear rising to the point of our becoming a repressive society. I feel that our state legislature may have acted in this climate during its recent special session on crime. I hope news analysts will cut back on the "headline hysteria," and that we can invest more money into looking at some of the root causes of crime and address problems of poverty and education with generous funding. It is troubling to note that major crimes are being committed by children of younger and younger ages. I am glad that we have reached a point in America when we are unwilling to tolerate mindless violence, but I agree with Senator Bradley who said, "We cannot simply replace a violent society with a repressive one."

Dear Mr. Seymour—The third-rate pap you wrote in your June 3rd column is an embarrassment to you and an insult to whoever in the reading public receives this low-level newspaper. Such generalities! No evidence! No data! Shame! *Anonymous*

CHAPEL HILL

WORSHIPING IN GERRARD HALL

Since the founding of the University of North Carolina, few changes have been more dramatic than the attitude toward religion and its practice on campus. On the occasion of its opening, one of the principals said in an address, "May this hill be for religion as the ancient hill of Zion." The second building constructed was a chapel, and for many years, all students were expected to attend regular worship. And can you believe that as late as 1972 every graduate of UNC was presented not only with a diploma but also a Bible?

Compare that to the proposal now under consideration to restore Gerrard Hall to its original intended use as a chapel on campus. There is some concern that this may precipitate legal protests if it is even called a chapel. However, there is an emerging consensus that if it is seen as a secular, multi-purpose place—including voluntary, non-sectarian worship—it may be possible to move forward with the renovation.

Actually, Person Hall was the original chapel. Gerrard was constructed later in the style of a New England meetinghouse. Its designation as a place for worship is indicated by the inscription over the doors, which reads, "To do Justly and to Love Mercy, and to Walk Humbly with Thy God."

Although today a Department of Religion offers the study of religion from an academic perspective, worship is another matter. We have moved from an era when no one would have questioned the propriety of praising God on campus to a time when many are vigilant to keep the public sphere completely secular. More and more, religion is relegated to the sidelines of modern life. Indeed, many people in universities across the country hold religion in low esteem and judge it to be bigoted, closed-minded, and backward looking.

Yet we are witnessing a resurgence of interest in spirituality, and students seem more ready to wrestle with existential questions about the meaning of human life. Some would welcome a place where they can meditate and worship, either privately or communally. Gerrard Hall could once again become such a place.

In so far as I am aware, the ongoing discussion about the project has not taken note of the fact that in the 50s and 60s, Gerrard Hall was a place where regular worship occurred every Sunday. In anticipation of the projected rapid growth of the university, the chancellor made the hall available to new congregations prior to their establishment off campus. The university recognized the desirability of increasing the number of local congregations to serve the exploding student population.

Many churches were born there, including Binkley Memorial Baptist, which worshipped there for nearly five years, starting in 1958. Before Binkley, The Church of the Holy Family began in Gerrard Hall, and following Binkley, it housed the Chapel Hill Bible Church.

As the first pastor of Binkley Church, I have many fond memories from our days on campus. Up front in Gerrard was a large paining of St. George slaying the dragon, one that we judged inappropriate as a focal point for Sunday worship. Each week we concealed the dragon with a covering and a cross. I recall one Sunday when the service proceeded on the stage set of *The Solid Gold Cadillac.* Already, the hall was being used for a wide range of events as a multi-purpose building. (You may recall a major scene there from the film, *Patch Adams.*)

Binkley's tenure on campus coincided with the arrival of an increasing number of black students. We saw an opportunity to reach out to them, reasoning that black students from North Carolina were either Baptists or Methodists or someone had been tampering with their religion! Fifteen to twenty African Americans were often in the congregation. One Sunday a reporter from *The London Illustrated News* photographed our integrated fellowship to appear in the British publication as evidence of a New South emerging.

While we were in Gerrard Hall, we welcomed a black seminarian to serve as a summer intern. His name was James Forbes, and he grew up in eastern North Carolina. Forbes is now the Senior Minister of the Riverside Church in New York City, where I had the pleasure of being his pulpit guest one Sunday last August.

One motivation for restoring Gerrard Hall is to provide a place on campus for such rites as funerals and weddings. I do not recall any weddings, but memorial services were held there for former Mayor James Wallace and Professor George Holcombe.

As long as the facility is available for worship on a non-sectarian basis and can also be used for some secular events, the principle of separation of church and state will probably not pose a problem. Indeed, there is already a precedent for a non-sectarian chapel on campus. It is located in UNC Hospitals. Christians worship there on Sundays and Muslims on Fridays. Thomas Jefferson, who is credited with the "separation" phrase, also worshiped in public buildings. Several other state universities have chapels, as does the Air Force Academy and West Point.

I hope we can call Gerrard Hall a university chapel. After all, this is CHAPEL HILL. Or should we remove the ecclesiastical association and heed Roland Giduz's tongue-in-cheek suggestion that we change the name of our Town to Hoggtown, in memory of the founding commissioner, James Hogg? He gave a large sum of money to build UNC and secured pledges of 1,386 acres of land for the university location. Or we could call it "Hogg Heaven"!

WCHL MAY RETURN TO CHAPEL HILL

February 10, 2002

People who have settled in Chapel Hill in the past five years are probably unaware of a great loss suffered by our town. I am referring to the sale of our formally locally owned radio station, WCHL, at 1360 on your radio dial. When it happened, there was no public protest because most people felt that little would change, but the change has been catastrophic. We lost "non-stop Chapel Hill." The station has virtually deserted the community and has also lost most of its listeners.

Symbolically, the station still calls itself a Chapel Hill station, but it is based in Durham and broadcasts from a studio located in the Durham Bulls Athletic Park!

It used to occupy the building where The Home Team is now located, across from Eastgate. It was a welcoming place to the entire community, and few things happened in Chapel Hill without WCHL letting us know.

Now all we get is a morning show from 6:00 to 9:00 A.M. with the familiar long-term voice of our own Ron Stutts. But until recently, even "The Morning Show" was insensitively compromised by being a simulcast morning show for Durham, too. We heard not only about the Tar Heels, but were forced to listen to news of Duke University teams! Fortunately, this has changed. The General Manager realized the awkwardness of the arrangement, and now "The Morning Show" focuses on Chapel Hill alone.

The good news is that things may be moving in the right direction, for there is mounting sentiment to establish a broadcast studio in Chapel Hill. Then "The Morning Show" could not only be aired here, but also be more accessible to local radio guests.

It is ironic that our town boasts of having three radio stations, yet not one of them covers the news of our community! WXYC is the station on the University of North Carolina campus that is primarily a non-stop music station for students. Of course, WUNC is located here, but it is a regional station and does not cover local news

There is an emerging interest to try to persuade the present owner, Mr. Don Curtis of Raleigh (who owns not only WCHL, but also other stations in the area), to let WCHL come back home. Most of us had no idea he would move it or that he would serve up canned programs instead of what we were accustomed to hearing. Mr. Curtis graduated from UNC and is an avid Tar Heel fan, so he should be sensitive to our sense of loss.

I had lunch with Ron Stutts the other day, and he believes that if a location can be found, at least a part of WCHL might return to us. He also believes that there is a possibility the entire operation may eventually move back. Meanwhile, more local programming will be scheduled. A new sports show premieres tomorrow and will be called "The Carolina Connection." Jones Angel will host it from 4:00 to 6:00 P.M. Also, the audio from the People's Channel's weekly program, "In Praise of Age," will be available on Sundays in the near future. Ron would like to hear from you with any suggestions or input you may have for the future. He has been greatly encouraged by the initial response to what is happening as people are rediscovering the station.

I am convinced that the old WCHL was primarily responsible for maintaining the mystique of the "Village." It nurtured a sense of community and contributed to the illusion that Chapel Hill is still a small town, even though it is an emerging city. The station also generated a sense of pride in this special place where we live. It played a role in our corporate life that nothing else has been able to fill.

I am especially aware of the absence of WCHL at election time. In the old days, all candidates for municipal elections were on the radio with campaign advertising spots and question-and-answer sessions. And on election night, we could always count on WCHL to give us immediate reports from the polls and to interview winners and losers. I think we had a better-informed local electorate back then.

I also miss our local station when we face the threat of a dangerous storm or are blanketed by a foot of snow. WCHL gave us a continuous update on local road conditions and a listing of all the closings caused by the weather. Housing projects for senior citizens require that all residents own a battery-operated radio to get such information, but currently it is not available locally.

The station was accessible to everyone. Announcements of local events were always welcome and without cost. Citizens were encouraged to offer their commentaries about any issues that concerned them. There were daily interviews with people from every segment of our community. In short, it was a community station. So much so, that people felt the radio station belonged to them.

You could also depend upon WCHL to get out of the studio and be on hand for many local events. Not only would it help publicize them; it would be there to let everyone in town know what was happening on the scene.

Apparently, the station was sold because it had become unprofitable. Other small towns in our state have also had difficulty supporting their radio connections. Now that the Chapel Hill/Carrboro Chamber of Commerce boasts of an unprecedented surge in membership, wouldn't it be wonderful if our business community would offer the promise of substantial advertising revenue. I hope Aaron Nelson, the new executive director of the Chamber, will have as one of his primary goals the luring of WCHL back to Chapel Hill. Ron Stutts said, "I want us to have the kind of station we used to have and to serve the community the way it should be served."

I am sure I am one of thousands in our town who are nostalgic to hear that often- repeated familiar phrase on the radio, "Thank you, CHL, for caring about our community."

Hello Ron: I was delighted to read Robert Seymour's article in Sunday's *News* about the possibility of WCHL returning to its home. As a resident (most of the time) since 1974, I really miss the radio station, for all the reasons Bob mentioned. While my boys were growing up, I relied on the station for school news, closings etc. As a performer, I was invited to publicize local events and there was a real sense of community, which is disappearing fast. Although I realize that we can't stop growth, we can continue to foster community spirit, and WCHL is definitely the way to do it. I feel Chapel Hill is not well served by any of the so-called local radio or TV stations. If we didn't have *The Chapel Hill News*, we wouldn't know what was going on locally. *J.S., Chapel Hill, NC*

To Robert Seymour: Thanks for your article about the local radio stations. We have only lived in the area coming on three years, and I have often wondered why the coverage for Chapel Hill/Carrboro/ South Orange County has been so poor. Now I know. I had stopped trying the station, but will sample it again. *J.S.B., Chapel Hill, NC*

WHY WE NEED SENIOR CENTERS

October 17, 2001

Orange County has some catching up to do. All across North Carolina, new senior centers are sprouting up like mushrooms. There is one in Pittsboro, one in Cary, and Durham has designated a prime downtown site for a groundbreaking soon. By contrast, the Chapel Hill Senior Center and the Carrboro Center both occupy leased space at an annual cost to the County of nearly $175,000. It is time for us to invest in our own buildings and prepare for the future.

Already, Orange County's senior population is one of the highest in the state. The census reports nearly fifteen thousand, about the same number as there are children in the public schools. The number is steadily increasing. When the baby boomers reach sixty-five, the growth will be 131 percent! A crisis is emerging which senior centers can help avert. The current facilities are far from adequate, with serious limitations in space and insufficient parking.

North Carolina has determined that this large segment of our population can best be served by a network of senior centers where older adults can access a wide range of assistance, and from where social workers can go out into the community to reach the homebound.

Unfortunately, many citizens have the impression that senior centers are primarily for leisure and recreation activities. Nothing could be further from the truth. In fact, they are, first and foremost, wellness centers. Every attempt is made to keep older people functional for as long as possible and to steer them through the possibility of disabilities and offer help in critical decision making as age advances.

Many people have the false impression that senior centers are only for those who are frail and dependent. This, too, is erroneous. Happily, nearly seventy-five percent of older adults are well and fit, and the senior center's main mission is to keep them that way and to perpetuate a high quality of life beyond what has been the case in the past. Incredibly, the fastest growing group in the elderly population is those who reach their one hundredth birthday! If we live long enough, aging eventually takes its toll on everyone, and senior centers will make this transition easier.

The range of health-related services offered is impressive. There are various levels of exercise and strength-training classes. Competitive, statewide senior games help seniors stay active in athletics. There are regular blood-pressure checks, cholesterol counts, and screenings for hearing loss, medications taken, and problems related to podiatry. A dozen or more support groups are available for seniors who suffer from debilitating diseases or who are caring for a disabled spouse. A staff of social workers offers both case management and referral advice.

In an attempt to keep seniors healthy, nutritious meals are available at noon. Recognizing that older people who live alone are less likely to eat well-balanced meals and to be isolated from socialization, the Older Americans Act subsidizes inexpensive lunches.

The centers also encourage older people to develop their creative skills through art and craft classes, writing groups, music, and drama. Intellectual stimulation is provided by a wide variety of programs such as the Village Elders, offering an on-going dialogue with university lecturers.

Senior volunteers assist other seniors in dealing with medical bills and in filing taxes. Last year, over twelve hundred older adults were assisted in paying their taxes electronically at the Chapel Hill Senior Center. Seniors are also eager to keep up with the latest in computer literacy. The computer lab has enabled a host of older adults to surf the internet and to correspond with their grandchildren by e-mail.

The Retired Senior Volunteer Program challenges retirees to put their skills to good use by volunteering in Orange County, where there are many opportunities to invest one's time and skills. Currently there are approximately six hundred older adults in volunteer positions throughout our community.

And finally, of course, there is recreation. Bridge playing is continuous. There is a regular Monday tea and a movie on Tuesdays. Men gravitate to the ping-pong and billiard tables. There are occasional dances, many trips, and potluck suppers.

The forthcoming election holds the promise of providing new facilities for senior centers. The commissioners have placed on the ballot the prospect of two new buildings, one to be located in the Chapel Hill/Carrboro area and to be called The Southern Orange Senior Center, and the other in Hillsborough, to be called The Central Orange Senior Center. They are asking for a total of four million dollars for a 25,000-square foot structure here and a 15,000-square foot structure for Hillsborough. Obviously, additional funding may be required from other sources if this vision is to become a reality.

Increasingly, middle-aged people are facing a pressing need for the long-term care of their aging parents. So, in a very real sense, senior centers are not only for older adults, but also for other family members who need help in formulating plans for their loved ones. As we try to get the word out about the November 6th bond-issue vote, someone has suggested an appropriate bumper sticker which would read, "PROTECT YOUR CHILDREN'S FUTURE; VOTE FOR SENIOR CENTERS."

ROAD RAGE ON THE RISE

May 21, 2000

It happened at the intersection of Willow Drive and the Highway 15/501 bypass while I was waiting for the red light to change. My mind was in neutral, and I failed to notice that my car had slowly rolled forward. Almost imperceptibly, it barely tapped the bumper of the vehicle ahead. Whereupon, the driver suddenly leaped out of his car and appeared at my window, shouting obscenities. I was stunned to total silence. If he had had a gun, this column might never have been written!

As more and more automobiles hit the road, and as the pace of our lifestyle quickens, road rage has become a more common occurrence. People who are normally of good temperament sometimes react in surprising ways. The frustration of the traffic triggers anger that puts our nerves on edge. It is a dangerous condition that can lead to ugly and occasionally tragic consequences.

Most of us must plead guilty. Is there anyone not riled, when, at the very moment a light turns green, the driver behind us blows his horn? Is there anyone trapped by passing traffic in a lane that is ending who is capable of wishing a good day to the motorists who refused to let you in? Is there anyone who has been blinded at night by bright headlights approaching who has resisted the temptation to reciprocate?

You are a prime candidate for road rage when you are in a big hurry to get someplace. You leave Chapel Hill at 8:30 A.M. to make a 9:00 A.M. meeting in Raleigh, but, repeatedly, the bumper-to-bumper traffic slows to a complete stop. You feel totally helpless because all you can do is steam and mutter invectives to yourself. Finally, the gridlock loosens, and you dart from one lane to another in a desperate effort not to be too late. Then your pent-up steam is likely to be directed toward anyone who impedes your progress. It is a daily scenario.

Trucks often kindle my road rage. I resent their rushing up behind me while I am in the passing lane and pushing me to exceed the speed limit. (I have long suspected that trucks have an agreement with law enforcement about driving faster than the rest of us.) I barely missed being a victim in a major accident with a truck recently. I had stopped at a red light and saw from my rear-view mirror a truck barreling down behind me at breakneck speed in the lane to my left. He sped right through the intersection, blowing his horn, apparently not having seen the light and unable to stop. Fortunately, no one was entering from the side street, for it would have been "curtains" for us all. I was left trembling with rage.

Further down the highway, I suddenly realized that I was behind that very same truck. Painted on the back was, "Our drivers are the best in the industry." And below the sign was printed a telephone number for anyone to call who had a complaint. I followed close enough to write down the 800 number and then pulled over to the shoulder to dial it. My anger was intensified when I was answered by an interminable menu telling me to push numbers ad infinitum, listing all the divisions of the corporation, no one of which seemed relevant to my call. I finally gave up in frustration and concluded that the number on the back of the truck was merely a public relations ploy no one was expected to use.

Nothing makes me more angry on the highway than to comply with "Road Work Ahead" signs by merging into the designated lane, only to have countless other cars ignore the signs and speed past me to the head of the line, where they nose in while I am still waiting much further back. I feel penalized for obeying instructions while those who ignore them are rewarded. I think a law enforcement officer ought to be stationed where the final merging occurs to issue tickets to all those who race to the front of the line, assuming they should have privileged access.

Several places in Chapel Hill/Carrboro incite road rage regularly. The main Chapel Hill Post Office is one of them. You get trapped as cars line up and compete for a parking place. Another is at the intersection of Highway 15/501 and Erwin Road, at the Sheraton Hotel. If you are coming up the bypass in the far right lane, you have to cross two lanes of traffic quickly in order to turn left on Erwin. More often than not, those lines are full and drivers persistently refuse to let you enter. I see near-misses there every day. The entrance and exit to Ram's Plaza is another impossible place, but fortunately, plans call for redesigning the traffic pattern sometime soon. Carrboro Plaza also poses problems, with access lanes like a labyrinth.

Nearly all of us have suffered frustration at the airport, where, with mounting anxiety, we have searched in vain for a parking space. Happily, the new deck is at last completed, and road rage there may diminish. Maybe the same thing will happen eventually at UNC Hospitals where construction never ends and parking always requires driving around and around and around.

Another situation I deplore is the proliferation of these huge SUVs. If you park a compact between two such vans, you must back out blindly. As you ease out into approaching traffic, it is impossible to see what's coming.

How should we cope with all of this? Soothing music on the radio may help. Also, give yourself plenty of time to get where you are going, and expect to be delayed. Conscientiously practice civility. And, of course, seriously consider the alternative of public transportation. Unfortunately, however, most of us are so accustomed to our cars that we assume buses are meant for other people.

HOSPITALITY FOR THE HOMELESS

July 16, 1999

Predictably, when the Interfaith Council made known its request to build a new administrative office building on a site next door to the community shelter, the on-going debate about the best location to house the homeless surfaced with a renewed intensity. Since the proposal carries with it a request for a twenty-five-year lease, it is an appropriate time for both the IFC and the town to engage in long-range planning. There is an urgent need to find a new site for the offices of the IFC, since the present facility on Wilson Street has been purchased by a new owner who wants to occupy the building by spring. As a member of the committee responding to this crisis, I concurred that it would be desirable to have the IFC staff and the shelter side by side. This would help insure the continuation of good management and retain the symbolism of hospitality for the homeless in the center of our community, and hence, our compassion.

Just prior to the Town Council's scheduled public hearing on this request, an alternative proposed location for the shelter in northern Chapel Hill on Homestead Road was put forward. It has precipitated broad-based discussion, and, in response to this, the IFC announced to the community gathering that it was not intransigent about its initial proposal and would be open to a careful consideration of any other location.

The IFC Board concedes that a strong case can be made for the north Chapel Hill site. It would be decidedly advantageous to have the shelter near the new Southern Orange Human Services building, and it would facilitate easier IFC management if the offices and shelter could be in proximity to the IFC's new family shelter (Project Homestart), which is already located on Homestead Road. Transportation and access to the noonday shelter meal are major concerns, though a number of ideas suggest that these potential problems might be surmountable. Clearly, the center of gravity of Chapel Hill is moving north. Both a new courthouse and main post office are already on the drawing board, not to mention UNC's projected new campus on the Horace Williams property.

There is also the question of the adequacy of the current shelter for the future. Already there are occasions when people must be turned away (which led to the building of Homestart for families). On winter nights, it is often necessary to put mattresses on the floor to accommodate the guests. If there were an economic downturn approaching, the present facility would not be able to provide for the needs of an increase in the number of the people it serves.

Whatever the outcome, I am pleased that our mayor and the IFC board have agreed to work with a taskforce to weigh the pros and cons and that all parts of our community will come to the table together to recommend a final decision. I hope this process will give to everyone a better opportunity to become informed about the need and that a consensus can be reached about the best way to meet it. I hope we can avoid polarizing the community and not yield to the simplistic temptation of assuming that those who want the shelter moved are any less compassionate than those who want it to remain downtown.

I also hope we can clear up some persistent misconceptions about the shelter. People who come to the shelter are not people who are unwilling to work. In fact, most of those who reside there find jobs in the community and are best described as the "working poor." Nor is the shelter population the "criminal element." Homelessness is not a law-and-order problem; it is an economic problem. Repeatedly, citizens have accused shelter guests of downtown crime at night. This has not been the case, because the people who stay there must be inside the building by early evening.

Furthermore, there is the widespread erroneous assumption that the panhandlers on Franklin Street are coming from the shelter. Typically, these are folk who refuse to enter the shelter. Indeed, I think we can predict with some degree of certainty that the moving of the shelter away from its current location will not rid Franklin Street customers of this irritation.

There is another minor misconception that deserves correction. Let's stop calling the community kitchen a "soup kitchen." Guests are served full, hearty meals—sometimes the best meal in town! The generosity of our community in providing an abundance of food and the willingness of congregations to recruit an army of volunteers to prepare three meals a day every day of the year is an impressive indication of the compassion of our citizenry.

The newly appointed task force has been asked to report back to the town and the IFC by mid-September. I believe they will present to us the best answer to the question that mandates primary consideration: *Where can the homeless in our midst best be served for an indeterminate future?*

UPDATE ON THE SWEET TEA CRISIS

June 20, 1999

Some of you might recall that several years ago I wrote a tongue-in-cheek column about the threat to one of our cherished Southern traditions, the inability to get sweet tea in many of the new restaurants. One of my most vivid childhood memories of the Old South, which signaled the arrival of summer, was to find large pitchers of sweet tea on the dinner table. On a hot day, nothing quenched the thirst like a tall glass of ice-cold sweet tea with a wedge of lemon and a sprig of mint.

I was surprised by the response to the column. It called forth a deluge of comments and correspondence, primarily from those who had also experienced the disappointment of ordering sweet tea in a public place and being told that only unsweetened tea was available. Then insult is often added to injury as the waiter points to the container of artificial sweeteners, as if they were an acceptable substitute.

Ted Vaden, the Editor of *The Chapel Hill News*, tells me that seldom has anything ever appeared in the newspaper that provoked such attention. Later, he perpetuated the interest by printing and distributing bumper stickers, which read, "I LOVE SWEET TEA." They can still be seen around town. Recently Ted cornered me and asked if I would consider writing a sequel. And so today I share with you an update on the sweet-tea crisis in Chapel Hill.

The original article precipitated two positive responses. I received a letter from the new manager of the Carolina Inn (which was about to re-open following its extensive renovations) assuring me that sweet tea would always be served there. Some weeks later, I was invited to lunch at the Carolina Brewery to sample the sweet tea they had just added to their menu. It was somewhat innovative, with a touch of ginger added. Thus, their tea is not authentically Southern, but it is very tasty indeed.

At the Fourth of July celebration in the summer following the appearance of the column, there was a sweet-tea competition that many of the local eating establishments entered and which I had the privilege of judging. The Rathskeller won the blue ribbon, so I went to lunch there the other day to test their quality control. Before I could say Jack Robinson, the waiter set before me not only a glass of tea, but a whole pitcher just for me. On a scale of one to ten, I would still give it a ten.

In some of the more expensive restaurants, you get the impression that it is considered almost boorish for anyone to request sweet tea. As a general rule of thumb, sweet tea can nearly always be found in "down-home restaurants", but is seldom found where there is nouveau cuisine. If barbecue is served, you can count on it, but it is rarely offered where fettuccini is featured. Expect it at Red, Hot, and Blue, but not at Aurora.

I feel sorry for Southern waiters who work in places where you can't get sweet tea. They frequently seem apologetic for its absence when you ask for it. After the Pyewacket waiter informed me they didn't serve sweet tea, I said, "Well, just bring me water," and he replied with empathy, "I understand, sir."

Occasionally, I have yielded to the unsweet and tried the artificial sweeteners, but inevitably, I regret it. It never measures up. The only sweetener that comes anywhere close to achieving the desired transformation is Equal, but I do not recommend any of them. Of course, ordinary sugar is no good because it refuses to dissolve in cold water.

A sure bet for sweet tea is the fast-food chains. They have adapted to Southern culture. Usually you will find two large canisters, one labeled "sweet" and the other "unsweet," but symbolically, the one containing the unsweet tea is sometimes smaller. At Subway there is a canister for sweet tea only, and a small pitcher of the unsweet alternative sits dwarfed beside it.

Other old reliables for wonderful sweet tea in Chapel Hill are such places as Dip's, Breadman's, and Dry Dock. Also, the K&W Cafeteria, with its large indigenous clientele, serves more sweet tea than any other beverage. You can even find cold sweet tea in local Chinese restaurants, a commendable accommodation from their hot-tea heritage.

The Carolina Club of the University perpetuates the Southern tradition (as indeed any eating establishment bearing the name "Carolina" should!), but its commitment is compromised at large events. I made this discovery at the recent Mother's Day buffet where only unsweetened was offered. Whereas, the Friday Center served nothing but sweet tea at the May RSVP luncheon for Orange County senior adults. Huge pitchers were at the center of every table.

I found only two places where the sweet tea provided was disappointing. It was so weak and watery at Darryl's that I asked the waiter for another glass, but the second was about the same as the first. The other place was McDonald's where I took my grandchildren for a "Happy Meal," but I was unhappy because the tea was so sweet I could hardly drink it. Maybe it is better on most days.

The surprise find of my tea-tasting tour was with a meal at the little Persian Parvaneh Cafe in the Galleria. The sweet tea there is superb, served in a large glass clinking with ice cubes and brewed to perfection.

My wife and I traveled through South Carolina last month and stopped for lunch at a mom-and-pop restaurant (Bill and Fran's) just off the Interstate. When I asked for tea, I said to the waitress, "I'll bet you don't even serve unsweetened tea here." But they did, and she explained why: "Since we are right on the highway, we have people stopping in from all over the country, and they think we are real funny down here for liking our tea sweet." There goes the South!

If you wish to become a member of The Society for the Preservation of Sweet Tea, accept no substitutes. The next time you are told that only unsweetened tea is available but that sweeteners are on the table, respond with your best Southern manners and say real politely, "Thank you, but I prefer water."

DO YOU KNOW YOUR ABCs?

May 8, 1998

You need to know your ABCs in order to function in American society. I am not referring to the alphabet in the usual sense, but to the way we abbreviate names by the use of letters and acronyms. They appear everywhere and are a part of our everyday speech.

I attended a planning meeting of the United Way recently, and the agenda listed MDC, FGI, and RTI as possible sources of help for researching information about Orange County. The chairman assumed that everyone understood, but I asked for a clarification. The listings were Manpower Development Corporation, Four Guys Incorporated, and the Research Triangle Institute.

After a consultation with a physician at UNC Hospitals, my doctor recommended that I have a MRI and an EEG. He assumed that I knew what these tests were, but I would have been hard pressed to say "magnetic resonance imaging and an electroencephalogram!"

Such vocabulary shortcuts are common in inter-office communication. Employees understand that FYI means, "for your information," and that TBA means plans are not yet complete but are "to be announced" at a future time. Your supervisor may leave on your desk a task to be completed ASAP, "as soon as possible." I learned a new one from a computer chat room conversation the other night when my correspondent signed off with TTYL, which I deciphered to mean, "talk to you later."

Have you noticed how frequently such abbreviations occur in the press? In a recent single issue of *USA Today*, the following headlines appeared:

"NTSB Wants Prompt Check of 747 wiring"

"Border Jams NAFTA's Fault?"

"ETS Answers Test of Time"

"Early Ejections Upset MLS Players"

It is often necessary to read the accompanying article in order to understand the headline! Would you have recognized the National Transportation Safety Board, the North American Free Trade Agreement, the Educational Testing Service, and Major League Soccer?

Surely, everyone in North Carolina knows that ACC stands for Atlantic Coast Conference, and in the minds of most people, it refers primarily to basketball. The name "United Nations" has succumbed almost completely to the ubiquitous use of "the UN" instead.

Alphabet soup is daily jargon in Chapel Hill. If you have a problem with your water supply, you contact OWASA. The DOA operates the Chapel Hill Senior Center. People in Orange County who need financial assistance go to the DSS, or to the IFC, or to OCIM. Area-wide transportation is provided by the TTA. JOCCA is the local legacy of Lyndon Johnson's war against poverty. (Orange Water And Sewer Authority, Department On Aging, Department of Social Services, Interfaith Council, Orange Congregations In Mission, Joint Orange Chatham Community Action.) You may belong to such local organizations at the UNA or TIA or CIS. (United Nations Association, The Interfaith Alliance, Communities in Schools.)

Baptist denominations in the U.S. have call letters that sound like national radio and television networks: ABC, NBC, and SBC (American Baptist Convention, National Baptist Convention, and Southern Baptist Convention). The Ecumenical Movement seeks to move all Christian bodies toward unity through COCU (Consultation on Church Union).

Ironically, several familiar national organizations persist in using shortcut abbreviations even though the letters no longer strictly apply. The YMCA, for example, is no longer confined to the young, nor is it for men only. And the NAACP is the National Association for the Advancement of Colored People, even though the word "colored" reflects an earlier era.

In the business world, we recognize what ATT stands for, but what about MCI? We also remember NCNB, but can you give the full name of BB&T? CNN is Cable News Network, but I confess to not knowing the name behind ESPN. A common synonym for the chief executive officer is "the CEO."

Sometimes capital letters are used to convey clever messages. Several senior adult groups call their organization XYZ for "extra years of zest." Teenage boys use the same letters to alert their peers to "examine your zipper."

When the initial letters of an organization create a word, we call it an acronym. These have proliferated in our culture. World War II women remember the WACS and the WAVES, and most of us are now familiar with NOW (National Organization for Women). The police department offers the public schools an educational program about drugs called DARE (Drug Awareness Resistance Education). The telescope being built by UNC in Chile is called SOAR (Southern Observatory for Astrophysical Research).

Imagine how all of these letters look to newcomers to this country who have a limited use of English. It must be mystifying and seem like another foreign language. Personally, I think it is rude to use in-house abbreviations and to simply assume that everyone understands to what they refer.

The other day, my seven-year-old grandson was with me in the car when we passed an ABC store. I asked him it he knew what ABC stood for, and with only a moment's reflection, he replied, "alcohol, beer, and coke." I was impressed by how close he came!

If you have persevered to the end of this column, I consider you a VIP and wish for you one of life's essentials, a generous portion of TLC.

POSITIVE SPIN ON THE GROWTH OF CHAPEL HILL

October 8, 1997

"Growth" is not a bad word. In fact, in most contexts it conveys very positive connotations. Yet, when we talk about the future of our community—especially among candidates at election time—growth becomes associated with everything undesirable and something to be avoided at all costs.

I am, of course, sympathetic with the legitimate concerns that continued growth raises, but I am not willing to condemn growth per se, as if it were responsiblc for all of our problems. Growth can also be the source of much good.

We are tempted to look back upon the past as an idyllic time and to bemoan our loss of "the village" we once knew. I have been in Chapel Hill almost forty years and have witnessed many changes in our town, but I do not want to return to the sleepy, provincial, racist community of the 1950s. I much prefer Chapel Hill as I know it today. The "good ole days" were not as wonderful as our nostalgia recalls.

Chapel Hill was a company town; we were an appendage to the university. The university owned all of our utilities: water, power, and telephone. We had very little independence from the academic community, and town government did not exercise nearly the autonomy that we enjoy today. It was only when Chapel Hill began to experience rapid growth that the relationship to the university began to loosen and "town and gown" became two separate entities, enabling us to work together as partners.

We had the reputation for being a liberal community, but it was a reputation that we did not deserve. University President Frank Graham once said that Chapel Hill was like a lighthouse that sent forth its powerful beam of light into the far distant darkness but was dark at its base. The early liberal image could be accounted for largely by Dr. Howard Odom, who did the first definitive sociological studies of the Southern Region, but Chapel Hill was a typical Southern town and rigidly locked into the mores and legalisms of segregation.

The dramatic growth of our town can be illustrated by the founding of Binkley Church, where I served as pastor for thirty years. The congregation was called into being because of the projected growth of the University, and we purchased property at our present site at the incredible price of $7,000 for almost five acres! People said to us, "Why do you want to build way out there?" No one then could have anticipated that some day we would be next door to the University Mall.

When my wife and I settled here, there were very few shopping opportunities in Chapel Hill. We made regular trips to downtown Durham to buy at Sears and Ellis-Stone. Finally, Eastgate Shopping Center came into being, but it was a disaster in urban planning until its more recent up-grading transformed it to the more attractive place it now is.

Mayor Howard Lee was one of the first citizens to challenge the "village" mythology, urging people to accept the reality that Chapel Hill was rapidly becoming a city. In the awareness of such growth, he urged that we establish a public transportation system. We have him to thank for bringing the bus transit to our town.

Consider what else growth has brought to us. We are now a cosmopolitan place with a world-class university. We enjoy ethnic diversity, and people from all parts of the nation now call Chapel Hill home. Though we still possess some of the graces of the Old South, we have transcended the traditional provincialism of the area and are judged by many to be one of the best places to live in America.

Growth has also given to us a major medical center, providing access to superior health care. When I arrived here, Memorial Hospital (as it was then called) had just been completed, and a fledgling new medical school was getting established. Subsequently, medical research has mushroomed, and UNC boasts superior dental, public health, nursing, and pharmacy schools, as well.

The growth of Chapel Hill was a major factor in the rapid enlargement of the Raleigh/Durham Airport. Many of us recall a rather dinky facility there, which had very few flights each day. Now we have easy access to a major airport with connections that can take us anywhere in the world.

Other amenities that are directly related to growth are the delightful range of restaurants now available to us and exciting opportunities for entertainment. Would anyone want to give up the Smith Center and our expanded recreational offerings? And we no longer have to go to New York to see the best and the latest in contemporary theater (although some of us still miss the community theater that preceded the repertory). Growth has also given us a commodious new public library and, more recently, a Chapel Hill Senior Center to serve a burgeoning senior adult population.

Today some people who worry about our growth talk as if they would like to lock the gates to our town and not let anyone else enter. Ironically, these are often folk who are relatively recent arrivals and have bought into the mythology of our idyllic past. I am sure I am not alone in celebrating the new Chapel Hill and in my willingness to face the inevitability of its continued growth. Obviously, our choice is not between growth and no growth. Our choice is to oversee the growth and to seek ways to minimize its downside, such as our bumper-to-bumper traffic.

We have been very fortunate in the past to have able civic leaders who have steered us through steady emerging change. I am confident that we will be blessed by a continuation of such leadership and that we will be successful in preserving the best of our past even though we no longer reside there. It may be something we prefer not to face, but the reality is that we are witnessing the appearance of a large new metropolitan area on the horizon, and we cannot stop it. We need to move more rapidly in working closely with Durham and Raleigh as this new "Triangle City" takes shape. (The Triangle United Way has taken this bold new step already.)

Continuing growth will mandate our being more willing to have faith in that future by preparing for it before it arrives. For example, we are about to vote on a large bond issue that, for the first time, includes something more than catch-up for our schools. This time we are also including money for more parks, affordable housing, and other public facilities to better serve our citizenry.

Since the word "growth" has fallen into some disfavor, another word has surfaced, one which all of our political candidates endorse as a desirable goal. The word is "sustainable." We want Chapel Hill to become a sustainable community, meaning that we want to become a more self-sufficient community and one that does not diminish our present resources so that they will be available to those who follow us. This involves more than trying to preserve our beautiful trees. It means broadening our tax base and providing better shopping opportunities so that Chapel Hillians will buy at home instead of nearby Durham. It means finding ways to provide a broad range of housing options for all those people who hold service-related jobs here but who come by bus into our community from Burlington, Pittsboro, and Durham because there is no place in Chapel Hill where they can afford to live.

It may not be a politically correct conclusion, but it just may be that Chapel Hill needs more growth if it hopes to become sustainable.

HABITAT BUILDS MORE THAN HOUSES

May 7, 1997

I attended the recent tenth anniversary celebration of the construction of Orange County Habitat for Humanity's first house, upon the occasion of their completing their fifthieth project. It was held at their primary building site in Chestnut Oaks, several miles out of Carrboro. In this brief time, Habitat has made a substantial contribution toward meeting our most pressing local need: low-cost housing. It is an astounding achievement to have provided a place to live for fifty low-income families!

The celebration occurred in the yard of the house currently under construction, one that will provide a home for a Hispanic family, people who are relatively new arrivals to our area. The event ended when a long line of "hard hats" lifted the sidewalls and pushed them into place. The building began to take shape before our eyes.

For me, however, the composition of the crowd was even more impressive than the new house. People from all walks of life were there and from every segment of our population. The privileged and the poor, the old and the young, students and townsfolk, Baptists and Episcopalians, blacks, whites, and Hispanics stood side by side. All were gathered together around a common cause, united in a tangible expression of love and a commitment to equity and justice. It occurred to me that Habitat not only builds houses—it builds community

Although Habitat describes itself as a Christian housing program, it is inclusive and non-discriminatory, welcoming all participants and uniting people from all social, ethnic, religious, and economic backgrounds to work together. It is the kind of project that invites everyone of goodwill to act on his or her finer instincts.

House building for Habitat has become a major catalyst for forging strong relationships in Orange County. Predominantly black and white congregations are joining hands in partnerships to construct a house, and a by-product of the shared task is better racial understanding. The intergenerational participation is also impressive. Although we live in a community composed of many young people and many retired people, there are few places where the two groups come together as acquaintances and friends. Habitat affords a unique opportunity for the old and the young to know each other.

Local churches have discovered that Habitat opens a door for an expanded campus ministry. Twenty-seven different student groups, most of them fraternities and sororities, have become involved and work hand-in-hand with eighteen local congregations. Habitat has given to these young church folk a vision of how to relate their faith to people in need in a very practical way. It has confronted them with the conviction that decent shelter should be a matter of conscience and action and to understand that the universal appeal of Habitat is rooted in the Judeo-Christian tradition of social justice.

The goal of Habitat is ambitious. It is no less than to completely eliminate indecent housing! Beginning in an inauspicious way in Americus, Georgia, it has now spread to all fifty states and boasts of completing one new house every forty minutes! Last year, over twelve thousand dwellings were finished and made available to those who needed them most.

Now the movement is swiftly spreading to overseas sites, already located in over forty countries. (I had an opportunity to visit a Habitat project in Hungary last summer and witnessed firsthand the great pride of young families as they showed us their attractive and solidly built new homes.)

Habitat is not a giveaway program. All prospective homeowners become partners and are required to invest a minimum of three hundred hours of "sweat equity." No-interest mortgages are issued over a fixed payment period, and small monthly payments are repaid over an average of twenty years. The money which comes in is then recycled to make possible the construction of more houses. The concept is as simple as it is brilliant. It recognizes that people in inadequate housing need capital, not charity, and instead of offering a handout, it extends a hand. Thus, Habitat is engaged not only in building houses but also builds self-reliance and self-esteem, as the new homeowners learn to stand on their own feet and to lift their heads high in the awareness that others have cared enough about them to make possible what had seemed an impossible dream.

Opportunities are available for any volunteer who wishes to become involved.People with little or no experience in construction can learn quickly and can soon discern the difference between shoddy and quality workmanship. Volunteers are needed not only for handling a hammer, but also for family outreach screenings to select the occupants for the new homes and for the never-ending tasks of publicity and fund raising. If you are a candidate for an overseas working vacation, there are opportunities for from one-to-three week's involvement in places like Bolivia or India or Zambia.

A significant by-product of the widespread support of Habitat in Orange County is the motivational value of seeing and experiencing first-hand the deplorable conditions under which many low-income families are forced to live. Hopefully, this will lead to collaboration with county and town officials to make possible other initiatives for people of limited financial resources to have a decent dwelling. The growing number of participants in Habitat will guarantee a ready-made constituency to support all such proposals.

✉

Reverend Seymour, Thank you for writing the wonderful article on Habitat of Orange County. You captured all of the great things Habitat does for housing, community and relationship building. Very well done!! *J.L.T. for Orange County [NC] Habitat [for Humanity]*

CHAPEL HILL'S MOST UNDER-USED RESOURCE

January 31, 1996

Did you know that there are over eight thousand senior adults in and around Chapel Hill? They have gravitated here from all over the country, and they come with impressive experience and expertise in nearly every area of knowledge. Many of them came because they want to live in proximity to a major university and be able to enjoy the intellectual stimulation it affords, as well as the feast of fine arts in music and drama.

Yet, surprisingly, while always generous in welcoming seniors to what it has to offer, the university has yet to discover and significantly use the talents of this large segment of our citizenry. Insofar as I am aware, there is no designated point of entry for potential volunteers to become involved in the educational mission of the university as it seeks to shape the future of the next generation.

Recently, I was invited by a group of students to be a resource for a forum on the civil-rights movement. The forum was held in the lounge of the Hinton James Dormitory. It was a wonderful experience both for me and, I hope, for the young people. It was one of those rare occasions when an opportunity was offered to a senior adult to interact and share ideas with the student population.

I came away from that event wishing a way could be found to structure such intergenerational exchanges more often. Chapel Hill 's retired population contains countless persons who have excelled in nearly every academic discipline or who have reached the highest levels of leadership in their chosen vocations. Just think what it could mean to students to have access to such persons as mentors or to counsel them as they contemplate their own career-development plans.

Not long ago, an attempt was made by the Senior Center to convene all retirees in our area who had had careers in foreign service. Nearly fifty men and women showed up! Imagine what their insights might mean to a political science department or in those university disciplines that impart knowledge about other cultures.

Ironically, instead of finding opportunities to share their expertise with the younger generation, many local seniors are involved in teaching each other. There are two large local organizations called "Peer Learning" and "Shared Learning" where seniors sign up for classes from a syllabus that looks like that of an institution of higher learning. Of course, such mutual stimulation is desirable and much appreciated by those who participate, but I wish there were some way to make it available to others beyond those of us who are old.

The Chapel Hill public schools have recognized the potential volunteer pool of capable seniors in our midst and have employed a volunteer coordinator to recruit them and to offer support for their involvement. The contact person is Pam Bailey in the General Administration Office. She tells me that there are more than fifty older adults who are on regular duty in elementary school classrooms to assist teachers and give individual instruction to children who need special help.

The high school has not yet tapped into the senior resource to any significant degree, but an opportunity for this to happen may be shaping up with the construction of the new East Chapel Hill High School. It is located on Weaver Dairy Road, adjacent to the Carol Woods Retirement Community, where some of the residents have expressed an interest in working with their new neighbors.

There are several groups of seniors who are joined together to make available their expertise for those in the community who request it. One of these is called SCORE (Senior Corps of Retired Executives), which counsels new small business ventures. Another is SHIIP (Senior Health Insurance and Information Program), offering guidance about policies and billing for health coverage for older adults. Then there is VITA (Volunteer Income Tax Assistance). This last group has a week's training each January to qualify as helpers to low- and moderate-income people who need assistance in filing their taxes.

The main place in the community to let it be known when you have a need for a senior volunteer is RSVP (Retired Senior Volunteer Program), which is located in the Chapel Hill Senior Center. This is where the majority of local seniors go to list their availability and register where their interests lie. Currently, RSVP has placed over six hundred older adults to work with nonprofit agencies in Orange County.

The United Way is another place where requests for volunteers can be made and where seniors step forward. It is located in the United Way office in the NationsBank Plaza and is called "The Volunteer Center for Orange County." About ten percent of their volunteers are senior residents of the area.

You can find senior volunteers in many places in our community. They are visible at the reception desks of the shelter, the library, the Interfaith Council, and the Senior Center. They can also be seen in the halls of the hospital. Some of them have accepted appointments to municipal advisory boards.

Chapel Hill is fortunate to have so many older adults who want to contribute toward the well being of our corporate life. But given our numbers, we still represent an under-used resource, especially by the university.

THE HOUSE THAT CHARLES INSPIRED

September 1, 1995

Hats off to Beppie Bradford, whose hard work and perseverance have established a much-needed new institution in our community. Beppie is the founder of Charles House and served as executive director for its first five years. She has just announced her retirement, effective in October.

Her dream of a facility such as Charles House was intimately related to her relationship to her father, the Reverend Charles Jones. In his later years of failing health, he was confined at home. Beppie realized that he needed the stimulation of interaction with other people and believed that his well-being would be improved if more structure were added to his daily life. Hence, the name "Charles House," an adult day-care center.

The adult day-care concept has enabled many older adults to remain at home with their families. It has provided a safe place for them to be while other adult family members are away at work. It has also enabled care-givers to have some regular respite. In many cases, an adult day-care center provides an alternative to a nursing home, where the expense for full-time care would be much greater.

But Charles House is far more than just a place to be. It offers a well-planned and varied program that stimulates continuing interest in life and brings great pleasure to the participants. For example, a day's schedule might include sharing the headlines of the newspaper, games, exercise, music, crafts, or enjoying the care of pets and the visits of young children. All such activities serve to prolong the independence of moderately impaired adults and, no doubt, to extend their lives. The goal of the professional staff is to understand both the limits and the capabilities of each guest and to enrich their lives in every way possible without creating stress.

Charles House is literally a house, and it maintains a warm, home-like atmosphere. Located in Carrboro on Hillcrest Street, it is in a quiet neighborhood surrounded by trees. The house is bright, with many windows, a glassed-in porch, and even a greenhouse for participants to plant and grow flowers. The facility is certified to serve sixteen participants, though more than twice that number may be served in any given week, since not everyone comes every day. The Charles House family includes men and women from sixty to one hundred and three years of age!

Because of the need for a high ratio of staff to guests, financial support for Charles House is always a major concern. In order to keep rates low enough to be within the reach of those who need care, there is an ongoing effort to raise funds to subsidize the cost. It is a non-profit institution and has secured generous support from many sources in the community.

The greater Chapel Hill area now boasts of a population of over ten thousand senior adults, and that number is steadily rising. Most of these are retirees who have settled here from all over the country. As these older adults continue aging, there is likely to be a growing need for the kind of intermediate care available at Charles House, and the future is likely to require establishing other similar centers.

Unfortunately, the name "day-care" has some negative associations. Immediately we think of children, and this tends to suggest that adult day-care is for those in their second childhood. Every attempt is made to overcome such denigrating stereotypes. Perhaps eventually another more appropriate name for such centers will surface. Charles House is widely recognized as being a model facility for other communities where similar centers are on the drawing board.

Here are the kinds of things people are saying about Charles House. A woman who needed to continue working and was worried about leaving her husband at home alone said, "Knowing that he is at Charles House has made it easy for me to be away from him, as I know he is happy, challenged, and safe. Having time apart is not only essential for both of us, but adds quality to our lives." A participant says, "My health has improved since being at Charles House, keeping my mind off my hurts and pains. And being with friends has helped me to enjoy living." And a physician remarked, "It has been a great help to several of my patients."

I was present for the celebration of the fifth anniversary of the founding of Charles House, and it was a joyful, upbeat affair. Board members, volunteers, professional care-givers, and family members of Charles House guests were all saying how fortunate we are to have such a place for older adults.

Charles House will not seem the same without Beppie Bradford there each day, but she is leaving a solid organization with broad-based community support. And Beppie will continue to be involved in the ongoing development effort. Now is the time, however, to say congratulations to her for accomplishing what she set out to do and to wish for her a much-deserved latitude of leisure and change of pace.

ARTSCENTER DESERVES COMMUNITY SUPPORT

December 7, 1994

A celebration is in progress at the Chapel Hill/Carrboro and Orange County ArtsCenter, marking the twentieth anniversary of its founding. This should be a source of considerable community pride, for no other such center in our state can match its ambitious program, which includes all the arts and encourages creative expression within every age group.

This anniversary is an indication of the strong commitment and perseverance of the staff, the board, and a dedicated core of our citizenry. It is no secret that the ArtsCenter has done well to survive, primarily because of the high overhead required to maintain its location. Yet, despite severe cutbacks in operating budgets since 1990, the same number of programs have been offered and the base of support continues to widen.

Recognition of the quality of its achievement has come from outside our community. It has received the *Reader's Digest* National Jazz

Network Award and the Governor's Award for family programs. Last year, nearly forty thousand people attended musical events, dramas, and various classes offered in painting, writing, photography, etc. It is an impressive agenda.

A particular achievement that benefits all of us is the social bridge-building the Center enjoys, embracing all segments of our population. Blacks and whites team up for both administrative chores and creative endeavors. A special outreach program targets teenagers who need a place to go and who have dormant talents yet to be tapped.

The creative expression of children is another priority goal. Someone has said that all children are innately artistic, but culture often fails to provide an opportunity for them to discover their creative abilities. A stated aim of the ArtsCenter is to "free the spirit."

Let it be said clearly that the ArtsCenter does not cater to professionals. It is committed to the concept that every person has the potential for artistic expression. Those of us who may doubt this are provided a chance to be proved wrong by signing up for a class. Amateurs are welcomed. The primary goal is not to produce celebrities but to enrich the lives of all of us by giving us permission to make music, paint, or dance.

A stated goal for ArtsCenter programming is that it will provide a forum to express diverse artistic traditions and various cultural heritages. It includes the international community and provides a place for people from other parts of the world to display their talents and art forms.

Education in the arts is central to everything the Center does. This happens not only in-house, but on occasion in the public schools, such as providing special workshops to help teachers introduce art forms into their curricula. Family programs bring to children a balanced series of educational and entertaining arts for the enrichment of their lives.

The Center is also committed to providing new visual artists a place to show their work. They are on year-round display at the Center gallery. Indeed, novices in music or painting or drama or dance are provided an opportunity to present their creations and to receive valuable feedback about their creative efforts. Young artists may find further assistance in writing grants to find funds to support their continuing activities.

For the past two years, the private/public partnership behind the ArtsCenter has returned from visits to other communities covetous of their performing arts facilities. Indeed, it would be great if the Chapel Hill/Carrboro area had such a building, but surely it is more important to have in place already a program that encourages and cultivates the arts. Who knows where this could lead us in the future?

Meanwhile, the ArtsCenter has an opportunity to put its operation on a more secure footing by purchasing its present facility. A sound financial plan has been projected and approved by the Major Campaign Review Board of the Triangle. Leading the effort are two of our foremost citizens: Ida Friday and Phillip Nelson, former interim president of the North Carolina School of the Performing Arts. They both stand ready to offer personal tours of the Center to any persons who request it.

The Town of Chapel Hill, the Town of Carrboro, and Orange County all judge the ArtsCenter to be one of our most valuable community assets and are offering continuing support. Also, a number of foundations are pledged to help, but a main portion of the funding must come from broad-based community support. Therefore, an effort is now underway to find 250 citizens who will contribute $1,000 each. But any gift of whatever size will be welcomed to meet the required $575,000 to secure ownership of the current building.

In order to further the cause and to demonstrate faith in the Center's future, the Mary Reynolds Babcock Foundation has forgiven a loan of $133,000. Another index of emerging health is the steady increase in revenues during the last two years as the number of participants increases.

We live in a special kind of place, and one of the joys of residence here is the smorgasbord of offerings in the arts. Your support of the ArtsCenter is a tangible way to guarantee the perpetuation of this legacy.

SUPERSTORES SHORT-CHANGING US ON VALUES

October 2, 1994

I did a quick double take en route to Durham the other day when I noticed that the church once located off to the right just beyond Interstate 40 was no longer there. In its place I saw a massive building under construction, which I have since learned would house another new mega-store, Home Depot.

Mega-stores seem to be emerging as the latest marketing trend. Soon Wal-Mart will anchor another shopping area on the boulevard, and at South Square we already have such giants as Office Depot, Home Quarters, and Toys R Us.

The pacesetters, of course, have been the grocery stores. We have had supermarkets for so long that we can hardly remember when we were without them. Banks have also been merging at a rapid rate, so fast that the small, locally owned institution has become a rarity.

I feel very ambivalent about all of this. Of course we all like the convenience, the choices of goods and services offered by these huge commercial establishments, and also the promise of lower prices. But we have lost something in our society, and I see little possibility of ever regaining it. Traditionally we Americans have assumed that bigger is better, but I am not sure this is really the case with the advent of the superstores.

In the process, we have sacrificed some human values. Many merchants used to take pride in owning their own small businesses, but now we have legions of people working for an owner they will never even meet. We have lost the personal relationships many of us once expected when we shopped with the same clerk repeatedly, someone who knew us personally and enjoyed passing the time of day with us when we came into the store. The butcher knew what cuts of meat we preferred, and the clothier knew the size of the suit we wore. But now the values of convenience and low cost have eclipsed the personal values, and for me, at least, shopping has become more of a chore and less a pleasure.

In most places in Europe, there has been an attempt to keep out the superstore. When you shop for food in most English towns, you must make the rounds of the baker shop, the butcher shop, and the greengrocer. Tourists tend to think this is all very quaint, but our overseas friends have kept something we are fast losing. Not only are personal values on the block, but the very viability of our small towns is at issue. Travel all over the South, and in countless communities you will see a superstore on the edge of town and blocks of vacant buildings on Main Street.

Nearby Hillsborough is struggling to survive just such an assault.

It is significant to note that the maga-store is sensitive to the accusation that something is missing. One of the big banks advertises the availability of "your personal banker." And Wal-Mart employs a professional greeter to stand at the door and tell you how pleased he is to see you. But do not be deceived. These people who try to preserve the personal touch are not the ones who make the big decisions about the company. Generally they're made by groups of strangers in boardrooms in a city far away.

Another downside to the advent of the mega-stores is the difficulty in securing their support for activities within the local community. Your Chamber of Commerce will tell you that the businesses most willing to provide for hometown needs are those whose owners live here. I can testify to this. In local efforts to solicit contributions for good causes, it is sometimes impossible to get through the bureaucracy with your request to the management, and often the response is a polite letter of refusal, nothing more. They take huge amounts of money out of the community, but frequently put precious little back into it.

Generally, Chapel Hillians have resisted attempts by mega-stores to locate here, but we are facing a painful dilemma. They are staking out places on our periphery where they know many of us will shop, but Durham County will benefit from the tax revenue, not Orange. It is no accident that Wal-Mart and Home Depot will be just across the line.

Maybe my resistance to this new marketing trend is related to my generation. It is natural for those of us who are older to be nostalgic about the past. But I am sure we have lost something important, and it saddens me.

Furthermore, I must confess that I feel intimidated by these monster establishments. I wander up one aisle and down another in a daze and usually cannot find what I am looking for. Or worse, I end up buying something I didn't come to get and really didn't need. I also get lost in these stores. They are like labyrinths to me, and when I finally negotiate my way back to the entrance, I have trouble remembering where I parked my car as I view the gargantuan parking area.

Could there be any symbolic significance in Home Depot's demolition of a relatively new church building to secure their site? Perhaps not. But I fear human values are being eclipsed by materialistic ones.

Dear Dr. Seymour, I like competitive prices as much as anybody, but I think we've lost more than the price savings in the demise of small family businesses. *E.G.C., Chapel Hill, NC*

SENIOR CENTER OFFERS MANY OPPORTUNITIES

September 4, 1994

It is surprising that in a community that prides itself on being such an excellent place to retire that an adequate senior center was so late in being established. The response to the new Chapel Hill Senior Center on Elliott Road has very quickly demonstrated the need. Last year, more than twenty-five thousand contacts were made with the center, and the number of participants and the programming continue to grow.

The September schedule offers a wide range of opportunities, including physical-fitness classes, intellectual stimulation, and health-maintenance services. There are craft and painting classes and a wide range of special-interest groups, including drama and opera. Bridge is a never-ending activity, with introductory instruction for those who want to learn to play.

This fall, the center is adding a third luncheon series on Mondays that will feature programs on music and the arts. The Wednesday series includes speakers on a variety of topics, and on Friday the emphasis is international issues, under the theme "World Perspective." The meals are a part of a federal program to foster socialization and nutritious food for seniors.

Unfortunately, most of the original senior centers in our country targeted only low-income seniors and neglected the majority. Now it is widely recognized that the aging process generates special needs for everyone, regardless of their economic or ethnic background. One of the goals of the new Chapel Hill Center is to reach seniors from every level of our community and to provide opportunities for all older adults. Thus, activities as diverse as bingo and lectures from UNC professors take place simultaneously.

To ensure access to everyone who would benefit from the center, an outreach program is in place. Interns from the School of Social Work are knocking on doors of seniors in the area to make sure they are aware of what is available to them and to arrange transportation where needed. It is gratifying to see a broad mix of people from every level of our common life participating and relating to each other.

From the outset, another goal of the new center was to make it a teaching senior center for young health professionals at UNC, especially those in geriatric curricula. With the cooperation of the Division of Health Affairs, an advisory board of professors and retired health professionals is committed to expanding the services and screenings available to local seniors. A new staff person, a nurse, has just been employed to direct this component of the center's program. Already, multiple support groups for persons living with various infirmities are meeting regularly, including pulmonary disorders, prostate cancer, and those with visual or hearing diminishment. Also, young medical students are assigned to the center to take medical case histories of seniors, thus giving them a more balanced view of the older population and an opportunity to improve their communication skills across the generation gap. The center is committed to recruiting local older people for geriatric research at UNC.

Not only is the senior center a place to serve seniors; it is a place where seniors can volunteer to serve. The Retired Senior Volunteer Program has an office in the center and matches the interests and talents of older adults with a broad range of placements. To date, more than six hundred seniors are involved as volunteers in Orange County.

Although the new center is spacious, lack of space is a primary problem. To ease the pressure, construction of a stairway to the mezzanine is underway to permit putting offices upstairs and free more room for groups on the main floor. Parking has also become more pressed because of the next-door opening of Montaldo's. This necessitated the Center's relinquishing twenty parking places. Fortunately, Squid's Restaurant has offered its parking area for spillover during the day, since the restaurant is only open in the evenings.

The Center's operation is made possible by a public/private partnership. The major player is Orange County, which provides staff from the Department on Aging and funds for two-thirds of the lease. The Town of Chapel Hill has increased its commitment with an allocation designated primarily to take care of utility costs. The private sector is represented by The Friends of the Chapel Hill Senior Center, an advisory group of local seniors who raised all the money for the up-grading of the facility and continue to pay the cost for a third of the lease included in an annual budget of well over $50,000. Yard sales, bridge tournaments, and fashion shows are undertaken regularly to make money available.

A current project is a signature quilt. By the end of September, it is hoped that two hundred people will have each contributed ten dollars to have their names inscribed on a handsome quilt that will hang at the Center. Another on-going opportunity is the Chapel Hill Legacy Wall, where the names of deceased seniors are remembered for a one-hundred dollar contribution.

The new Chapel Hill Senior Center has quickly become an integral part of our community. If you have not yet had occasion to visit, we hope you will do so. Drop in for a cup of tea any Monday afternoon from 3:00 to 4:00. And pick up a copy of *Senior Times*. You will surely find something listed of interest—from line-dancing to chess. We are preparing a place for you!

WE HAVE MADE PROGRESS IN RACE MATTERS

July 13, 1994

I appreciated the new president of the National Association for the Advancement of Colored People sharing his views about discrimination in Chapel Hill in his recent "Village Voices" column. I am sure the Reverend Eugene Hatley will serve both the organization and our community well.

I am the pastor he referred to who made the statement about Chapel Hill being a much better place for black people today than it was in the 1950s. We had visited together a few days before the article appeared, and I recall making such a comment. This was not a "causal observation," for I was in Chapel Hill during the twenty-seven years when Mr. Hatley was away, and I have seen major changes that I feel should not be belittled.

I believe we have made substantial progress despite continuing problems. I know it is not politically correct to be optimistic about race relations, but I am convinced that we are moving toward an inclusive society in which race will become increasingly irrelevant. Whereas Mr. Hatley considers the changes achieved thus far to be "slight," I think we are light years away from the rigidly segregated community we once knew. Indeed, in the 1950s, Chapel Hill was a typical Southern town, doubly shameful because of the liberal reputation of the university.

I agree that there are still major areas in our community life where discrimination remains, and it is clear that covert prejudice is far more difficult to eradicate than overt prejudice. I also acknowledge structural racism and understand that the struggle for equality still faces a challenging agenda, especially on the economic front.

I am not willing, however, to trivialize the significance of the victories already won. In fact, I would argue that we would not be in a position to push further had we not first removed the more visible and blatant practices of segregation.

One of the most hopeful signs is the openness of our political system, which in our own community has brought black citizens into places of effective leadership and influence. The chairman of our county commissioners is black. Our district attorney is black. Until recently, the superintendent of our public schools was black. The head of the Department of Social Services is black. We elected three black members of the school board. We were one of the first towns in the nation to elect a black mayor, who now represents us in the state senate. The new president of the UNC student body is black. They are all positions of power and influence and demonstrate that our citizenry is able to look beyond race to elect people who are capable regardless of color.

The recent school board tragedy has been painful to all of us. It strikes me as unfair, however, for anyone to claim that the attempt to remove Ms. Burnette is racially motivated. She was elected by a strong coalition of both black and white voters, and two school board members who are black have been involved in all the proceedings. (I regret Mrs. Royster's resignation.) Ironically, if race had been a factor, it was the reverse racism of those who voted for her *because* she is black! I doubt seriously whether many whites that cast their ballots for Ms. Burnette would have voted for a white candidate from a similar background with such limited credentials. People saw Ms. Burnette as a promising young woman whose courage, character, and commitment would make a valuable contribution to the community. I personally feel that she could serve all of us best by resigning and securing the college education she desires.

Many white people also deplore the slowness of the university to employ more black faculty, but what can the university do? The fact is that the number of black Ph.D.s available in America is very small, and the demand for them makes it difficult to compete in recruiting. Even Duke University has lost several of their stellar black professors to Ivy League schools. There are several options. We could employ blacks without the Ph.D., or we could steal Ph.D.s from predominately black institutions. Or we could pay black professors more than white professors in order to bid at a higher level. Obviously, the one thing we must do is to enlist more young blacks for graduate education and offer the strongest possible support to those on the Ph.D. track in every academic discipline.

The controversy over building the Black Culture Center has also been agonizing for many white people. Those of us who marched with blacks in the 1960s find it difficult to support anything that looks like racial separation. Initially, the Black Culture Center looked more like a step backward than a step forward. I am aware that integration is no longer considered a desirable goal among many blacks and that the current emphasis is on equality. I can support this in so long as the equality goal is not to separate. I lived long enough in the Old South to learn that anything separate is seldom, if ever, equal. I can support the Culture Center only if it is intended for all.

I cannot applaud the NAACP's embracing Mr. Farrakhan, for this seems contradictory to Mr. Hatley's stated desire to see all black organizations "that believe in justice and equality for all people" to join hands and work together on a united front. How can someone who has made anti-Semitic remarks be affirmed as a brother committed to justice?

I am also troubled by the endorsement of the opinion that white America still thinks of every black as a "nigger." This strikes me as an unfortunate stereotype of white people. I also hope it is not true that the "silent majority" of local blacks consider Chapel Hill to be "the northern part of hell." These are disturbing indictments of white sisters and brothers who live here.

I have supported the NAACP throughout my adult life, and I will continue to do so. I judge it to be an optimistic organization, for it believes in the "advancement" of black people. It not only takes just pride in what it has already achieved, but also is committed to the emergence of a genuinely inclusive society.

CHARITY STILL BEGINS AT HOME

May 4, 1994

Every organization I belong to needs money. Almost every board of non-profit groups in our community devotes an inordinate amount of time to trying to think of ways to do fund-raising. One Saturday in April, I went to three fund-raising events on the same day! And in addition to the multiple local appeals, every mail delivery brings at least a half dozen other requests for innumerable good causes solicited nationwide. There is a continuous, competitive struggle as all these groups seek simultaneously to tap the wellspring of American benevolence and generosity.

In recent years, we have seen a proliferation of players in this money-raising marathon. The public's incessant cry that taxes not be increased has left many government agencies without adequate resources to offer services people demand. As a result, we have witnessed a concerted attempt to close the gap by asking the citizenry for voluntary contributions over and beyond their legal assessment. Many of these new non-profit organizations begin with the word "friend," as in Friends of the Library, Friends of the Department of Social Services, Friends of the Department of Parks and Recreation, and Friends of the Chapel Hill Senior Center. We label all such alliances as "public/private partnerships," indicating that an agency functions by virtue of government money being supplemented with voluntary contributions.

We deceive ourselves about holding the line on taxes as long as we are expected to give over and beyond our legal requirement to accomplish what should properly be a government responsibility. It is also inherently unfair. It means that people who are unwilling to accept cutbacks have no choice but to add to the government's inadequate funding with money from private sources, thus providing services for community needs while many others are not paying their part.

A classic illustration of this is the Interfaith Council (IFC) of Chapel Hill, our community's main social service agency. For years, the IFC has been supplementing the County Social Services budget for people in crisis—to the tune of about $10,000 a month! Also, the IFC raises large sums from the private sector to support the shelter and community kitchen, services which local government might otherwise be forced to manage and pay for in full.

Another illustration is the torturous and seemly endless appeal for financial support for public television and public radio. We have just completed the PBS marathon, and we are now being bombarded by daily repetitive requests from the airways "to keep the telephones ringing" and call in our pledge. Isn't it sad that these technological miracles of mass communication must be subsidized by voluntary contributions to survive? You would think that any enlightened government would be eager to make possible the use of such educational media with generous grants.

There is also "double-dipping" within churches. Nearly every congregation in Chapel Hill has line items in it annual budget for the support of IFC, Habitat for Humanity, and other such worthy causes. Thus, members of these churches make a corporate gift, but that is not the end of it. The same members are also approached as individuals for a gift over and above that which their congregation designates. This means that the actual amount given by each worshipping body is in fact considerably larger than the figure listed in the church budget.

I will not soon forget Ronald Reagan's suggestion for solving the homeless problem in America. He said that if each church did its part and people tithed their income, that the problem would go away, and it would not need to be on the government's agenda. Somehow this advice seemed hollow, for I knew that Reagan almost never attended church, and his tax return indicated that he gave less than two percent of his income to charity. He was willing for others to absorb the cost while he abstained.

I am glad we Americans are judged to be generous people who support many worthwhile endeavors, but I sometimes think we might be more effective if we exerted more pressure on our government to provide adequate funding for basic services instead of constantly scrambling for money from private sources to do the things that get neglected. There are times when I feel considerable ambivalence about being asked to give money to so many good causes which have the effect of allowing our government to appropriate considerably less than is necessary. There are occasions when I feel it might make more sense to picket the legislature or Congress than to dig deeper in my pocket. Realistically, however, I am sure the answer must always be "both/and"—to continue being as generous as we can while at the same time being advocates within the body politic for those whose needs are not yet adequately met.

[To the Editor]: After having read his wonderful guest column, I deeply regret that I never got to hear the Rev. Robert Seymour preach during the years that he occupied the pulpit at Binkley Church.

In these times when political conservatives—Democrat and Republican alike—dominate the nation's economic policy, it takes great courage for a public figure like the Rev. Seymour to say, "...We might be more effective if we exerted more pressure on our government to provide adequate funding for basic services instead of scrambling for money from private sources."

...If America's worshipping populace, clergy and laity alike, truly wish to provide for the hungry and the homeless, we can accomplish a great deal more with letters to those who are supposed to represent us in Congress—to the David Prices and the Jesse Helmses—than we can with a contribution to a Christmas collection for the poor, needed as such collections are. It is members of Congress, after all, who have the power and the purse strings to provide homes for all the homeless and to feed the hungry if we demand that they do it. A small fraction of the billions they spend on the military-industrial complex would be more than enough.

It is indeed time for the members of Congress who just gave themselves a $100-per-week salary increase to do their part for all of us. And it is my sincerest wish that we can all share in Bob Seymour's wisdom and compassion. *A.S., Chapel Hill, NC*

TRAVEL

SPRING SKIING AT STEAMBOAT SPRINGS

April 19, 2000

I was in Steamboat Springs, Colorado, in March for five days of spring skiing. The conditions were perfect: deep snow, bright blue sky, and mild temperatures. Every year I wonder if I should "age out," but the lure of the scenic beauty and the exhilaration of schussing downhill always wins out over my better judgment.

An additional draw is the opportunity it affords to be with my family. My children and my grandchildren met me there, and we shared the joy of trailing one another all over the mountain. It does my elderly ego great good to keep up with my progeny on the slopes as they often look backward with a surprised expression to see me following close behind.

A further attraction is that anyone over seventy can ski free, so for five years I have avoided the fifty-dollar-a-day lift tickets! This policy of free skiing for seniors is in effect at most major ski resorts in the U.S., and the number of older adults on skis is steadily increasing.

For the younger crowd, the new thrill is snowboarding. This is the fastest growing sport in America. When it was first introduced, many resorts regarded snowboarders as a hazard and confined them to special areas, but now they are everywhere, my son and grandson included. The equipment is less costly, and they say it is easy to learn.

The town of Steamboat Springs is seven thousand feet above sea level, higher than Mt. Mitchell. The vertical drop is thirty-five hundred feet, from a mountain height of just over 10,500 feet. Skiing came early to the area, introduced by Norwegians who excelled in ski jumping. This year the town is celebrating its 100th anniversary and boasts of sending more skiers to the winter Olympics than any other resort town in America. The locals call their white blanket "champagne snow."

I was fortunate to return home with only minor bruises from several falls, but I did have one emergency that proved quite exciting. At mid-mountain one of my plastic molded boots split in two, so I was stranded until a Good Samaritan summoned the ski patrol to my rescue. A snowmobile arrived and zipped me back to the lodge where, in deference to my years, the rental shop issued me new boots without cost. My grandson was intensely jealous of my having had the descent on the snowmobile .

A luxury at the end of the day is soaking in the outdoor pools, which are fed by natural hot springs at the foot of the mountain. A feature at one of these was an enormous tubular water slide that twisted and turned from a height of at least a hundred feet. My grandchildren demanded that I give it a try, so I finally relented. Access required walking up a steep staircase, and when I reached the top gasping for breath, the attendant said, "Mister, if you climbed all those steps, you can go down free." (Everywhere I turned, age had an advantage!) I have never felt so totally out of control as I did going down that slide, and my family laughs every time they recall my expression as I emerged with a splash at the bottom.

The mountain at Steamboat was originally called Storm Mountain, but the name was changed to Mount Werner in 1964 in memory of three-time Olympic champion Buddy Werner, who was killed by an avalanche in Switzerland while still in his twenties. The Werner family is still regarded as the "first family" of the town.

Safety is a growing concern at ski resorts. Helmets are now considered standard gear for children, though most adults would still rather risk skiing without them. It is surprising that Colorado law does not yet require safety bars on all of the ski lifts. Sometimes you are swinging over ravines to a fifty-foot drop below. Those who ski recklessly are prohibited on the mountain.

Steamboat is a booming community. I chanced to meet a member of the town board, who said that their major municipal agenda was how to control growth and how to make housing more affordable for the workers they need. It sounded very much like Chapel Hill. Already the labor shortage has led to a creative solution. The resort goes to Australia and New Zealand to recruit students for winter jobs here while it is summer vacation time "down under." We heard the Aussie accent everywhere.

A huge hotel, to be called Grand Summit, is under construction and will tower over the base village. Many local residents deplore what is happening, but now that modern jets can fly into a nearby airport, providing easy access to the area, the boom is not surprising. It has become a world-class destination, and one of the joys of the lift ride up the mountain is the opportunity to visit with people from everywhere, not only from the U.S., but from abroad.

Steamboat Springs is also succeeding in becoming a choice place for a summer holiday. Ski trails become trails for mountain bikes, and area ranches, where there are genuine cowboys, provide horseback riding into the spectacular surrounding country.

A VISIT TO VICKSBURG AND NATCHEZ

April 9, 1999

My wife and I have just returned from a spring visit to the old Mississippi cities of Vicksburg and Natchez, where the azaleas were in full bloom and the fragrance of wisteria filled the air. This is the time of the annual "pilgrimage" when many of the magnificent ante-bellum homes are open to tourists. The trip was sponsored by the North Carolina Museum of History and was like a journey into the nineteenth century.

I was surprised to learn that both Vicksburg and Natchez voted not to secede from the Union, but the State of Mississippi overruled them. These towns were wealthy from the cotton trade and had many northern connections from the river. Sadly, many of the old buildings in Vicksburg were destroyed in the Civil War, but Natchez suffered no damage at all. In Vicksburg we had the pleasure of staying in Cedar Grove, one of the magnificent homes (now a hostelry) that was spared because the owner's wife was a cousin of General Sherman.

Because of Vicksburg's strategic location as the "Gibraltar of the South" on a high bluff overlooking a bend in the Mississippi River, Union forces judged that its fall was essential for the control of the river. When attacks from gunboats on the water failed, a land army under General Grant surrounded it from the east, and after a forty-seven–day siege, the city surrendered on July 4, 1863. Because of the somber associations with this date, the people of Vicksburg refused to celebrate the Fourth of July with the rest of our nation until after World War II!

We traveled the sixteen-mile road through the National Cemetery where one of the bloodiest battles of the Civil War was fought. Over thirteen hundred monuments—some of them grandiose—line the route, remembering the regiments and officers from every state that participated in the conflict. Illinois alone sent thirty-six thousand men, while the entire Confederate garrison totaled only thirty thousand.

My great-grandfather, whose family name was Sproles, was killed at Vicksburg, so I particularly wanted to see if there was any record of his death at the reception center. I was surprised when the computer printed out the names of thirty soldiers named Sproles, three who had the identical name of my grandfather.

At Vicksburg, we also enjoyed an hour's cruise on the river, which at that point merges with the Yazoo River and is over a mile wide. The appearance of the waterfront was compromised by shabby buildings and warehouses, with the exception of the sleek new Harrod's Casino, one of Mississippi's newest industries. I recalled Mark Twain's description of the river as being "too thick to drink, too thin to plow."

Natchez is an hour south of Vicksburg and is the oldest civilized settlement on the river, preceding even New Orleans. The Natchez Indians were there first, then the French, followed by the British and Spanish. Before the Civil War, it was one of the wealthiest towns in the nation with more millionaires per capita than any other place in the country. That wealth was lavishly spent in constructing huge homes that were furnished with the best china and furniture available in Europe and elsewhere.

In the early 1930s, the Women's Garden Club of Natchez came up with the idea of renovating some of the homes that had fallen into disrepair and opening others to tourists for a tour of antebellum homes. Today there are thirty-two mansions on display, and every spring and fall the city is almost overrun with visitors. Add to this the proliferation of bed-and-breakfast places, restaurants, and antique shops, and you now have one of the community's main sources of revenue! Unfortunately, about a fourth of the downtown stores are still boarded up, having long ago succumbed to the suburban sprawl of mega-stores and malls, but the restoration continues, making Natchez a magnificent national treasure, so designated by the Department of Interior.

Unlike Vicksburg, Natchez has succeeded in transforming the riverfront into a green bluff park with a number of monuments and historical markers. One of these commemorates a horrendous tragedy, a deadly fire at the African-American Rhythm Club, where moss and crepe paper ignited and led to the deaths of 230 people in 1940. Another poignant historical marker honors the novelist Richard Wright who was born in Natchez. It reads (in part), "His life-long quest for freedom led him to Paris, France, where he died in 1960."

You can visit these Mississippi towns and hear almost nothing about the slave culture that created them. One guide began her remarks by commenting that the Civil War was about economics and had nothing to do with slavery, as if the two were unrelated! I noted a sign in front of the old post office that indicated that it was slated to become a black-culture center. I predict that in the near future the realities of plantation life will also go on tour as more and more visitors ask questions. The life of luxury and leisure could not have been sustained without its accompanying shadow of human bondage and oppression.

If you have not visited these cities, I highly recommend it. It was rather nice to drop out of the twentieth century for a few days!

MONTANA: AMERICA THE BEAUTIFUL

November 20, 1998

When Tony Bennett was asked to sing the national anthem at the opening of the World Series at Yankee Stadium, he chose to sing instead, "America the Beautiful." I applaud his action. It is easy to sing and the lyrics celebrate our magnificent country. The words praise our "alabaster cities" and "amber waves of grain" and voice gratitude for our living in a land of both "liberty and law."

These words resonated in my mind in August when my wife and I took a vacation trip to Montana. We had seen the film, *The Horse Whisperer*, and we were so impressed by the magnificent scenery in the movie that we impulsively decided to go see it. I had also recalled an article in a travel magazine entitled "The Most Spectacular Drive in America," and it was in Montana, and we followed its recommended route by flying into Billings (Montana's largest city), where we rented a car. Then we drove south on Highway 220, which dips into Wyoming and through Yellowstone National Park before intersecting with Montana's Highway 89, a route with little traffic that runs north all the way north to Glacier National Park. We were awed by the endless "spacious skies" and the "purple mountains' majesties." It was America, the beautiful.

The first part of the journey took us through the Bear Tooth Mountains, where the road rises to eleven thousand feet and runs along the top of the ridge across grassy meadows where patches of snow were surrounded by a panorama of purple and yellow wild flowers. It was breathtaking. Twenty-five–foot high poles lined each side of the road to enable finding the roadbed after heavy winter snowfalls.

Montana is our nation's fourth largest state, but it has a population of less than a million. Its east and west are almost like two different states because the east is relatively flat and less interesting, while the west offers great variety in scenery, including what the Blackfeet Indians call "the backbone of the world." (Meaning, of course, the Rocky Mountains.) The name "Montana" is Spanish for mountain. There are also huge ranches, forests, and vast windswept plains where the horizon seems to extend infinitely into space. You can see weather patterns approaching from miles away.

Montana is proud of the Lewis and Clark Expedition, which opened up the West, because over a fourth of the territory explored is within the state's boundaries. The railway penetrated the area in 1891, and in 1910, sixteen hundred square miles were designated to be protected as Glacier National Park. Soon thereafter, efforts were underway to bring tourists into the region. This prompted the building of the famous Big Tree Lodge, where an enormous lobby is secured by giant Douglas-fir pillars.

Pearl and I spent two nights in the lodge and especially enjoyed traversing the surrounding park in one of the vintage "jammers," a fleet of specially built cars dating back to the late 1930s (but recently reconditioned). They are bus-like vehicles with rollback canvass tops. We had a scary drive up "Going to the Sun Road" with a venerable senior adult driver from Mississippi at the wheel.

We had planned to do some hiking in the park, but were intimidated by ubiquitous signs warning would-be hikers about the danger of bears. An estimated two hundred grizzlies inhabit

Glacier, plus five hundred black bears. They are highly unpredictable in their behavior. They emerged from hibernation early this year because El Niño reduced the annual snowfall by two hundred inches. One staff member was killed by a grizzly in May, and several tourists have been mauled. All hikers are advised to carry pepper spray for protection and to whistle while they walk so as not to surprise a bear by coming upon one suddenly.

Glacier Park extends to the Canadian border, where it is contiguous with Waterton, a similar park in Canada. In 1932, they were symbolically joined by the shared name, Waterton-Glacier International Peace Park, and in 1995, the United Nations designated the whole area as a World Heritage site.

We continued our journey by traveling west of Glacier and then back south until we completed a fifteen-hundred–mile circle back to Billings. Driving in Montana is an adventure because there is no daytime speed limit.* Signs simply read, "Be Reasonable and Prudent," judging your speed by the weather and the condition of the road. We tried to keep our speed at sixty-five, but were among the slowest on the highway.

Montana has become known as an area where right-wing militias flourish, groups that talk about seceding from America the Beautiful, but everywhere we went, people were gracious and friendly. However, we were a little disconcerted whenever we saw an occasional T-shirt that read, "If it's tourist season, why can't we shoot them?"

Don't be intimidated. It is a spectacular place to visit.

* *This has since changed. Now a designated speed limit is enforced.*

Dear Rev. Seymour: I am originally from South Carolina and have not traveled much. But in September I had a business meeting in Whitefish, Montana, and wound up spending a week at the Grouse Mountain Lodge.

What a treat! We spent three days hiking in Glacier National [Park]. We watched the sun rise at Granite Peak and set on Avalanche Lake. We saw chipmunks and bighorn sheep. We met new friends from Vancouver and Valdosta.

But mostly it was just the overwhelming beauty of it all. The majesty of the mountains. The snowfall and incredible silence while standing on the Continental Divide. Up that high, a whisper can travel for miles. A prayer can float on the clouds. *J.R., Chapel Hill, NC*

A RAILROAD RUNS THROUGH IT

November 7, 1997

You may have seen the Public Television program shown repeatedly in recent months entitled, *The Last Train Across Canada.* It left the false impression that it is no longer possible to travel across the world's largest country by rail. The journey is still available, the only difference being that now you must make several changes of trains in order to complete the forty-five hundred mile trip from Halifax to Vancouver.

My wife and I signed on for a segment of this trans-Canada trek and traveled from Toronto to the west coast in September as participants in a Smithsonian Study Tour. Just before leaving, however, we received a telephone call informing us of a train derailment, and, ironically, we had to fly around the accident and meet the train in Winnipeg, thus missing the first leg of the rail trip. This afforded an extra day in Toronto, which enabled us to see more of that celebrated city, famous for its ethnic diversity of four million, and for staging the third-best in theater, after London and New York.

The train trip included not only a guide, but also a specialist in rail history who gave a series of lectures en route (sometimes telling me more about trains than I wanted to know!). We learned that the east-west connection was completed on the first week of November in 1885, after incredible hardships on the part of a largely Chinese-immigrant work crew as they carved their way through the formidable Canadian Rockies.

The impetus for the project was not only to foster access to the interior and trade across the nation, but also to bind the country together in a solid union. Some feared that the Far West might be tempted to become a part of the United States.

Another motivation emerged when the president of the Canadian Pacific Railway became convinced that the spectacular scenery of the Rocky Mountains could become a major tourist mecca. "If we can't export the scenery, we'll import the tourists," he said. Obviously, this required adequate accommodations as well as train tracks, so the railway entered the hotel business and built two of the most magnificent resorts in western Canada, which are still in operation and world famous for their luxury facilities: the Banff Springs Hotel and the Chateau Lake Louise. After Yellowstone, the Canadian Rocky Mountain National Park was the second such designated park in North America.

Pearl and I drove to Lake Louise on our honeymoon over forty years ago, and the changes we saw on this recent visit were dramatic. The Chateau Lake Louise has vastly expanded, and multitudes of tourists (mostly Japanese) swarm the grounds and lobby. Sadly, the magnificent view of the glacier was not quite as spectacular as we remembered because it has receded noticeably up the mountain, probably because of global warming. Banff has become a boomtown, and its famous hotel now includes a world-class conference center, with seven hundred guestrooms and a staff of over a eleven hundred! Both Banff and Lake Louis have added ski slopes, so the resorts are open for the arrival of visitors all year.

The once-graveled road that leads from Banff to Jasper is today a major highway. Not surprisingly, there is considerable controversy about the threat to wildlife and a need to more carefully manage the number of people who can enter the area at any one time. Park residents and environmentalists share a common goal: to establish a balance between use and preservation that maintains the values and beauty of nature while at the same time providing the means to enjoy the recreational opportunities available in the surroundings. Some innovative experiments are in progress to protect the animals—such as digging tunnels under the roads and building bridge paths over them, in the hopes that deer, elk, moose, and bears will learn to cross at these places. Elk roam freely all over the city of Banff, and it is not unusual to see black bears along the wayside and bighorn sheep on distant ridges.

A major highlight of our trip was a stop at the Columbia Ice Fields. Discovered in 1878, they cover 130 square miles, making them the largest such natural ice fields south of the Arctic Circle. The fields feed hundreds of glaciers flowing down from high altitudes to form a network of exquisite turquoise lakes. We were able to ride up to the canopy of ice on specially made "snow-coaches," vehicles with enormous tires built especially to traverse the treacherous terrain.

We moved on up into the Northwest Territory, which was opened originally by trappers and fur traders, many of whom worked under the auspices of the Hudson's Bay Company, formed in 1670! Amazingly, the company is still in business, with a chain of over one hundred stores located all across the nation. While we were there, newspapers headlined stories about the possibility of the firm's impending bankruptcy. Ironically, today the Hudson's Bay Company sells nearly everything except furs!

The most spectacular part of our journey was aboard a privately owned tourist train called the Rocky Mountaineer that makes the two-day trip from Banff to Vancouver from April through October. It offers "Gold Leaf Service," which includes a seat in a comfortable glass-domed car with a gourmet restaurant on the first level. Panoramic views enable you to appreciate the full glory of peaks that rise to over twelve thousand feet. Another wonderful feature is that the train stops at Kamloops for the night, and passengers are transferred to nearby lodgings, thus not missing any of the scenery by overnight travel.

To learn more about this outstanding journey, write to Smithsonian Study Tours in Washington, D.C. and consult the Rocky Mountaineer Rail's web site at: www.RkyMtnRail.com.

UNITED KINGDOM DIVIDED OVER FUTURE MONARCHY

January 26, 1997

My wife and I were in London over the New Year with the Playmakers Theater tour. As we entered the heart of the city en route to our hotel, our bus had to stop at an intersection in order for the Royal Horse Guards to cross the street in front of us. They were elegantly mounted on huge horses and were wearing flaming red capes to protect them from the bitter cold. Cameras surfaced quickly, and there was excitement over this unscheduled encounter.

Our hotel faced Green Park and was only a short walk from Buckingham Palace, which fronts the park on the opposite side. Several people from our group braved the cold weather to watch the changing of the guard, a major tourist attraction. Indeed, the pageantry associated with the royal family is still one of the best shows in town.

I remained in Britain for several days beyond the tour in order to make a nostalgic visit to Edinburgh, where I was a graduate student for two years in the early 1950s. One of my most vivid memories of my residence there was the occasion of Queen Elizabeth's visit to Scotland shortly after her marriage to Philip, when he was named the duke of Edinburgh. The royal party was to be welcomed upon arrival at a public hall located only several blocks from the divinity school, so I walked over to witness the proceedings. I approached the building by a circuitous route of alleyways and emerged to find myself near the entrance surrounded by photographers who were wearing press passes. Since my own camera was conspicuously visible, I pretended to be "legitimate" and remained with the professionals. It was a perfect spot where I could see everything, looking out toward the crowd and the regiment of honor guards.

Imagine my surprise when the limousine finally arrived and the queen stationed herself in proximity to where I was standing while her husband inspected the troops. Then she turned and began visiting with the photographers, myself included! My picture appeared the next day in *The London Illustrated News*! There I was, talking to the queen of England! Needless to say, this was a most exciting event and my mother's primary topic of conversation in my South Carolina hometown for weeks following.

On this recent return visit, I was struck by the fact that at the end of each theatrical production, the audience no longer stood and sang, "God Save the Queen." I learned from a number of people to whom I spoke that there was mounting controversy about the future of the royal family. Many felt that the behavior of some of the "royals" had made the monarchy the laughing stock of the world, like the script of a royal soap opera.

Quite by accident, as I scanned television channels, I stumbled upon a major national event on the evening of January 11th. There was a three-hour debate about the future of the monarchy before an audience of three thousand people from all walks of life, brought together in Birmingham from twenty different locations. The question before the assembled crowd and the country at large was, "Do you want a monarchy?" The discussion began in a very civil way but soon deteriorated into a shouting match.

The debate was billed as the biggest public forum ever in Britain. Fourteen thousand telephone lines had been installed for people to call in their responses, to register "yes" or "no." An astounding total of two and a half million responded!

In the course of the telecast, various aspects of the issue were discussed, and then the audience was asked to vote their opinions by holding up either red or blue cards, indicating their approval or disapproval. The most resounding response came in answer to the question, "Should Charles be king?" More than ninety percent rejected him and felt he had compromised his future not simply by the divorce, but by admitting to an adulterous relationship.

A representative from the Church of England insisted that if Charles did become king the church and state would have to separate. He felt it would be intolerable for the national church to be headed by one who had so brazenly violated the church's teaching.

Another main consideration was the cost of the monarchy. The overwhelming majority thought the royal family should pay its own way since their wealth is among the highest in the world. There was indignation over the Windsor Castle fire and the initial assumption that it would be re-built at taxpayers' expense. Although the queen finally agreed to pay for its restoration, she added to the indignation by opening Buckingham Palace (owned by the people) and charging admission to cover the cost. Over eighty percent of the British citizens interviewed in a recent poll could not name three good things the royal family does, and more than half felt they were not worth their upkeep.

Much of the debate centered on the inability to reconcile democratic ideology with a monarchy.

Why should people rule by accident of birth instead of by a vote of the people? How can a queen whose dwelling has two thousand rooms be expected to understand homelessness? There was little serious discussion about the advantages or disadvantages of becoming a republic with a president. Instead, most of the discussion dwelt upon the bad press, the personal scandals, and the parasitic "hangers on."

The tabloid press received scathing criticism from the supporters of the monarchy. Some chided that the press would have nothing to write about if the monarchy ended. Others judged the public to be at fault for putting the royal family on a pedestal and forgetting that they are human beings like everyone else. Still others recalled the outrageous behavior of ruling monarchs at earlier periods in English history.

The fact that this debate took place at all is in itself significant. There was a time when even raising the question about the future of the monarchy would have been considered an act of treason, but now there seems to be mounting sentiment to hold a national referendum on the matter in the near future.

When all the telephone responses were tabulated, however, it appeared that the monarchy remains reasonably secure despite widespread disaffection. Predictably, the majority of the Scots want the monarchy to end, but sixty-six percent of the English favor its continuance. Many people are pinning high hopes on Prince William as the most likely heir to the throne.

Ironically, one of the principle arguments for preserving the monarchy is its marketability as a tourist attraction. As an American who has talked to the queen, I can understand its value!

AUSCHWITZ CONVICTS MANY VISITORS

July 19, 1996

I have just returned from Poland, where I made a pilgrimage to Auschwitz, the infamous death camp operated by the Nazis. As I traveled there from Krakow on an air-conditioned bus, I thought of those thousands of innocent people who made the journey packed in stifling cattle cars, arriving from all over Europe. It was a bright, sunny day, but appropriately, the skies turned gray as we approached our destination, and the rain that followed reminded me of the tears of the doomed.

I was in the company of Jewish friends whose presence intensified my apprehension about my ability to even survive the sight of where so many people were executed. I felt slightly nauseous as we approached the place, a feeling which worsened upon seeing at the entrance a snack bar selling hot dogs and Coca-Cola. It seemed offensive for anyone to stop for food in a setting where enforced starvation was a daily routine.

Auschwitz had been a Polish prison before being taking over by the Germans to house political prisoners there, but soon followed their gassing of Jews, gypsies, and homosexuals. The site worked so well that it was expanded to nearby Birkenau (Auschwitz II), which was constructed primarily for the genocide of the Jewish people. Grim looking barracks stretched as far as the eye could see. Some arrivals were allowed to live for a while in order to be a part of the labor force, but the majority were sent directly to the gas chambers and crematoria.

One building was referred to as "the death house." Here prisoners who were reprimanded for even some minor infraction of the rules were systematically tortured in the most heinous ways imaginable. Some were packed into small underground cells to suffocate. Others were deprived of food and water until they died. Groups of workers were forced to stand up all night and then required to do hard labor the day following.

This building was also the place where ghastly medical experiments were performed on living prisoners, especially young children. Sets of twins were forced to stand barefooted in deep snow for long hours to observe how their bodies reacted to prolonged exposure to the cold.

Executions took place daily, usually by a single shot in the back of the neck as the prisoner stood naked awaiting his or her fate. Gallows were also used, and hanging bodies were left visible at the center of the camp to strike terror in prisoners who were still alive.

The horror of Auschwitz was so overwhelming that we were numbed to silence as we entered one of the gas chambers where human beings were herded like sheep being led to the slaughter. We also saw the large ovens where operators boasted about the number of bodies they could dispose of in one day's time.

A nearby museum displayed mountains of human hair and specimens of cloth woven from it. Large rooms full of the shoes, luggage, and toiletries of victims spoke loudly of the magnitude of the murders committed, estimated at one and a half million in this camp alone. (The Nazis had twenty-three other extermination camps, located primarily in Poland and Germany.)

Several days later I went to Prague where I visited the renovated Pinkus Synagogue in a neighborhood which had for centuries been the site of the Jewish ghetto. The synagogue now serves as a memorial to seventy-five thousand Czech and Moravian Jews who lost their lives under Hitler and whose names are inscribed on the walls, covering the entire interior of the building. The Jews in our group found their family names there.

How could such a monstrous tragedy as the Holocaust have ever happened? The German people say that most of them did not know about the camps, and here in America our leaders refused to believe the rumored accounts of what was occurring. I was troubled by recalling how the United States did so little in receiving Jewish refugees, at one point turning away a ship crowded with them from the port of New Orleans. We made it very difficult for people fleeing from the Holocaust to find a home here. Lady Liberty's lamp burned low.

Even more disturbing to me is the fact that the prejudice and hatred that led to the Holocaust were rooted in centuries of church history, as Christians judged Jews to be lost to God and persistently discriminated against them. It is painful to learn that even Martin Luther was anti-Semitic.

Contemporary German Christians are so sensitive to this issue that they have insisted that all references to the Jews be deleted from the script of the famous Oberammagau Passion Play. Also, a powerful prologue has been added to remind the audience of the potentiality for evil in each of us.

At the execution wall in Auschwitz, numerous bouquets of fresh flowers are brought by visitors day after day, and burning candles are left in loving memory of the dead. It is deeply moving to see these symbols of beauty and light claiming the last word over the darkness and death that once prevailed there.

The philosopher George Santayana writes, "Those who cannot remember the past are condemned to repeat it." These words reverberated in my mind when I read in the newspaper upon returning home that Southern Baptists had voted to launch a major effort to evangelize the Jews. I could identify with the reaction of Jews who remember from centuries past that frustrated attempts to accomplish such missions often led to persecution, expulsion, and executions. As a Protestant pastor, I distance myself from any such evangelizing efforts, preferring dialogue with my Jewish friends and respecting the vibrancy and vitality of their faith.

✉

Dear Bob, I read and re-read your very sensitive and insightful piece in the *CHN* about Auschwitz... I just wanted to tell you how much I appreciate the conclusions you drew from this experience.

The history of Christian proselytism is extraordinarily painful for our people. You can imagine how the Southern Baptist Convention's attitude toward Jews appears to thoughtful members of the Jewish community. How reassuring to read that you and like-minded, sensitive Christians want to "distance myself from any such evangelizing efforts, preferring dialogue...." I wish that all religious people could understand that one cannot have dialogue and, at the same time, "evangelize your dialogue partner."

So, Bob, thanks sincerely for your very considerate, clear, and heartfelt words. They mean a great deal to me and the Jewish community. *Rabbi John Friedman, Durham, NC*

SKIING, A SPORT FOR PEOPLE OF ALL AGES

March 22, 1996

I am one of a rapidly growing number of senior citizens who can be found on the ski slopes all across the country. I am not over the hill, but on the hill and going downhill fast.

I stumbled into this sport quite unintentionally. One Christmas, our teenage children were invited to Stowe, Vermont, for a ski vacation with their cousin, and his mother suggested that Pearl and I come along to enjoy the après-ski ambiance. Once there, however, we decided we should at least give skiing a try, and with considerable awkwardness at middle age, we finally managed to get our equilibrium. We haven't missed a winter since.

I know of nothing more exhilarating than being out of doors on a snow-covered landscape and seeing the awesome beauty of this nation from some of its highest peaks. This year our view was from Snowmass, an alpine resort in central Colorado, and only ten miles from Aspen, where we skied from twelve thousand feet. Our flight to a nearby airport was canceled because of a heavy deposit of fresh snow, so we landed in Denver instead, where we arrived on the first anniversary of the opening of its controversial, tent-like airport. From there, we had a five-hour drive by van over the continental divide, along ice-patched roads heaped high with snow on both sides.

Conditions for skiing were ideal. Four feet of snow had accumulated, and the last top layer of packed powder had been perfectly groomed by snowcats (large-tractor like monsters that crawl all over the mountain each evening). Trails marked green are for beginning skiers, blue is for intermediate, and black designates expert runs. I can manage those in the middle category fairly well, but attempts to negotiate a black one inevitably lead to a palpitating heart and predictable spills.

Even though the temperature may be in the teens, generally you do not get cold. Long underwear is essential, and layers of clothing are topped with down-filled jackets and padded trousers. People sometimes complain about cold hands and feet, but thick gloves and heavy socks are usually sufficient. (Electrically-heated socks are available!) Goggles and protective sunscreen are necessary to prevent sunburn.

Restaurants are located at various altitude levels on the slopes, where steaming hot soup, chili, and hamburgers are top-selling items. Hot chocolate or cider also affords a welcome respite when your legs begin to complain.

Après-ski takes over when the lift lines close. Usually, the day's end includes a leisurely soak in one of the heated pools, which offer much-needed balm for sore muscles. Afterwards, choices for dinner at the village base range from short-order places to elegant French cuisine.

My son and his family were with us, so we had the joy of skiing with our grandchildren, ages five and seven. They learned how to ski last year in the excellent ski school for children, and now zip down from the very top of the mountain with absolutely no fear.

People who do not ski often think it is highly dangerous, but this is really not the case. Once you learn how to control your speed and are willing to accept your level of ability, you can protect yourself and avoid embracing trees. I have been fortunate in never having had a serious injury. (Though on this last trip I managed to get a huge bruise from falling on a sheet of ice in the parking lot!) Every resort is also carefully monitored by a ski patrol whose jobs are to make sure there are no reckless skiers and to be available when accidents occur.

I have seen many changes in skiing in the past few years. Now every resort has snowmaking equipment in case nature does not respond on schedule. The painfully slow two-person chair lifts are being replaced with fast "quads," enabling four people to ascend together at a rather rapid pace. Most resorts have at least one gondola (imported from Switzerland), which can transport as many as fifty skiers at a time to the top. Boots and skis are also greatly improved in design, making them much easier to put on and much safer to use. The equipment with which I learned to ski was cumbersome, but the new gear requires much less hassle.

Another recent innovation on the ski slopes is the introduction of snowboards. These look very much like skateboards and require considerable skill to master, but they have become a popular challenge to many of the young, even though most conventional skiers feel threatened by the possibility of a collision with them.

I especially enjoy the opportunity to meet many different people who share my lift rides. I have had conversations with skiers from all over the U.S. and have been surprised to discover that one of the largest groups at nearly every resort is from Florida! More recently, people are coming to ski in the States from many parts of the world. The West has become particularly attractive to South Americans, and it is not uncommon to ski with new friends from as far away as Australia. Year after year it is also apparent that an increasing number of skiers have graduated to senior status and intend to stay on the slopes as long as age permits.

A major drawback to skiing is the expense. Equipment is costly, though it is possible to rent it on a daily or weekly basis at a reasonable price. Lift tickets have also skyrocketed in cost. When we began skiing, we paid less than twenty dollars a day, but tickets are now up to over forty dollars. If you are a senior adult, however, you get a special deal, for when you reach seventy, you can ski FREE—and that means me!

SEASONS

ON BEING "GOOD FOR GOODNESS SAKE"

December 23, 1998

He sees you when you're sleeping;
He knows when you're awake;
He knows when you've been bad or good,
So be good for goodness' sake!

A phrase from this secular seasonal song lends itself to ethical reflection. It raises the fundamental question of morality: Why be good? During the year-end holidays, many of us feel motivated to multiple acts of thoughtfulness and kindness. What prompts us to do this? There may be many reasons.

Imagine yourself leaving a shopping mall weighed down with an armful of presents. You pass a Santa Claus ringing a bell for the Salvation Army, asking for a contribution. You hesitate for a moment, but then you fumble for your money and drop a ten-dollar bill in the kettle. Why did you do it?

Consider the possibilities. Your motive may have been prompted by a twinge of guilt. Having spent money all day on friends and the people you love, you may have made the gift to offset feeling a little selfish. Or you may have given out of a strong sense of duty, remembering that your parents taught you to share. Or perhaps you are impressed by the Salvation Army's reputation for assisting the needy, and you wanted to have a part in it.

There are other possibilities, less altruistic. You could have given out of a sense of pride, to bolster your self-image as a caring person. Or maybe the person playing Santa Claus happened to be someone you know, so you felt the pressure to respond to his appeal with a sizable bill. You want him to remember you as a generous person.

But there are better reasons. Your act of charity could have arisen out of a sense of gratitude for all that has been given to you. You might have felt thankful when you compared your privileged circumstances to the plight of the poor.

And there are worse reasons. Such as acting on the advice of those television evangelists who say that if you give, you will get much more in return. "Cast your bread on the waters, and it will come back to you ten fold," they promise.

The lyrics to "Santa Claus Is Coming to Town" suggest one further motive. It is fear. Somebody's watching to see who's "naughty or nice." Someone knows whether you've "been bad or good." So "you better watch out!"

Any of these multiple reasons could account for your having contributed ten dollars to the Salvation Army. Goodness is seldom "for goodness' sake" only. Psychiatrists tell us that even our highest motives are generally mixed and seldom pure, yet all of the world's religions call us to purity of heart and singleness of purpose. Most of us can identify with the whole range of possible motives suggested by the above analysis.

Have you noticed that an increasingly common way to raise money for charity is to plan a "benefit" event? Special social functions offer pleasurable evenings to participants with a portion of the proceeds for admission being designated to some worthy cause. What a shrewd way of serving ourselves while serving others! The motivation is murky.

An appropriate resolution for each of us as we move into the new year is to relinquish lesser motives for doing well to higher motives. "Being good for goodness' sake" becomes a matter of prioritizing our reasons for the good we do, like ascending a ladder from its lower rungs to higher ones.

I would label the bottom rung on such a scale the giving that is prompted as expiation for guilt, suggested by the phrase "conscience money." Substantial contributions to good causes are often made because the donor feels some discomfort about how the wealth was acquired. For example, did you know that the Nobel Peace Prize comes from a family fortune amassed from the sale of explosives?

We move up a rung on the ladder if we give from a sense of responsibility, when we understand that the well-being of our communal life depends upon everyone supporting a broad spectrum of good causes. At this level, the gift is simply recognition of what a person perceives to be his or her fair share.

Near the top of the ascending ladder is the motive of thanksgiving. We give out of a sense of gratitude for all that has been given to us. Indeed, gratitude is recognized as a primary mainspring of ethical living.

The results are the same for the Salvation Army no matter what may have motivated our giving, but what a difference it makes to the giver if the reasons are right! Remember that couplet from T.S. Elliott's play, *Murder in the Cathedral*?

The last temptation is the greatest treason:
To do the right deed for the wrong reason.

The temptation is always there even though our ideal in life is to possess consistency between our inner motivations and our outward actions. Nobody wants to be called a hypocrite, and that is what a hypocrite is: someone who acts from a false motive. Integrity exists where outward goodness reflects genuine goodness within, "good for goodness' sake."

THE MIRACLE OF RENEWAL

April 2, 1997

Is there anyone who does not stand in awe of the renewal we see around us in nature at this season of the year? It is as if the world has been asleep during the winter months and is awakening again. The fresh morning air and the floral beauty lift our spirits and seem to offer to each of us a new lease on life.

It is not surprising that in nearly every culture where this dramatic transformation occurs there is some festival or ritual to celebrate the return of spring. It is an understandable impulse, for it appears that the whole world around us is being miraculously re-created. Nor is it surprising that such celebrations often have religious associations, for the faithful return of spring suggests the faithfulness and dependability of God.

Though the rhythm of renewal in nature is especially vivid in this season, it is not confined to it. Every morning, even in winter, gives us a fresh start, and it sometimes seems that the world is being re-created day after day as we move from light to darkness and sunset to sunrise. The Hebrew Scripture promises that "God's mercy is new every morning" and invites us to greet every dawn with the affirmation, "This is the day which the Lord hath made."

We also experience the miracle of renewal in the perpetuation of our physical health. We can be "dead on our feet," as we say, but after a good night's sleep we can be up and ready to go again. The recuperative power of the human body is something we take for granted, but it is truly amazing how we can be transported from exhaustion to refreshment day after day after day.

The miracle of renewal is further apparent in the healing process. Physicians can set the conditions for it, but it is not they who bring it to pass. Illness may strike us down, but gradually a reversal begins to stir within us as we move from sickness to health. We live in the assumption that the possibility of renewal is always present, and so we pray for it and try to find ways to work with the process.

Perhaps even more miraculous is the spiritual renewal we experience and the renewal of personal relationships. A favorite biblical verse from that most familiar 23rd Psalm is "He restoreth my soul." We have all suffered those debilitating dark hours of depression and discouragement and despair, as if we had fallen into some deep well from which no escape was possible, but for reasons beyond our accounting, the cloud starts to lift, and life gradually looks inviting again.

Here are a husband and wife who have come to a low point in their life together and are about to conclude that their marriage is over, but slowly a new relationship develops, less stormy and more stable. Or here are two friends who have suffered the pain of alienation because one has wronged the other, but when the party who has committed the injury finds the grace to ask for forgiveness, the barriers come down, and they are drawn closer together than ever before.

Another way we experience the miracle of renewal is in the creative process. Anyone whose livelihood depends upon their being constantly creative can attest to those long, dry periods when nothing seems to be taking shape or coming together, when we give our best effort to bringing something new into being and yet feel drained and empty and without inspiration. An artist may sit before a blank canvas without any vision to share, but gradually, as if from nowhere, the well of creativity begins to flow again, and the imagination becomes alive with imagery that demands expression. Or a researcher may sit before a mass of information that seems unrelated month after month, but then one day a of flicker of light ignites a new theory that brings all the material together with enlarged understanding. Both the artist and the scholar are recipients of the miracle of the emergence of new life.

As a preacher, I am especially sensitive to this kind of experience. Sunday after Sunday, for forty years, I needed a new sermon and fresh insights, and there were times when I would sit for hours before a blank page, anxiously wondering if I would be able to come up with something in time. Not infrequently, an idea invaded my consciousness in ways I could never account for. I felt visited from outside myself with newness of life.

I submit that this is the story of each of our lives. The principle of renewal sustains us, and we depend upon it in faith. We are always being called into being from beyond ourselves.

This reminds me of the four sculptures Michelangelo carved for the tomb of Pope Julian. They look unfinished, for the figures seem to be emerging from the rough stone, as if being torn out of non-being into being by the hammer blows of the sculptor. So it is with us. We are sustained, day after day, by resources of renewal and creativity that call us into being and shape our lives. The return of spring reminds us of this and prompts us to expressions of wonder and gratitude.

Among Christians there is an understandable temptation to associate the coming of spring with Easter, since they coincide on the calendar, but both Scripture and Christian theology resist this conclusion. The doctrine of the resurrection has to do with God's intervention where real death has occurred, not dormancy. It is important to make this distinction, for no matter what our personal faith may be, the return of spring is a primary witness of the principle of renewal that pervades all of life, and for which we can all be grateful.

REVOLUTIONARY REVERBERATIONS OF CHRISTMAS

December 25, 1996

My earliest memory of Christmas is of noisy explosions on Christmas Eve all over town. In my native South Carolina, Christmas is still a time for fireworks. I recall looking out of my bedroom window and seeing the dark skylight up with multi-colored Roman candles. Children did not consider Christmas complete unless Santa had left a veritable arsenal of rockets and blockbusters under the Christmas tree. And the ruckus would continue all day and the night following.

It never occurred to me to question the appropriateness of all of this, but in retrospect, I see it as having been more appropriate than the merrymakers realized. For it was the sound of revolution! And that is precisely what the original Christmas ignited.

Christians are so accustomed to associating Christmas with beauty and sentimentality that it comes as a surprise to discover revolutionary rhetoric in the biblical account of Jesus' birth. But look at these words of Mary's song as she cradled her baby:

"He has scattered the proud, put down the mighty from their thrones,
and exalted those of low degree;
He has filled the hungry with good things, and the rich he has sent away empty."

Instead of a lullaby, Mary sings about a radical reordering of life that reverberates like thunder!

An abbreviation for The New Testament is TNT, an explosive book! Wherever Scripture is faithfully preached, the seeds of revolution are planted.

We Southerners should understand this well because of the civil-rights movement, which so radically changed Southern life. Blacks discovered from the outset that their most effective weapons were quotations from the Bible and that white Christians were helpless in their attempts to fend off the Scripture they professed to believe. Consequently, we witnessed one of the most dramatic social upheavals of all time.

Hopefully, another revolution is spawning in response to the Christian acclamation of Jesus as the Prince of Peace. There has always been a strong pacifist tradition within Christendom, but conscientious objectors have generally been regarded as a radical minority. Maybe that is changing. Recently the man responsible for our nuclear strategic defense throughout the Cold War made a public plea for the abolition of all nuclear weapons and voiced his fear that the military could not be trusted to contain them. Also, last week *The New York Times* noted that sixty retired generals and admirals from more than a dozen countries signed a statement pleading for the removal of all nuclear warheads. Modern warfare has become too horrible to contemplate, not to mention the excessive cost of military hardware, money desperately needed to meet the social needs of humankind. Christmas calls us to take the revolutionary risk of reversing our faith in power to relying on the power of faith.

The reference to filling the poor with good things and sending the rich away hungry sounds like a severe judgment upon the wealthy, but if the gap between the haves and the have nots continues to widen, revolution may eventually be inevitable. Salaries of many CEOs have reached obscene levels of greed, such as the dismissed head of Disney who was just awarded a ninety-million-dollar severance package! (Compare that with minimum wage of the average teacher's salary of just over $22,000.)

Another interpretation of Mary's prediction of the reversal of fortunes of the poor and the rich may be a simple statement of a spiritual reality. People who have everything may be slow to realize what their deep needs actually are. Self-sufficient folk find it difficult to admit their needs. A full hand may be forced to go away empty of those very best seasonal gifts of love, hope, and faith, while people who know their poverty are generally more ready to receive.

In our own time, the values espoused by Jesus have been seen as being so out of step with the world as to be judged ridiculous, and thus, he has been portrayed as a clown. *Godspell* has become a classic. Consider what a revolutionary lifestyle He proposes:

"Bless those who persecute you."

"Return good for evil."

"Forgive seventy times seven."

Putting such principles as these into practice would turn the world upside down. Yet, at Christmas many people pause to pay tribute to the One who summons us to live this way. It is a time when Christians who celebrate Jesus' coming would do well to pray for courage to risk a commitment to His revolutionary leadership.

IN EVERYTHING GIVE THANKS

November 20, 1996

As Thanksgiving approaches, there is some evidence that as a society we may be taking more seriously that biblical admonition to "always give thanks for everything."

Indeed, there are signs that we may be becoming more civil in our relationships to each other, for ubiquitous expressions of gratitude greet us nearly everywhere we go. The words "thank you" are very much "in" these days.

Seldom does a day pass without hearing them or seeing them somewhere. "Thank you for using AT&T." "Thank you for choosing American." "Thank you for shopping at Wal-Mart." And when I turn on my computer, the first thing I hear on the audio from my server is "Thank you for using Compuserve." Obviously, the corporate world wants us to know that we are appreciated.

Recently, "thank you" signs appeared on the doors of the Chapel Hill post office. I wasn't sure why I was being thanked until I saw credit-card logos printed beneath. I presume this means that we can now pay for our postage with Visa or Mastercard and that the post office is grateful for our business.

There are some situations where I am thanked inappropriately. After waiting on the runway for a forty-five minute delay of my flight, an attendant announces, "Thank you for your patience." By then my patience has long since run out and been replaced by frustration and anxiety about making my next flight connection.

Some of this is a proven psychological ploy that is called positive reinforcement. At many of the fast food restaurants, for example, there are trash bins visible in all directions with the large letters "THANK YOU" inscribed on them. Maybe we should replace all of those threatening signs that say, "$100 Fine for Littering" with "Thank You for Not Littering." Someone should do a study to see which message gets better results.

No doubt the most common "Thank you" that we see today is, "Thank You for Not Smoking." I laughed out loud when I saw a cartoon that showed the reception desk at Phillip Morris, above which was posted the sign, "Thank You for Not Suing."

Gratitude gets expressed in some surprising places. When an official at a tennis match wants the crowd to be quiet as a player prepares to serve, he simply says, "Thank you." In the Old South, polite table manners dictated that when you wanted another biscuit, you said, "Thank you for a biscuit." This was a euphemism for "Pass the biscuits, please."

I can think of many places where a "thank you" might be helpful. In a church bulletin, for example, it might be effective to print just before the sermon, "Thank You for Your Attention." Or even better, "Thank You for Not Sleeping."

The cartoon character, the Reverend Will B. Done, proposes that we reflect the current trend by issuing a new translation of the Ten Commandments. Instead of saying sternly, "Thou shalt not commit adultery," he suggests, "Thank you for not committing adultery."

The Department of Transportation is another place where some changes could be made. We could replace all of the current highway signs with a more positive approach to the traveling public. Stop signs could be replaced by ones that would read, "Thank You for Stopping," and prohibitive signs about parking could be improved by the more gentle reminder, "Thank You for Not Parking Here."

We might have more success in reducing the violence in our society if we posted signs in public places saying, "Thank You for Not Shooting." Or in the courtroom witness box, there could be a sign for the person giving testimony that would read, "Thank You for Not Lying."

By now you realize that much that I have said here is with tongue in cheek. But, seriously, is there not a danger that what at first may give the appearance of our becoming a more civil and grateful society is in reality only a superficial expression?

How do we distinguish between genuine gratitude and a perfunctory remark? I submit this as a worthy topic for consideration as we observe Thanksgiving. To whom are we really thankful?

As we approach the end of the year, there are two people who will be leaving the political scene that I would like to thank. They are Anne Barnes, who has served us so effectively in the State Legislature, and Don Willhoit, who has given us twenty years as an Orange County commissioner. All of us owe to them a great debt of gratitude.

Of course, the One to whom thanks is meant to be directed at Thanksgiving is God, the Creator and Sustainer of our lives. Yet, we are living in such a secular time that very few people find their way to worship on Thanksgiving Day as did our Pilgrim forefathers and mothers. Let me encourage you this season to consider all the blessings that are yours and to express your gratitude with something more genuine than a mere nod to God.

I had better stop now lest I be accused of preaching. Thank you for reading this.

RELIGIOUS CORRECTNESS FOR THE HOLIDAYS

December 3, 1995

Today is the first day of the Christmas season.

You may have the impression that it began on Thanksgiving Day, for Macy's Santa Claus parade distracted attention from the aroma of roasting turkey. Furthermore, on the Friday after, millions of Americans participated in the biggest shopping day of the year, as merchants tried to convince us by their alluring sales that Christmas was well underway.

The religiously "correct" know that Christmas never officially begins until the first of the four Sundays prior to December 25th. The ecclesiastical calendar calls this period Advent, alerting us to the approaching of Christmas and calling us to prepare. And that first Sunday is today, Advent I.

There are two ways of celebrating Christmas, the sacred and the secular, and it is often difficult to separate the two. As each year passes, secular customs seem to be more and more dominant, so much so that the religious significance of the season is almost eclipsed. This is all very confusing, especially to children, who are highly vulnerable to an inability to distinguish between what has religious significance and what does not.

Much of this change is directly related to marketing, for nothing fuels our economy more than Christmas. Some merchants expect to do at least forty percent of their annual sales during the year-end holidays. Last year, Christmas shoppers rang up a whopping 233 billion dollars in purchases! Celebrating Christmas has become critical to our economy, and in order to assure a huge response, the secular accretions to the holiday have become increasingly pervasive.

Having discovered that the ancient Jewish festival of Hanukkah conveniently occurs during the holiday season, the business world has had some success in encouraging the Jewish community to celebrate in ways similar to that of Christians. It is now not uncommon for Jews to send Hanukkah cards, to decorate their homes, and to give more gifts to their children. Merchants are eager for everyone to participate in the seasonal celebration, including unbelievers. And so, in order to include everyone, religious symbolism is deliberately downplayed.

A further factor that has accelerated the secularization process is our sensitivity to the Constitutional restraint about the appropriateness of religious expression in the public arena. In an attempt not to appear supportive of any one religious group, and to be impartial toward all religious groups, we have been prompted to remove both Christian and Jewish symbols from the marketplace. With similar policies affecting public schools and government buildings, the holidays have been made to look like little more than a meaningless orgy of consumerism.

The greatest asset to keeping the cash registers ringing is Santa Claus. Although there has been some attempt to canonize him by remembering an ancient bishop who went about giving to the needy, the religiously "correct" judge it to be bad form for Santa to appear at church functions. His image is altogether secular, catering to those who already have much and who want much more.

Visit any typical shopping mall and you may see absolutely no evidence that Christmas has any relationship to religion. Customers are lured inside by colorful wreaths and garlands, reindeer and candy canes. More than likely, all the background music will be secular songs, such as "Jingle Bells" or "I'm Dreaming of a White Christmas." Even in card shops, most of the messages circumvent religious themes in favor of "Season's Greetings."

The situation is aptly satirized by a wonderful cartoon that shows two women looking at a beautifully decorated store window filled with merchandise. In the center of the display is a simple manger scene. Upon noticing this, one of the women says to the other, "Of all the nerve! The Church is trying to horn in on Christmas!"

We are moving toward a totally secular event that might more accurately be labeled a winter festival, similar to what occurred in Russia during the Communist era. It is a festival stripped of virtually all religious connotations. This may lead to literary changes even in some secular classics, such as, "'T was the night before the winter solstice, when all through the house..."

Decorating policies in the public sector generally permit such things as wreaths, candles, and lighted trees. Recently, however, the use of the tree has become somewhat controversial, for we persist in calling every decorated tree a "Christmas tree." Actually, the emergence of the tree as a sign of Christmas has occurred in recent times and has no ecclesiastical significance in and of itself. A tree is like a cake, which, until it is decorated, remains only a cake, but it can be transformed into a wedding cake or a birthday cake. Similarly, a tree without Christian symbols, adorned with just baubles and tinsel, is not a true Christmas tree. The religiously "correct" understand that the only trees appropriate for the church are decorated with Christmons, the traditional symbols of the Christian faith.

One of my rabbi friends thought that a wreath was also a Christian symbol, suggesting a crown of thorns, but I am not aware of anyone in the Church who sees a wreath as anything more than a secular decoration.

Perennially, some Christians are outraged by what they judge as sacrilege in the use of the abbreviated "Xmas" sign in the marketplace. Yet, the truth is that "X" (a cross) represents Christ and has a long history of use within the church. It is a cryptic, but legitimate, way of spelling "Christmas."

The colors associated with Christmas also have both sacred and secular meanings. Most people think red and green are the colors of the season, for they represent the winter landscape with red berries and evergreens, but the ecclesiastically "correct" know better. The colors of Christmas are purple and white. Purple dominates Advent and symbolizes penitence, while white is reserved for Christmas Day and two Sundays thereafter, symbolizing purity.

One thing further. Secular wisdom warns that it is bad not to have your Christmas decorations down by New Year's Day, but Christians celebrate for a longer season. The religiously "correct" keep their decorations in place until January 6th, the day that marks the arrival of the Magi at the manger.

To my secular friends, I say, "Have a pleasant winter holiday!" To my Jewish friends, I say, "Have a happy Hanukkah!" To my Christian friends, I say, "Have a joyful and blessed Christmas!" And to everyone, I say, "May the holidays bring to you personal renewal and a resurgence of hope."

Robert Seymour has demonstrated, both through his writings and his actions, that he will lead in the direction that his conscience dictates. That is why he has become the conscience of our community.

KEVIN C. FOY
Mayor of Chapel Hill

Robert Seymour has dedicated his life to helping others, as is evident in his writings. We first met in early 1990… I had lived in Europe and South America for more than twenty years before settling in Chapel Hill and had met many people in my travels, but no one quite like Robert. I was immediately impressed with his dedication, leadership, and human compassion. Chapel Hill is fortunate to have Rev. Robert Seymour.

LEE PAVAO
Former member of the Chapel Hill Town Board

To be a champion of both civil rights and iced tea can only occur in the South—and only in a south that has changed and continues to change. The witness of Bob Seymour is one of the reasons this area changed for the better. Whether his pulpit was at Binkley Baptist Church or the Senior Center or through the "Village Voices," Bob speaks with courage, conviction, and humor.

THE REVEREND RICHARD EDENS
United Church of Chapel Hill

Robert Seymour, Minister Emeritus of the Olin T. Binkley Memorial Baptist Church in Chapel Hill, North Carolina, served as the first Pastor of the congregation from 1959 through 1988.

He was the founding President of the Interfaith Council for Social Service and the principal founder of The Chapel Hill Senior Center. Since his retirement, he has been involved in many community endeavors and has especially enjoyed writing a regular column for *The Chapel Hill News.* Mr. Seymour has published three previous books: *Celebrating Christmas as Christians*; *Whites Only—A Pastor's Retrospective on Signs of the New South*; and *Aging Without Apology—Living the Senior Years with Integrity and Faith.* A graduate of Duke University and Yale Divinity School, he also holds a Ph.D. from the University of Edinburgh.